EMERSON´S GHOSTS

Emerson's Ghosts

Literature, Politics, and the Making of Americanists

Randall Fuller

OXFORD
UNIVERSITY PRESS

2007

OXFORD
UNIVERSITY PRESS

Oxford University Press, Inc., publishes works that further
Oxford University's objective of excellence in research, scholarship, and education.

Oxford New York
Auckland Bangkok Bogotá Buenos Aires Cape Town Chennai
Dar es Salaam Delhi Hong Kong Istanbul Karachi Kolkata
Kuala Lumpur Madrid Melbourne Mexico City Mumbai Nairobi
São Paulo Shanghai Singapore Taipei Tokyo Toronto

Published by Oxford University Press, Inc.
198 Madison Avenue, New York, New York, 10016
www.oup.com

Library of Congress Cataloging-in-Publication Data

Fuller, Randall, 1963–
Emerson's ghosts : literature, politics, and the making of Americanists / by Randall Fuller
    p. cm.
Includes biographical references.
ISBN: 978-0-19-531392-5
1. Emerson, Ralph Waldo, 1803–1882—Criticism and interpretation—History. 2. American literature—
History and criticism—Theor, etc. 3. Criticism—United States—History—20th century. 4. Politics and
literature—United States—History—20th century. 5. Emerson, Ralph Waldo, 1803–1882—Influence.
I. Title.
PS1637.3.F86 2007
814'.3—dc22   2006037233

9 8 7 6 5 4 3 2 1

Printed in the United States of America
on acid-free paper

For Julie

PREFACE

My subject is the construction of Ralph Waldo Emerson by some of the most influential American literary critics of the twentieth century. Van Wyck Brooks, F. O. Matthiessen, Perry Miller, and Sacvan Bercovitch have each relied on Emerson to further their critical projects—projects which in turn have reflected their wider social and political engagements with "America." More broadly considered, this book attempts to provide an institutional history of American literary studies—and its disciplinary cousin, American Studies—throughout the twentieth century and occurring against the sweeping backdrop of national and cultural history.

As a result, I am less concerned with a teleological account of Emerson studies than with the changing models of doing American literary and cultural studies during its brief history. My contention is that Emerson's vision of the nature and significance of intellectual work, especially as set forth in "The American Scholar," has provided a fertile challenge to would-be (re)mappers of American literary and cultural history. My study accordingly demonstrates the rich heterogeneity of our critical heritage through a focus on what I take to be its central aspect, the complex involvement and identification with Emerson. It emphasizes certain critical "paradigm-makers" in the belief that close attention to their practice can deepen our understanding of the persistent aspirations and difficulties attending any effort to think through and express American literary history; and its analysis centers on the interaction of personal urgencies, professional requirements, and cultural politics in an attempt to trace the subterranean and often hidden sources for our obsessive concern with Emerson as a tutelary spirit who promises to connect the literary with the world, poiesis with praxis—the long foreground to our beguilingly hopeful and yet deeply vexed efforts to become public intellectuals in the United States.

The first chapter explores the enormous imaginative influence Emerson has exerted over readers, and the second examines Emerson's early cultural construction by critics at the end of the nineteenth century. The next four chapters comprise individual treatments of critics of central importance to American literary history. These four critics had unparalleled influence on the emerging and intersecting fields of American literary scholarship and American Studies; it is not too much to say that without their work both fields would be strikingly different, unrecognizably so. Ranging from Brooks at the beginning of the twentieth century to Bercovitch at its conclusion, each critic's work is situated within personal circumstances, local institutional politics, and finally a broader twentieth-century intellectual and cultural history.

In limiting my focus to those figures who may be said to constitute the very origins and emergence of American literary scholarship and American Studies, I have revealed much of that history to be white, male, and Harvard-connected. My final chapter seeks to acknowledge the most important development in both fields during the past three decades or so: the fact that what was once known as a national literature and its critical reception have become extraordinarily diverse, contested, plural. This means, among other things, that any question involving Emerson for now and for the immediate future must ask to what extent he can be reshaped or even reenergized for a transfigured social and academic context. In the final chapter I treat this question and touch on the extraordinarily rich and diverse work on Emerson that has followed in the wake of the New Americanists before attempting to answer some of the questions raised by that work.

"Friendship," writes Emerson, "like the immortality of the soul, is too good to be believed." This book could not have been written without the warm friendship and generous collegiality of many, many people. In trying to recapture the historical and intellectual contexts of Emerson's most insightful twentieth-century critics, I have benefited especially from discussions with and comments by Henry Abelove, Jonathan Arac, John Ashbery, Sacvan Bercovitch, Peter Carafiol, Stanley Cavell, Wai Chee Dimock, Lyndall Gordon, Sam B. Girgus, Bruce Greenfield, J. C. Levenson, Leo Marx, Edmund S. Morgan, Lawrence Rosenberg, Cushing Strout,

Shira Wolosky, and Rafia Zafar. Donald E. Pease and Daniel T. O'Hara read portions of the manuscript in its early stages, offering invaluable suggestions and comments that not only helped in revising the manuscript but contributed to my thinking in ways that continue to reward. Both exemplify generosity of spirit coupled with intellectual rigor. And the group of colleagues at the 2005 Dartmouth Summer Institute on the Futures of American Studies who responded to an early draft of chapter 6 not only improved that portion, but made this a better book overall. Lawrence Buell offered timely and searching comments that greatly improved the final chapter. I owe a special debt of gratitude to Ken Egan, Chair of the Department of English, colleague and friend, who not only found ways for me to write and present my work, but who has read the manuscript in its various permutations more than once, always improving it with his insights. I am grateful to Charles Taylor, Dean of the College and Vice President of Academic Affairs at Drury University, for financial support that enabled me to conduct research. I wish to thank the staffs at Harvard's Houghton Library, Yale's Beinecke Library, and the Van Pelt Library at the University of Pennsylvania for their unfailing patience and help. My greatest intellectual debt goes to Robert Milder, interlocutor and friend, whose seemingly inexhaustible fund of learned and intelligent suggestions recalled for me, time and again, why Emerson might continue to matter. I wish to thank my parents for their boundless support and encouragement; I am most fortunate to have in-laws who offered the same. Above all, I am grateful to my wife, Julie, for her sympathy and discernment, her infallible sense of what matters most, her incandescent self.

ACKNOWLEDGMENTS

C hapter 2 first appeared in "Emerson in the Gilded Age," *ESQ: A Journal of the American Renaissance* 45 (1999): 97–129. Reprinted with permission. Copyright 2000 by the Board of Regents of Washington State University.

Chapter 5 first appeared as "Errand into the Wilderness: Perry Miller as American Scholar," *American Literary History* 79 (Spring 2006). Reprinted with permission.

A slightly different version of chapter 6 appears in "Aesthetics, Politics, Homosexuality: F. O. Matthiessen and the Tragedy of the American Scholar," *American Literature* (June 2007). Reprinted with permission.

CONTENTS

ABBREVIATIONS

EL   *Ralph Waldo Emerson, Essays and Lectures*, ed. Joel Porte (New York: Library of America, 1983).

JMN   *The Journals and Miscellaneous Notebooks of Ralph Waldo Emerson*, ed. William H. Gilman et al. (Cambridge: Belknap of Harvard University Press, 1960–1982). Cited as *JMN* with volume and page numbers.

EMERSON'S GHOSTS

CHAPTER I

The Haunting of American Literature

Enter GHOST . . .
Thou art a scholar; speak to it, Horatio.
—Hamlet

The ghost is not simply a dead or missing
person, but a social figure, and investigating
it can lead to that dense site where history and
subjectivity make social life.
—Avery F. Gordon, *Ghostly Matters:*
Haunting and the Sociological Imagination

Emerson and the Critical Imagination

This book calls attention to the ability of one author, Ralph Waldo Emerson, to exert tremendous imaginative influence over certain readers and critics—to *haunt* them, as it were. I use the term "haunt" advisedly, not only to conjure up Harold Bloom's description of Emerson as "our ghostly father" and that sense of belatedness Geoffrey H. Hartman evokes as "a haunting, ambiguous sense of living in the aftermath"[1] but also to suggest the always illusionary *literary* experience by which Emerson's writing has demonstrably effected psychological transformations upon individuals in ways that remain to some extent mysterious and unpredictable.

Emersonian hauntings are the result of energies that cannot be entirely explained by context—although history's impress etches itself indelibly upon the conditions of his authorial production and reception. Nor can such hauntings be explained entirely by the dense specificity of the text—though, again, Emerson's richly contrastive language plays a far greater role in the critical engagement it produces than has typically been

3

acknowledged. Emersonian hauntings are generated, rather, within the volatile transaction between readers and an aesthetic mode that encourages perceptual transformation while remaining multivalent enough to suggest numerous, and often conflicting, transformations. These hauntings achieve their most salient effects by suggesting ways of opposing or critiquing the often disappointing actuality of American modernity—a modernity that sometimes seems relentless in its efforts to colonize or limit thought and action.

Winfried Fluck has persuasively argued that since at least the late eighteenth century, the shared project of the humanities throughout Europe and the United States has been a struggle to countermand the consuming instrumentalism of modernity.[2] I would add the observation that crucial and somewhat distinct aspects of that instrumentalism achieved particular force and a commensurate sense of urgency in the United States from the antebellum period to our present day. Those aspects include (but are by no means limited to) aggressive industrialization, the conflation of laissez-faire capitalism with democracy (with democracy *as* commodity), the shift from production to consumption, the emergence of ever-more encompassing and connective communications technologies, mass media, the Manichean division of the world (at least for a significant portion of the twentieth century) between the United States and the former Soviet Union, and, with the end of that division, a global dispensation that has produced new networks of multinational interests, sectarian conflict, and a more contested notion of the nation-state.

The critics of my study—and the Emerson upon whose example they grounded their work—are of interest in part for the ways in which they criticize and at times imagine opposition to the challenges of modernity manifested in history. I am aware that to invoke the word *opposition* (or its close relatives, *dissent* and *resistance*) is to risk the celebratory gesture—the revolutionary bravado—that passes increasingly for action in the professionalized humanities. To counter this, I hope to show how and why particular acts of cultural and literary criticism might have felt *urgent* at a given time—how this admixture of history and inclination have shaped, among other things, our dynamic understanding of Emerson, so that it often seems, in Stanley Cavell's words, "as if we do not yet know what this man is and what he wants."[3]

Emerson's originary performance of cultural critique is so influential in part, I argue, because it is *literary*. Variously extolled and derided throughout his historical reception as a philosopher, a poet, and a cultural descriptor, Emerson might better be understood as an aesthetic or literary intellectual whose accomplishment is the endless troping of these (and many other) discourses to create what Oliver Wendell Holmes described as that "Emersonian atmosphere"[4] and what I am here calling a form of haunting.[5] That haunting might be critically situated somewhere between what traditional literary critics once referred to as "influence" and, more recently, subsequent theorists see as Derridean "spectrality,"[6] that sense of writing as capable of overwhelming the interpretations of literary-critical descendants through a forceful imaginative power unleashed in literary turns and conundra, in language that is often at odds with itself. Its effect, broadly speaking, is to excite perceptual habits within a space imagined to exist somewhere between raw, unmediated experience and those tendencies toward conceptualization designed and meant to order such experience. Emerson's particular and robust version of literary performance encourages eccentric reading and fosters sympathetic identification ("I contain multitudes," wrote one of the earliest haunted). It posits a speculative haven in which consciousness may enlarge itself through imaginative solidarity with the author or through adversarial overcoming of self and society. And it accomplishes these tasks in large part through aesthetic surplus: a surcharged dynamism created by the clangorous juxtaposition of words, images, and discourses—a *something else* that evades or extends beyond that which can be categorized. Like the Hamlet who mobilizes Derrida's spectrality with his lament that "time is out of joint," the haunting force of Emerson has centered upon the problem of how best, in times of rapid and disorienting historical change or crisis, to act.

American Scholars in the twentieth century have been keenly susceptible to Emerson's version of aesthetic surplus. Like Hamlet, they have been compelled to engage with a ghostly precursor whose illusionary presence challenges orthodox descriptions of reality while at the same time encouraging them to imagine themselves as potential actors on the stage of human affairs. More specifically, they have felt called upon to follow Emerson's project of realizing American politics and culture by resisting it through a disruptive linguistic movement juxtaposed with brief, shimmering narratives of wholeness and integrity. The good luck as well as the misfortune of these particular scholars has been their sensitivity to Emerson's appeals as well as their urgent sense that such appeals needed conversion into modes of action that would reshape or redirect culture.

I am aware that to speak of Emerson in such terms is to evoke claims on behalf of the aesthetic that until quite recently were suppressed by the past two decades of literary scholarship. It is to hint at the undertheorized significance of authorial intention, the powerful half-life of prior interpretations, and the readerly appeal of authorial biography (Van Wyck Brooks went to Harvard because it was close to Concord, for instance; F. O. Matthiessen regularly took students to Emerson's house). More important, it is to suggest that while the conjunction of idea and image may persuade individual readers to perceive their world differently—and thus to think and behave in ways that rub against the grain of more coercive or absolutist thought and language—it does so in ways that are radically, and necessarily, volatile. Like that "evanescence and lubricity of all objects" which Emerson laments as always "slip[ping] through our fingers when we clutch hardest" (*EL* 473), his own essays provoke in readers an almost overwhelming desire to grasp at solid concepts and propositions—to *theorize* themselves into a vantage whereby truth might be envisioned—only to leave them clutching at air. It is in this expression of sheer movement, sheer transpositional *power,* that Emerson most suggests a refusal to accept modernity's normalizing impulses. It is also where he characteristically refuses to offer prescriptions.

If this form of writing provides little solace or guidance for those who feel pressure to take practical action—and this has been a fairly constant lament by many of Emerson's most sensitive readers—it does afford the kind of salutary self-complication Murray Krieger sees as exemplifying the relationship between formal object and social engagement: "In the everyday world of action, of decision-making, literature, unlike other discourses, does not help us decide so much as it warns us to distrust the decisions we make. When we are required to choose one path rather than another, it reminds us to tread with a light foot and a heavy heart."[7] Put another way, if abstraction invites us to imagine the possibility of achieving a commanding mastery over various grounds of knowledge or experience, Emerson's literary language asks us to imagine the opposite: a position embedded within a ravishing, chaotic, and profligate particularity that *may* suggest activity—but in ways always open to revision. This is by no means to privilege the aesthetic realm over that of the historical-political—to adopt without question what Terry Eagleton calls "the ideology of the aesthetic."[8] It *is* to imply the necessity for self-consciously and simultaneously deploying *both* modes of textual reception and interpretation, for leveraging the two against one another in the hopes of postponing that which can never be indefinitely postponed: an instrumentalization of literature and thought. My contention is that in the momentary grace provided by this tense opposition, in the surprised interregnum that occurs when the aesthetic bumps up against history and history bumps back, we might discover new ways of perceiving and belonging, new potentialities for being, new methods of understanding that may (but only if we are extraordinarily lucky) be marshaled "out there" in the world. This position, which Emerson consistently encourages and which I wish to examine within the context of some of his most perspicacious and influential followers in the field of literary and American studies, nevertheless incurs costs, both psychic and social, to be paid by the public intellectual, the literary critic, the American Scholar.

Emerson, Politics, and Aesthetic Transformation

For Emerson, the literary would be an always fertile, sometimes communal, site where he might address and even mold perspectives, sympathies, and ideologies. As a practitioner of the literary, he aspired to provoke aesthetic transformation by summoning public feeling and mobilizing affect as well as thought. But in creating his palimpsests of dense particularity and bristling contradictions—palimpsests fashioned by mining his journals to create collage-like assemblages of apothegms as well as by deliberately eliminating transitions from thought to thought so that the reader is forced to construe meaning in the spaces between sentences—he ensured that the desire for closure or unity would be piqued and then thwarted, and that any gesture toward action would be complicated by self-awareness and doubt.

We can glimpse an early example of this process by pondering the year 1834—what Robert D. Richardson has described as Emerson's "year of wonders," marking the author's growth as a poet, his move to Concord, and the gradual receding of his well-known problem of vocation.[9] This year is of interest less because of any technical advances Emerson made as an essayist or for any insights influencing his philosophy than because it reveals him engaged with the issue of political discourse and with working out a way in which to enlarge and at the same time undermine the meanings contained within that discourse.

In 1834 the Whig Party had formed in response to the increasing consolidation of the Democratic Party, while a series of riots in Boston and elsewhere along the Eastern seaboard marked "the opening salvos . . . of a new period of civil disorder in Jacksonian America."[10] These events, especially as they were manifested in two disruptive New York electoral contests avidly followed (and in one case attended) by Emerson, allowed him to conceive of politics for the first time as a dynamic contest not so much over ideas as over the *verbal representation* of ideas. Noting in his journal that "the idea is deep & pervades the whole mass of men & institutions," Emerson concluded a post-election entry with a radically new understanding that it was "words the antagonist party oppose & revile & therefore on these . . . the battle is fought" (*JMN* 4: 430). This surprisingly modern insight, rich in its Foucauldian implication of language saturated by power, helped Emerson initially to conceptualize the means by which a dynamic cultural resistance could be mounted. It allowed him to join his notion of the soul to progressive rather than reactionary politics—to democratic individualism instead of the older politics of class deference and privilege endorsed by his family and his milieu of Unitarian Brahmins. But while this progressive impulse would inform such major reformatory treatises as "The American Scholar," "Man the Reformer," and "The Young American," it did so in a language that deliberately distanced and reduced "the battle" between "antagonist" parties by contrasting the paltry and instrumental aims of political rhetoric with the polysemous array spun from language's simultaneous knitting and unraveling. The contentious New York elections, in other words, eventually enabled Emerson to think about the literary as a mode capable of complicating and troping (complicating *through* troping) political representation, while at the same time holding out the possibility of transforming and even activating individuals.

In some rather striking ways, Emerson's position in 1834 prefigures that of many public intellectuals throughout the twentieth century who felt compelled by various cultural exigencies and opportunities to reshape a moment of crisis through an active imagination (a Hegelian *Vernunft*) felt to be threatened by the bureaucratizing forces of politics, commerce, or culture. Critics and public intellectuals such as Van Wyck Brooks, F. O. Matthiessen, and Perry Miller shared during disparate cultural moments a common sense that history had failed, that the present existed as crisis or upheaval and seemed, as a result, susceptible to change through cultural suasion. Unlike these subsequent (and largely secular American Scholars), Emerson, convinced that "men are convertible" and "want awakening," felt his aspirations to transform culture authorized by his religious sense that "the highest revelation is that God is in every man" (*JMN* 4: 84). His scholarly conception of calling as something both enriching to the self and additive to society—a conception he effectively ghostwrites for later public intellectuals who will displace the Over-Soul with formulations of America, democracy, the Other, or a fluid and flexible identity—is particularly apparent in a February journal entry: "A new audience[,] a new Sabbath affords an opportunity of communicating thought & moral excitement that shall surpass all previous experience, that shall constitute an epoch[,] a revolution in the minds on whom you act & in your own" (*JMN* 4: 266). In many ways, this emerging sense of vocational destiny and social conversion was brought into sharper relief by Emerson's confrontation with the obdurate fact of Jackson's Democratic Party—a party (according to Maurice Gonnaud's still excellent account) that resembled nothing Emerson "knew either from experience or from history, which scattered to the winds the great national tradition Washington had inaugurated and which seemed to be leading America into an abyss of disorder and violence."[11] Jacksonian democracy challenged Emerson's understanding of his historical moment by promulgating the inherent worth of the individual even as it encouraged the grasp and scramble of uninhibited materialism. In his response to the political party Emerson oscillated between millennial optimism in the approaching transformation of society and despair over the apparently insurmountable divisiveness of a covetous and distinctly uncivic life. While sympathetic to the conservative ideals of a patrician stewardship then in the process of being reformulated by the Whig Party, he began increasingly to investigate areas of overlap and correspondence in his conception of self-reliant individualism and Jacksonian democracy. In a typical gesture, he framed these efforts within the benevolent context of a higher "moral law," struggling to situate his lived historical moment in the progressive flow of Romantic philosophy and to realign the often disappointing *now* into a pattern of utopian process and telos. "There is a revolution in this country now, is there?" he complained during the spring of 1834 in a journal passage that abruptly shifts—metamorphoses, as it were—into an ameliorating historical perspectivism: "The Jackson men have made their fortunes; grow old; die" (*JMN* 4: 287). Emerson's effort to absorb the threat of the Democrats into a grander conception of organic growth is particularly evident in a contemporaneous passage that begins with a cancelled passage—"*I am sorry to*"—and then swerves into utopian endorsement: "Good is promoted by the worst. Don't despise even the Kneelands & Andrew Jacksons. In the great cycle they find their place" (*JMN* 4: 281).

In a similar vein, Emerson would tentatively link Democratic politics to his vocational aspirations, reconceiving the upstart party as a potential, if temporary, ally. "We all lean on England, scarce a verse, a page, a newspaper is writ in imitation of English forms, our very manners & conversation are traditional and sometimes the life seems dying out of all literature," he wrote in June. "I suppose the evil may be cured by this rank rabble party, the Jacksonism of the country, heedless of English & of all literature" (*JMN* 4: 297). In this speculative, even despairing, mood, he again abruptly changes course and imagines the Democrats as performing a necessary service by destroying ossified forms—social and aesthetic—and clearing the ground for individuals in a metamorphic process by which "Societies, parties are only incipient stages[,] tadpole states of man as caterpillars are social but the butterfly is not" (*JMN* 4: 308). Still, Emerson would not be nearly so interesting if he simply channeled historical obstacles into the optative language of denial. The mood of amelioration is in fact often colored by a darker, if complimentary perspective, as when he notes how the Jacksonian revolution threatens to clear away culture altogether—and with it any chance that a prophet-artist might initiate a transformation of the social, economic, and political system of individualism into the realization of an independent, autarchic self.[12]

For Emerson, this dilemma culminated during and after the November election in New York—an election that was part of a larger pattern of divisive politics and disruptive riots that swept up and down the Atlantic coast and seemed to signal, in Richard Hofstadter's words, "the pathology of a nation growing at a speed that defied control, governed by an ineffective leadership, impatient with authority, bedeviled by its internal heterogeneity."[13] Citing 1834 as a pivotal year in an era of rapid industrialization and urbanization, a year made even more fraught by a rising tide of immigration and a brief financial panic, Carl E. Prince attributes the rash of civic disturbances to the "huge gap" so often described as obtaining "between perception of the American dream and its untenable reality."[14] While Emerson sought at times to obscure this gap by airily dismissing "such disfigurements as Antimasonry or Convent Riots or General Jackson & the Globe" (*JMN* 5: 29), his developing politics, if not yet his aesthetics, were indelibly shaped by a social context in which, according to David Grimstead, "there was in some men's minds a sense of a real possibility of social disintegration."[15]

If the riots that accompanied New York City's 1834 elections indicate heated partisan conflict, they also mark the development of a Whig strategy to retain power by appropriating the discourse of democracy (*propaganda* might be a more accurate word) increasingly favored by a newly expanded electoral franchise. This strategy has since been seen as part of a larger trend wherein antebellum speakers, adjusting to the groundswell of Jacksonian sentiment throughout the country, increasingly jettisoned lofty eloquence and adopted instead a rhetoric of the "common" people. It caused American lexicographer Noah Webster to complain in 1837 that the prevailing commonplace that "the *people* can govern themselves and that a *democracy* is of course a *free government*" was voiced by political speakers who "have never defined what they mean by the *people* or what they mean by *democracy*."[16] Such strategies were particularly common to New York election politics, which Marvin Meyers portrays as characteristically "a war of words arraying hostile persuasions under rival party standards. The protagonists found a public eager to receive its own unformed sentiments toward social ways and institutions in pointed rhetoric, and to respond with votes and loyalty."[17]

The New York City Election Riots of April 8–10, while more violent and sustained than the election disturbances that revisited the city in November, provoked less of a response from Emerson for the simple reason that he was in Boston when they occurred. But the riots—and the political agons they violently emulated—were by no means remote to him, especially since his older brother William lived in the city. Political animosity between Whigs and Democrats were displayed in the New York streets with partisan parades and rallies that turned increasingly violent. By the third election day, matters had escalated to such an extent that a group of Whig voters captured the city arsenal and armed themselves with guns against club-wielding Jacksonians. Philip Hone, a prominent Whig and former mayor of New York, expressed patrician outrage at the volatile events by lamenting in his diary that "respectable persons were beaten and trampled in the mud" by "Irishmen of the lowest class." But he viewed the election results, which placed a Jackson candidate in the mayoral office but gave control of the city council to the Whigs, as "a signal triumph of good principles over violence, illegal voting, party discipline, and the influence of officeholders."[18] Addressing his brother William after the tumultuous elections, Emerson reiterated this party line by casting the Whig's political gains as a provisional victory for the party's moral politics: "Thanks from all good men to the patriots of your city & yet the times make the sanguine despair."[19]

Six months later, when Emerson visited his brother in order to serve as a substitute minister in Manhattan, his trip coincided with yet another election—this time to determine who would serve as governor for the state. Attending a number of preliminary campaign speeches and anxiously following the election, Emerson experienced firsthand a highly partisan contest characterized by Gay Wilson Allen as a "violence of words, noisy demonstrations, and, as the November election drew near, by actual rioting in the streets."[20] Once again, competing national ideologies were manifested at the local level; attending a "Merchants' Meeting at the Exchange," Emerson heard the upcoming election described as a mandate "to decide whether the principles of General Jackson are approved and ratified by the people, and whether Mr. Van Buren is to be his successor. . . ."[21] His initial response to the threat posed by the New York Democrats was to transform obstacles into opportunities: "Let the worst come to the worst & the Whig cause be crushed for a season & the Constitution be grossly violated[,]" he notes, "then you would see the weak Whig become irresistible" (*JMN* 4: 334). But he soon began to imagine an opportunity within the historical mistake of Democratic domination whereby the literary intellectual might make a difference. If civil discourse was disrupted by "the outrages of the mob," order would be restored by the poetic Seer who could peer beyond the present tumult and announce the promise of the future: "the best sign which I can discover in the dark times," Emerson wrote consolingly in New York, "is the increasing earnestness of the cry which swells from every quarter that a systematic Moral Education is needed" (*JMN* 4: 326).

To this point, Emerson has yet to register the Whig's accession to Jacksonian egalitarianism—or at least to its rhetoric of democracy. The party's willingness to invoke the cause of the people—a crucial tactic if it was to contend at all in the political arena redefined and controlled by Jackson—is nevertheless suggested in one of the resolutions adopted at the merchants' meeting attended by Emerson: "*Resolved,* That relying on the *sound sense of the people* to repel any such wicked attempt, to *respect the right of all citizens* and to preserve the public peace, we will, undismayed by such threats, exercise all our rights, perform our sacred duties at the poll, and use every legitimate means to insure a fair election and a successful result."[22] Hone, who spoke at this meeting, seems positively invigorated by the response to his newfound "egalitarianism"; as he recorded in his diary with the characteristic tone of priggish self-congratulation, his speech was "one of the few cases in which I succeeded in satisfying myself, and judging by the applause I received I was not alone in my opinion."[23]

For Emerson, the merchants' meeting elicited a far different response. He noted in private that it was "rather humiliating to attend a public meeting such as this New York Caucus last evening & see what words are best received & what a low animal hope & fear patriotism is" (*JMN* 4: 327). Dismayed by the boastful tone of Hone's speech, Emerson seems genuinely surprised to find the Whigs guilty of attempting "to secure the votes of that numerous class . . . of indifferent, effeminate, stupid persons who in the absence of all internal strength obey whatever seems the voice of their street, their war, their town, or whatever domineering strength will be at the trouble of civilly dictating to them" (*JMN* 4: 328). The entire political process, he now saw, was an amoral exercise in trying "to get the hurrah on our side. That is the main end" (*JMN* 4: 333). Of particular concern was the manner in which the Whigs, by courting the votes of "stupid persons," undermined the authority of a cultural elite and thereby jeopardized the ethical underpinnings of his vocational project.

Disappointed by the platforms of both parties, Emerson characteristically strove to sublimate his revulsion and discover the moral principles governing these proceedings. In what verged on a kind of cosmic despair, he wrote five days before the election, "I believe in the existence of the material world as the expression of the spiritual or real & so look with a quite comic & condescending interest upon the show of Broadway. . . ." Yet the November election continually recalled Emerson from the "condescending" speculation he craved, forcing him by its very concreteness to reassess contemporary politics within the immediate framework of his self-definition as a writer-lecturer. Much like the Whigs, he seems gradually to have understood that to reach an audience he would need to adopt the language of democracy to advance his transcendental conception of the self. Unlike the Whigs, this appropriation would be less in the service of acquiring power or in advancing up the social order than in resisting or at least subverting that power in order to offer an alternative version of society. Unable to discover tangible value in the actions of either parties once the election began, Emerson noted, "Whilst it is notorious that the Jackson party is the *Bad* party, . . . on all the banners equally of tory & whig good professions are inscribed. The Jackson flags say 'Down with corruption!' 'We ask for nothing but our Right.' 'The Constitution, the Laws,' 'the Laboring classes,' 'Free trade,' &c &c" (*JMN* 4: 332).

This conceptual shift—from concern with political process to concern with the *representation* of politics—marks a notable development in Emerson's conception of the literary intellectual. More than a recognition of the suggestive power of party sloganeering (though that, as well), Emerson's focus on the representation of political ideas suggests what Giles Gunn describes as "symbolic revisioning," in which "to reenvision America critically is not at all to remove this process from the realm of symbols but to reconceive the nature of the symbolic realm itself and of the potentially critical as well as expressive, not to say ethical, processes that go inside it."[24] If, on the one hand, it is to promote the imaginative realm over and above the narrowly political in the struggle to interpret and make meaningful the vagaries of daily life, it is also, on the other, and however unwittingly, to embue *culture itself* with the power of hegemonic coercion that would be discerned by subsequent critics of the twentieth century.[25] Recognizing the Jacksonian representation of human worth as potentially commensurate to his own belief in the primacy of the self, Emerson came to understand the actional possibilities inherent in this fluid yet powerful "realm of symbols." "Should the Whig party fail, which God avert!" Emerson wrote during the November elections, "the patriot will still have some confidence in the redeeming force of the latent i.e. deceived virtue that is contained within the tory party" (*JMN* 4: 332). As the election approached, the journal entries suggest that as the public sphere became saturated with various "good [if latent, or deceived] professions," notions of society and citizenship would be increasingly mobilized and even constituted by symbolic discourse. For a public speaker hoping to build upon the epochal reformation of society initiated centuries earlier by Luther and transposed to the New World imaginary by Puritan and Revolutionary forefathers, the redirection of public consciousness might occur once these popular symbols had been captured from their narrow usage and reinvested with the latent and generative virtue they formerly expressed or might express anew in variant modalities.

If we ceased our examination of Emerson's development at this moment, we might understand the author as little more than another polemicist in an antebellum version of the culture wars. But the truly

significant question about Emerson's awakening to the malleable power
of political discourse is not so much how effectively he marshaled it to
promote social change, but rather why he found it necessary, finally, to
aestheticize that discourse: to trope the language of Jacksonian sloganeering in ways that sought to undermine its more coercive and instrumental
designs and to enrich it in ways that opened onto indeterminate possibility. To begin to answer that question we must first recognize that for
Emerson, political discourse was always folded into a larger theory of
expression that thwarted the constrictive determinism of ideologies. The
power of multivalent symbols, he characteristically writes in "The Poet,"
"drives men of every class to the use of emblems." "The schools of poets,
and philosophers, are not more intoxicated with their symbols, than
the populace with theirs. In our political parties, compute the powers
of badges and emblems. . . . Witness the cider-barrel, the log-cabin, the
hickory-stick, the palmetto and all the cognizances of party" (*EL* 454).
For Emerson, the political use of symbolic language is disappointing not
only for its grotesque attempt at coercion but for its failure to recognize the power of open-ended language that might awaken the reader
from the drudgery of convention and rote behavior and into the assertive
awareness of a universe alive with soul-enlarging vitality.

Emerson juxtaposes the top-down hierarchical imposition of ideology with the literary's leveling capacity for sympathetic transformation in
terms of the parent-child relationship, noting that "all public ends look
vague and quixotic beside private ones. . . . If I put myself in the place of
my child, and we stand in one thought, and see that things are thus or
thus, that perception is law for him and me. We are both there, both act.
But if, without carrying him into the thought, I look over into his plot,
and, guessing it is with him, ordain this or that, he will never obey me.
This is the history of governments" (*EL* 567). If the force of his argument
is subverted by the substitution of one form of authority (parental) for
another (political), the salience of the passage remains in its conception
of an ethical *carrying of others* into an imaginative space of shared thought
and perceptions that will, in Emerson's cosmology, eventually lead to a
higher plane of consciousness and shared action. How to accomplish this
task is addressed, among other places, in "The Poet," which describes
the artist as one who "will *draw all men* sooner or later" (*EL* 448; my
emphasis), suggesting once again an imagined community conjured into
existence by the poet and capable of effecting a kind of conversion. If
this yearning for transformative communion is shaped by the Romantic poet's desire to alter the rational order of Western culture, it escapes
an overweening authoritarianism by continually shifting its emphasis to
the aggregate readers who are meant to *share equally* in the blessings of

vision, as well as to the "accidency and fugacity of the symbol" (*EL* 456). Discussing "a youth" who had "gone rambling" one day and "written hundreds of lines," only to discover that in the process "all was changed," Emerson recalls his own participatory reception of this aesthetic experience: "How gladly we listened! how credulous! Society seemed to be compromised" (*EL* 450–451). In the last sentence meaningful social change occurs, or *seems* to, not so much through the determined slogans of politics—what today we would refer to as the struggle to hegemonize a field or population, to administer or bureaucratize the imagination—but rather from the foundation-shaking properties of an aesthetic language that absorbs and tropes all slogans and platitudes in order to reveal their susceptibility *to change*.

"The American Scholar" is the example *par excellence* of an Emersonian effort to achieve transformation by means of the wildly destabilizing and contradictory energies of the symbolic and linguistic. This transformation, which relies upon the attentive reception of language, perspective, and tone, is designed less to direct behavior in any specific or actionable way than to create a cognitive-affective imaginary within which a person may feel perceptually exhilarated and empowered, goaded into a greater awareness that *may* lead to a sense of self-overcoming. By creating an impression of endless potential wherein available cultural materials are troped and in this protean troping made ever new, Emerson's writing offers to expand the reader's horizon, and in this hypothetical offering encourages that reader to factor this *newness* into his or her behavior.

Addressing the issue of action as it intrudes upon the practice of (and in) "The American Scholar," Emerson distinguishes between past and present deeds in a passage that can best be described as rhapsodic:

> The actions and events of our childhood and youth, are now
> matters of calmest observation. They are like fair pictures in the
> air. Not so with our recent actions,—with the business which we
> now have at hand. On this we are quite unable to speculate. Our
> affections as yet circulate through it. We no more feel or know
> it, than we feel the feet, or the hand, or the brain of our body.
> The new deed is yet a part of life,—remains for a time immersed
> in our unconscious life. In some contemplative hour, it detaches
> itself from the life like a ripe fruit, to become a thought of the
> mind. Instantly, it is raised, transfigured; the corruptible has put
> on incorruption. Henceforth it is an object of beauty, however
> base its origin and neighborhood. Observe, too, the impossibil-
> ity of antedating this act. In its grub state, it cannot fly, it cannot
> shine, it is a dull grub. But suddenly, without observation, the

selfsame thing unfurls beautiful wings, and is an angel of wisdom.
So is there no fact, no event, in our private history, which shall
not, sooner or later, lose its adhesive, inert form, and astonish us
by soaring from our body into the empyrean. Cradle and infancy,
school and playground, the fear of boys, and dogs, and ferules, the
love of little maids and berries, and many another fact that once
filled the whole sky, are gone already; friend and relative, profession and party, town and country, nation and world, must also
soar and sing. (*EL* 60–1)

This passage—energized by lurching perspectives, fleeting tropes, the
masterful use of halting phrasal rhythms that compel us forward even
as we have to read and reread in order to fully absorb the content, and
the variations on a theme of rebirth or metamorphosis—may stand as
an exemplary sample of Emerson's aesthetic, informed to some extent by
Coleridgean organicism but by no means susceptible to the modernist
pressures for closure that would later make his writings so troubling to
midcentury aestheticians. The passage's key figures of transformation—
insect metamorphosis and fructification—suggest the exuberant joy of
troping Emerson discusses in "The Poet," the fondness for imagery that
reflects his notion of how language develops within the sentence or paragraph. We see also in this passage the "mysterious & delightful surprise"
he elsewhere describes as "that pleasure we derive from literary composi-
tions" (*JMN* 5: 278). Part of this jubilance comes from adopting a stubborn, adversarial stance toward a society ("profession and party, town and
country, nation and world") imagined as indifferent and against which
indifference the self is honed. To the extent that oppositional pleasure is
expressed, Emerson can be said to engage in cultural politics. But those
politics are distanced here through an aesthetic mode of plenitude and
surfeit that reveals itself as paradoxically more lifelike, more vitally participatory in the construction of the self than in any mere ideological
commitments.

Any close comparison of passages from Emerson's journals with their
published iterations reveals just how carefully he altered sentences to create a rhythmic pulse designed to compel the reader onward. These orphic rhythms are then released in such a way as to then bring the reader
up short. The repeated use of the stately and Latinate words *observation*
and *contemplation* is strategically deployed in the passage above so as to
be undermined by the mysterious alchemy Emerson describes wherein
prior actions, "suddenly, without observation," are transmuted into wisdom. The substitution of *angel* for *butterfly*—derived primarily from
Dante's work of earthly transition, *Purgatorio*,[26] yet still satisfying in its

unexpectedness—suggests a fundamental tenet of imaginative writing: *Intention always transfigures itself.* Through the unexpected associative matrix created by word choice and image, by literary tradition, and through the temporal spaces that are always a part of composition and revision, authorial purpose is deflected and altered by aesthetic surfeit and thus becomes a model of indeterminacy and interpretive openness to be experienced as such by careful readers.

I do not mean to suggest that Emerson invariably subsumes the political into the aesthetic, or that in his writing the reader is allowed to escape into the realm of some transcendent ideality or linguistic pyrotechnics. (Emerson may at times seem to be precursor to the ungrounded free play of poststructuralism, but that by no means implies a shared purpose with its militant antifoundationalism.) Something other than escape is being modeled here—something we begin to see when we note that his writing is always a discursive hybrid, an admixture of the theological, philosophical, scientific, social, and aesthetic, each energized by transitionless juxtaposition, each incorporating another ad infinitum, each troping the forms in which these discourses find themselves delivered—and all this in ways that call such discursive modes into question even as it summons us to rethink or reimagine what we mean by *politics, religion, science.* "We can never see Christianity from the catechism," he characteristically announces, suggesting a literary predisposition interested not only in the shaping and reshaping of inherited, and seemingly fated, language, but in the experience imagined to precede language altogether (*EL* 409). The function of Emerson's poetics, finally, is not to substitute one ideology for another, but to assert the disappointing incompleteness of ideology itself.

Emerson admits as much in the passage of "Politics" that emerges directly from his earlier experience with the New York elections. If the nation is divided by "two great parties," he notes in the middle of that essay, an unfortunate reality is that "one has the best cause, and the other contains the best men." In a long string of negations that become hypnotic with repetition (the Whigs, for instance, do not "build, nor write, nor cherish the arts, nor foster religion, nor establish schools," etc.), Emerson leads us to his central assertion: "From neither party, when in power, has the world any benefit to expect in sciences, art, or humanity, at all commensurate with the resources of the nation" (*EL* 565). Such a statement may of course be interpreted as bourgeois mystification that substitutes a seemingly timeless or universal stasis for social change. Emerson's subsuming of politics within the "resources of the nation" might furthermore be taken as crucial evidence in the case for the author as entangled in exceptionalist ideology. But equally germane is the degree to which the sustaining narratives and contrastive language of this and other essays have demonstrably enlivened sentiment and electrified intellect for readers, creating responses where none before existed and in ways unavailable to the "political" or "social." "If we continue to require that literature save the world by becoming the new intellectual synthesis of morality, science, and politics," Daniel T. O'Hara has recently remarked, "then we are in danger of losing sight of what literature can really do"[27]—which is to grant us precisely the kind of idiosyncratic and contemplative experience Emerson repeatedly advocates.

"The American Scholar" as Disciplinary Ur-Text

With such thoughts in mind, we might turn again to "The American Scholar." It hardly needs repeating that Emerson's address has been received by generations of cultural workers as a call to action, a challenge to intellectual complacency, a provocation to more meaningful engagement with the world and the world of ideas—and as such it may be taken for one of the most influential utterances on this theme in American cultural and academic history. The essay's rapid perspectival shifts, its deployment of unusually coordinated images, even its martial pulse: many have attested to the work's combinative ability to leave one intellectually breathless and, paradoxically, self-validated. The way Emerson projects his presence into the essay, along with the manner in which this presence invites readers to participate in a utopian "work" that will result in "the conversion of the world" (*EL* 71), has made it a foundational text in American literary studies since the late nineteenth century.[28]

"Men such as they are," goes a typical passage, conjuring up the numbed and sluggish populace upon which the American Scholar will effect his or her work and then burlesquing the language of political warfare, "very naturally seek money or power; and power because it is as good as money,—the 'spoils,' so called, 'of office.' And why not? for they aspire to the highest, and this, in their sleep-walking, they dream is the highest. Waken them, and they shall quit the false good, and leap to the true, and leave governments to clerks and desks" (*EL* 66). Saturated with the same concerns that attended Emerson during the New York election, this passage invokes those "questions of language and representation" Eduardo Cadava describes as "inseparable from the transformative, and hence political, power at the heart of all of Emerson's writing."[29] It features Emerson's typical rapid shifts in tone (from derision and exhortation to apostrophe and rhetorical question) and the juxtaposition of competing vocabularies (the interpolated jargon of political spoils immediately offset by a hortatory language of aspiration that borrows from the political in order to supersede it). These three sentences further derive their power from Emerson's availing theme that human life is carried out on two separate planes of existence, the somnambulistic life "such as [it is]" and an infrequent but intense spiritual life imaged here as the "highest" aspiration imaginable, a "true[r]" perspective from which paltry politics and financial gain would dissolve in the blinding recognition of what, in "The Divinity School Address," Emerson calls "the moral sentiment." This bifurcated existence, this refractory "double consciousness" which he laments in "The Transcendentalist" and which forms nevertheless the core of his vision, is elsewhere parceled out between the Understanding and Reason, as in his journal elaboration of a "First Philosophy" written in June 1835 and comparing the "poet's personification 'Death in Life,'" or Understanding, with the vital, if intermittent, Reason, whose visitation is said to catapult us to "the top of our being; we are pervaded, yea, dissolved by the Mind" (*JMN* 5: 274). If it can ultimately be seen as a vestigial remnant from the Calvinist anatomy of grace, the soul-ravishing experience of God's inexplicable benevolence rushing undammed into the regenerate soul, it also has, as Cadava suggests, a specific social and political component.

In other words, the political situation observed firsthand by Emerson during the New York elections haunts the lineaments of "The American Scholar." If Emerson had viewed the rise of the Democratic party as ultimately contributing to an empowering individuality that might one day render political machinations unnecessary, so, too, in "The American Scholar" does he view the Panic of 1837 (the financial crash still unraveling while he composed his address) as an even more dire historical opening by which all Jacksonian striving for gain might be understood as the instinctual upward yearning by "[t]he sluggish and perverted mind of the multitude slow to open to the incursion of Reason" (*EL* 57). "Loud cracks in the social edifice," he would remark in his journal earlier in the spring, when "hard times" and "men breaking who ought not to break" were the result of a run on banks in New York (*JMN* 5: 304). "The world has failed" (*JMN* 5: 333), he notes several weeks later. In the social rifts created by crisis, Emerson viewed the possibility of progress—simultaneously a form of theological transfiguration and literary troping—linked to a broader moral development of the nation itself: an ascendance providing hope (one of the key words of the address) in an eventual "nation of men" that, as Emerson proclaims in the final sentence, "will for the first time exist, because each believes himself inspired by the Divine Soul which also inspires all men" (*EL* 71).

Emerson can speak so confidently, we know, because of his beliefs in the moral progress of the universe, in the correspondence of mind and benevolent universe, and in the deep connectedness of all humans by the

Over-Soul. The imagistic shorthand for these premises in "The American Scholar" is most evident, oddly enough, in the references to insects that run throughout the essay, an image he seems initially to have quarried in his journals shortly after the 1834 elections.[30] Time and again, the drowsing populace of a grasping U.S. are seen as "flies" (*EL* 66), as "young grub" (*EL* 59). "Men are become of no account," he elaborates. "Men in history, men in the world of to-day, are bugs, are spawn, and are called 'the mass' and 'the herd'" (*EL* 66). The force and aptness of this imagery lies not only in the "lowness" of its referent but in its potential for resplendent transformation—a transformation, moreover, that carries the experiential weight, as he hints in the address and, far more voluminously, in his journals, of having been glimpsed or intuited in his own moments of ecstatic transport.

The important point here is that Emerson's peroration has haunted generations of Americanists not only because of its convincing and performative suggestion that "the conversion of the world" might be practicable at times of social crisis but also because of its assigning a crucial role in this conversion to the literary intellectual.[31] The scholar, we are told, is "the world's heart. . . . [and] [w]hatsoever oracles the human heart, in all emergencies, in all solemn hours, has uttered as its commentary on the world of actions,—these he shall receive and impart. And whatsoever new verdict Reason from her inviolable seat pronounces on the passing men and events of to-day,—this he shall hear and promulgate" (*EL* 63–64). The vigor of Emerson's language derives in part from his effort to translate into syntax his deeply held belief that "[i]t is one soul which animates all men" (*EL* 67), and that hence, by "going down into the secrets of his own mind, he has descended into the secrets of all minds" (*EL* 64). But the suggestion coiled within that syntax—that America may fulfill its promise through the action of scholars "in all emergencies"—has remained of perdurable importance to the institutional development of American literary criticism and American Studies. It has consistently provided the American Scholar, imagined and putatively enacted by Emerson and, in turn, by those listeners and readers who continue the work outlined in the address, with a vocational role less concerned with the study or interpretation of "America" than with a mandate "to cheer, to raise, and to guide" that symbolic construction of national identity toward its ideal existence. This mandate accordingly would carry the greatest force during social and historical "emergencies" because, as Kenneth S. Sacks has noted, "At times of stress, idealism can offer hope and may carry the day. But at times of calm, few look for or wish to ponder so challenging a vision."[32]

Yet if Emerson's writing conduces to a sense of heightened purpose in those for whom the urgent work of cultural renovation is felt to result from perceived historical crisis, it simultaneously undermines any easy prescriptions for action desired by the reader. We get a sense of this by returning to the concluding sentence of Emerson's address: "A nation of men will for the first time exist, because each believes himself inspired by the Divine Soul which also inspires all men" (*EL* 71). If the reader has followed the vagaries of Emerson's argument up to this point and if the reader is susceptible to the unfolding rhythm and sound of Emerson's style; if the reader, perhaps discarding the theological underpinnings of the address, nevertheless glimpses an actional possibility tied specifically to a form of cultural work (the "hear[ing] and promulgat[ing]" of "the human heart, in all emergencies"); if the reader, moreover, promulgates his or her reading for a living; and if such a reader, finally, lives during a time of perceived cultural disappointment or alarm (and what reader won't?)—perhaps such a reader will see in Emerson's address a significant utterance to be appropriated and mobilized in ways suitable to the given moment. Certainly readers of the past have responded this way, as the subsequent chapters of this book shall reveal. But it is necessary to again take note of the language set forth in Emerson's final line: "A nation of men will for the first time exist, because each *believes himself inspired* by the Divine Soul which also inspires all men" (*EL* 71). At stake here is a temporal belief, a conviction of a future event not yet fully realized in the present, an eventuality that exists *textually* in Emerson's address as possibility and little else. That such belief is primarily textual can be discerned in the seemingly offhanded linkage Emerson assigns this belief and its apparently foregone ability to "inspire . . . all men," a claim that adroitly slips out of the future tense and into a confident present that has been belied by the address's repeated focus on the historical "iron lids" that oppress the soul's unfettered action. A hypothetical future, in other words, is endorsed by a groundless but rhetorically effective claim of inevitability that in turn becomes a device of closure. If this can be taken as an example of wishful thinking on Emerson's part, I take it also as part of the conceptual shift I described above by which the author became increasingly concerned not so much with political processes as with the symbolic representation of politics. I see Emerson, in this final sentence, attempting to rewrite or transvaluate the language of nationhood—a language previously contaminated by the "spoils of office"—in order to effect a cheering transformation in consciousness that will begin at the site of language and proceed in directions left to the vagaries of the future. Emerson is able to conceive of this project now because he understands the symbolic realm to be not only expressive but also critically self-reflexive. "The nation of men" Emerson envisions at the beginning of this sentence is an example of conventional political representation set in motion *not* to enact hegemonic coercion but rather to chip away at political authoritarianism by bringing to the attention of his readers the accidency and fugacity of all political symbols.

By now it should be apparent that Emerson's foremost accomplishment is textual, even literary. Yet if I ended my discussion of "The American Scholar" here, I would essentially be reiterating structuralist orthodoxy that sees in Emerson—in all writers—primarily a linguistic event. This approach would so heavily invest the ability of language to shape and order the world that all politics not constituted by language would dissipate in a vapor of unreality. Such a move would render a disservice to the recognition within Emerson's writings that we become open to the world at the moment we discern in our troping the limits of language. Put another way, access to worldly activity is granted in Emerson's writing only once we refuse to settle for the limits of language, to measure language against the world. This cautious measuring is visible, I believe, in those shifting verb tenses that prickle through the last sentences of "The American Scholar" and leave the reader conceptually upended, looking for support. "We will walk on our own feet; we will work with our own hands; we will speak our own minds" (*EL* 71), Emerson prophesies just before the final sentence, directing our attention toward future actions that currently exist only within the text, that have yet to occur. These actions, moreover, are formative contributions to that "nation of men" that "will for the first time exist." Yet for Emerson, excessive claims about the constructive aspects of language seem finally to cede too much control to a dominating other; more specifically, they replace God or the "Divine Soul" with language.[33] It is the final reference to this Soul, "which also inspires all men," that calls the reader up against the refractory moment in which "all men" are clearly *not* inspired, in which language's ability to forecast such an eventuality is called to account by the world's own claims and proofs. In this tense standoff, thought and action, language and reality, aesthetics and history are leveraged against each other in taut irresolution. "If . . . every aesthetic representation is skewed away from transcriptive realism by its own formal law, *and* by historical circumstance, *and* by individual psychology," Helen Vendler wisely remarks, then "no direct ethical injunction to life-action can be deduced from the apparent intimacy with the past [or a future] that a symbolic object seems to create."[34] In the final sentence of "The American Scholar," Emerson can be seen to haunt himself with the possibilities and limitations of social change as it is imagined through an aesthetic realm always conditioned by but always resistant to history.

The problem, then, isn't so much that successive generations of scholars have either heeded or failed to heed Emerson's call in "The American Scholar." Rather, it is that they have too often collapsed the aesthetic energies of Emerson's literary writing within their own instrumental readings or, conversely, granted those energies unrealistic capabilities that have suggested heaven on earth, teleology, and transcendence. Straining to coerce practical and predictable results from a mode of experience that can best be described as ontologically inessential and therefore, miraculously, absolutely essential to our well-being, they mobilized instrumentalism to attack a larger instrumentalism. They yearned to convert "America" into a fulfillment of its highest promises, and by doing so, Emerson's ghosts have found in "The American Scholar" the ur-text of their cultural projects and, at times, the founding document of their disillusionment.

Renewing American Literary Studies

The following book examines the cultural contexts of Emerson's construction from roughly the period of his death unto our own times, and it does so by focusing on a series of influential paradigm makers whose involvement with Emerson reflects wider social and political engagements with the idea of "America." Despite changes of emphasis in these critics' various readings of the Emersonian canon, the most important text for their activity *as* critics was "The American Scholar"—a figure they sought to reenact in ways that continue to structure the fields of American literary criticism and American Studies. Theirs is a story of how the interplay of culture and personality served to create new versions of Emerson, and how those versions became variously institutionalized as working frames of reference for others. More important, it is a story about the rise of American literary criticism and American Studies, about the way these fields have been activated and defined by efforts to oppose or critique the instrumental hegemony of American modernity.

The examples of critics such as Van Wyck Brooks, F. O. Matthiessen, Perry Miller, and Sacvan Bercovitch are compelling, I believe, for the way they prefigure and parallel our own critical moment—the way they suggest in different manners both the urgencies and the consequences of those urgencies to make literature matter in the world. What so haunts these gifted and perceptive critics should also haunt us—for each experienced firsthand the transformative experience of literature in general and of Emerson in particular. Moreover, their lives were radically altered by this encounter, which they variously experienced as Truth, Beauty, Action, and Culture. Their difficulties arose when they sought to reactivate that transformative experience in order to remake the world. Their haunting, in other words, stems finally from the inability of Emerson's forceful prose to enter as directly into the economic or political realm as it had into them. This inability to effect the social change they so urgently desired suggests, moreover, the inability of prose to affect diverse readers in precisely the same way.

I choose not to see this as a failure of either Emerson or literature—for while literature is deeply implicated in the political, and while certain literary works have demonstrably affected social progress, the literary *per se* by its very nature does not act directly on the political realm. Emerson's ghosts wildly overestimated the effects of literature on politics, but only because of literature's uncanny ability to produce such strong feelings in the first place. Still, if the literary exerts only the most attenuated pressure upon cultural criticism, what it manages far more convincingly is what Hartman describes as "its famous 'concreteness' or illustrative energy," which provides "counterexamples to disembodied thought and unearned abstraction."[35] Emerson's essays, despite their surplus of imaginative play and frequent linguistic zaniness, reveal that no writing remains untouched by ideology or power.[36] But within this writing contaminated by historical processes, within this wrought and figured language, exists a mischievous awareness of its own *poiesis*. This self-awareness hints at a susceptibility to change and suggests, moreover, the fabricated quality of all discourse—particularly those forms of communication that assert claims of authority through naturalized signs or totalizing concepts.[37] Emerson's essays, in their restless flight from sentence to sentence, their disjunctive and metamorphic ruptures, are really palimpsests of available and competing discourses arranged in such a way as to thematize their made-ness, their appropriable nature, their resistance to facile manipulation. The examples of the critics examined in these pages suggest, among other things, that modes of substantial being may accrue when interpreters "listen" to texts with patience and respect as well as with a commensurate wariness against overidentification, reckless impersonation, or frictionless co-optation. They also suggest the dangers of entering into a monological relationship with texts, hinting at the professionally repressed empathic reading that has so often underwritten literary studies' overestimations of its power to direct the political realm.

Literary writing enabled Emerson to create a self or persona characterized in part by the principled refusal to fully commit to any stance. This refusal, in turn, emphasized his sense that all such stances eventually invoke affiliation. Emerson repeatedly writes, thinks, and performs an absence of position, a centerless imaginative power that can never be fully domesticated. This absence of positionality is not analogous to the New Critic's apolitical stance, which as we know was politics by another name. Rather, it derives from the generation of multiple positions, none of which are allowed to predominate long enough to be resolved through dialectic sublation. And it constitutes one of the most durable models of cultural criticism we have.

"Pathology," Freud notes in *Civilization and Its Discontents*, "has made us acquainted with a great number of states in which the boundary lines between the ego and the external world become uncertain or in which they are actually drawn incorrectly."[38] If the aesthetic invariably calls attention to its artificiality, thus opening an illusionary space in which to gain distance from our commitments, instrumental interpretation runs the risk of eliding the boundary between ego and external world altogether—of triangulating the will of the critic, historical circumstances, and the perceived presence or absence of causal effect in literature's relations to those circumstances. Take, for instance, John Carlos Rowe's assertion, in *At Emerson's Tomb*, that "the liberal tradition of American literature," should be "evaluated in terms of the political and social achievements of specific historical movements."[39] In this formulation a demystified literature is judged by way of a simple algorithm: the goal of social justice × historical circumstance × literature's causal link to both = value. Such basic math gives short shrift to the literary's fulsome capacity to articulate experience while allowing us to experience articulation; it denies (or disapproves of) the experience of aesthetic interiority and dismisses the more difficult and indirect equation that attempts to factor in those forms of articulation that inspirit people.

The Emersonian revenant visiting American critics throughout the twentieth century is an admonitory presence that warns us, through literary language, that ideals, however seductive, always run the risk of pathology. For far too long American literary studies has historicized—always historicized—at the expense of more flexible approaches. (Previously, it followed the no-less instrumental edicts of the New Criticism.) If the fruit of this idealized praxis was the recovery of social contexts and marginalized voices, its rigidification into orthodoxy has become predictable and, too often, uninteresting, untransformative. "The grossest ignorance does not disgust like this impudent knowingness" (*EL* 475), says Emerson, writing about such determinism in "Experience," an essay I shall discuss in my final chapter as a work that might prove salutary for cultural criticism in the post-everything environment of current literary studies. The haunted past of American criticism suggests the need for a different approach from reflexive historicism or aestheticism, one that leverages the historical and the aesthetic against each other and forces its practitioners to ask themselves precisely what the two critical procedures might have to teach each other. It abjures us to strive for a fully contextualized account while simultaneously recognizing the aesthetic presence I have been discussing; it asks us to restore to the works we study both a refractory particularity that resists ideological critiques *and* a demystification that keeps us always mindful of those cultural objects that are the raw materials of the aesthetic.

In a letter to Perry Miller reflecting on the aesthetic creation of the self within a larger preoccupation with national identity, the poet Archibald MacLeish writes, "'A man is his decisions,' as you put it—and we Americans more than most. Or rather more *consciously* than most. From which consciousness flows that *self*consciousness as to who and what we are. And our awareness that we are not what we have always been . . . and not what we are inevitably becoming . . . but rather what we are going to *make* of ourselves."[40] The always quixotic effort to create a literary text may be of such compelling interest because it is so analogous to the always vulnerable process of forming a self, a personality, a viable subjectivity within a history that often seems disappointing. The experience of constructing such a self—the experience of chance-and-particularity, of metonymy and metaphor—may be precisely what leads the critic to adopt its inverse: those grand explanatory narratives that buffer the psyche made anxious by contingency and uncertainty. Whether such theories avow the autotelic artifact or the social efficacy of literature, they are designed to quell the fearsome doubts prompted by the abyss of living that is never fully teleological, never entirely comprehensible, never something we can satisfactorily fix or freeze within a critical framework. In this way, we might regard the critics described in the following pages as themselves aesthetic constructions, shaped by history yet struggling to create identities that might fund, however unpredictably, history-to-come; wavering, like the rest of us, within a ghostly realm bounded by untamed detail, on one side, and, on the other, reductive abstractions that nevertheless suggest actional propositions.

In truth, we still do not have a criticism supple enough to suggest how psychic needs and politics, interiority and the subtly felt but often contradictory pressures exerted by various cultural forces, intersect and vector in ways that make particular authors suddenly preeminent, suddenly powerful, suddenly *haunting*. In our determination to be determined—our drive to coerce literature into often predictable positions or politics that in turn take on the narrative of a fateful inevitability—we have rooted authors and readers in an only partial actuality. Many of Emerson's most perceptive critics grappled with the experiential openness mimicked by the aesthetic as well as with its countervailing opposite, the yearning for closure. Before we shrug off their exemplary responses to Emerson as the contextualized responses of minds entangled in the sticky web of ideology, we would do well to read their lives with close and sympathetic attention.

They are, after all, our critical ghosts. They are, to some extent, ourselves.

CHAPTER 2

Emerson in the Gilded Age

I n the decades between his death in 1882 and publication of his *Journals* in 1909–14, Emerson carried the weight of new and often contradictory meanings for contemporary artists, critics, and readers. During this period Emerson was reduced to a one-dimensional ideal even as his expressive and critical possibilities were broadened, enshrined as the originary spirit of American literature even as his literary and philosophical accomplishments were called into question. Speaking at Emerson's centenary celebration in 1903, John Dewey noted that while "literary critics admit his philosophy and deny his literature," philosophers "extol his keen, calm art and speak with some depreciation of his metaphysic."[1]

This statement is true for practically any moment in Emerson's remarkably long career in the American literary canon. But what makes the period immediately following his death especially interesting is the unprecedented cultural authority suddenly, almost spontaneously, attributed to him. During his life Emerson had been an enormously popular figure who spoke for the spiritual and literary beliefs, values, and attitudes of many nineteenth-century Americans. In death he became less a spokesperson than a symptom of cultural forces in struggle, a symbol in contention, an ideology susceptible to appropriation and alteration. Not yet a figure to be studied in academic sequestration, Emerson during the last decades of the nineteenth century was rather a *national* treasure.

Throughout the 1880s mass-produced engravings of his portrait hung throughout the nation's schools, colleges, and free libraries, each amply stocked with anthologies of an emergent American literature in which he invariably assumed an almost mythical role. His serene visage adorned magazine covers and the portico of the Library of Congress and became immortalized in marble at Harvard, the college he had scandalized half a century earlier with his "Divinity School Address." Hailed in 1882 as "the greatest of American men of letters"[2] and the figure who stood "preeminently for American literature to a foreign audience,"[3] Emerson officially entered the pantheon of "great" American authors when his essays were issued in the sumptuously prepared eleven-volume Riverside Edition of his *Complete Works* (1883–84). A decade later, the *Essays* were voted the nation's greatest literary treasure in the *Critic's* 1893 poll, and in 1903 an authoritative edition of Emerson's works, edited and annotated in a gesture of filiopiety by his son Edward Waldo Emerson, would commemorate the centenary of his birth.

Tracing the widespread sanctification of Emerson in the Gilded Age challenges schematic versions of canonicity that have arisen in the past two decades. For in fact the process of canonization as it was exerted on Emerson cannot properly be described either as monolithic or even consistently interested in enshrining the dominant culture. What his example suggests, rather, is that canonicity is best understood as the effort to establish a framework of accepted authors within which fierce cultural struggles may take place. Those struggles are the result of different parties with different agendas attempting to establish *their* version of an author as a "usable" ancestor capable of inspiring the present in order to create a desired future. And as has been the case more often than not, the desired future imagined through Emerson was one that resisted the materialistic basis of American modernity.

Emerson's ability to serve the interests of competing political and aesthetic interests is particularly apparent in those discussions of his personality and life that almost invariably overshadowed analysis of his writings.[4] These Gilded Age biographies of Emerson insisted on imagining his life as loftily detached from all social and historical references, containing, as Henry James commented, neither "the rapidity, or the complexity, that a spectator loves."[5] By focusing on an author so removed from everyday life, critics often managed to avoid the difficult task of interpreting his prose.[6] Critical analysis failed to adhere to an author whose works, in the words of a *Saturday Review* critic, were "more easily reflected upon than described, more easily felt than reflected on."[7]

Yet it was the very perception of Emerson's indefiniteness—both the eventless quality of his life and the uncategorizable nature of his writings—that enabled him to be made and remade by those who wished to shape and influence American culture and society during the last decades of the nineteenth century. We gain some sense of this in the Chicago *Dial*'s obituary, in which Emerson stands not so much for literature or philosophy as for having "done more than any other to hold in check the materialistic tendencies of the day."[8] Julian Hawthorne commemorated "the memory of him and the purity and vitality of thought and of the example with which he has enriched the world."[9] Versifying this sentiment in her lyric eulogy, "Concord. May 31, 1882," Susan Coolidge imaged Emerson "urging upward, year by year,/To ampler air, diviner light."[10] And in America's most influential periodical, *The Atlantic Monthly*, W. T. Harris described Emerson's importance to Gilded Age artists, critics, and readers in a simple formula: "All who saw him were inspired to live more ideal lives."[11]

The Emerson who emerges in late-nineteenth-century biographies, commemorative poems, and solemn frontispiece portraits is almost always a cultural ideal capable of acculturating and even improving individuals while at the same time justifying, and on occasion critiquing, institutional interests. This description is true of other authors as well: Richard H. Brodhead, in his discussion of the imaginative appropriations to which Hawthorne has been put, remarks that authors variously inspired by the novelist never simply confronted an enabling prior text but also faced "the institutional establishment that appropriated Hawthorne's texts and pressed their claims *and* the idea of literature that that establishment maintain[ed]."[12] What separates Emerson from Hawthorne—or from any comparable figure in American literary history—is the sheer range of appropriations, the prodigality of uses, to which Emerson's thought and writings were subjected. Oliver Wendell Holmes, seeking to describe the almost suffocating authority of his friend, imagined an "Emersonian atmosphere" engulfing American culture, permeating social discourse and limning art and its adjacent fields of philosophy, psychology, religion, and sociology.[13] If Hawthorne was an originary figure whom subsequent imaginative writers either imbibed or resisted for inspiration, Emerson is more properly understood as a figure of unparalleled *cultural* influence, an author whose far-reaching concerns and resonant vocabulary helped make available large tracts of late-nineteenth-century American thought to many who never even read his essays.

I.

In many ways, the biographies that helped create and transmute Emerson as a cultural icon during the 1880s and 1890s are symptomatic of an era characterized by a foreboding sense that once reassuringly finite boundaries of knowledge were becoming obsolete. New developments in scientific theory had undermined the foundations of theology. Cherished beliefs in personal autonomy and independence faced onslaughts from a wide range of sources, including expanding corporations, on the one hand, and populist and socialist movements on the other. Even the much vaunted sanctuary of Victorian domesticity suffered from strain and tension as men and women, enervated by what seemed increasingly barren gender roles as well as by a sense of powerlessness before large and impersonal forces, came to feel dangerously unmoored. Religious, moral, and political beliefs that legitimated cultural homogeneity and the authority of the family seemed increasingly beleaguered.[14]

Oliver Wendell Holmes's *Ralph Waldo Emerson* (1884), a best-selling volume in the American Men of Letters series and among the most influential book-length biographies of Emerson after his death, speaks to a historical moment in which the ideas and values that had once structured American middle-class life—and more particularly a declining New England patriciate—threatened to become detached from their meaning. Holmes's study seeks to shore up a vanishing era's waning ideals and values by attaching them to a conception of literature as an elevated repository of timeless truths that resisted the ambiguities of social process. As a result, the pantheon of great American authors in which Emerson is represented as the undisputed centerpiece—a pantheon that not incidentally includes Holmes and other Fireside Poets—is static and hierarchical, an immutable canon of taste and value imaged as shimmering high above changing political and economic actuality.[15]

To a great degree, Holmes's portrait follows a much larger pattern of literary sanctification established by the United States' genteel men of letters to enshrine Emerson as a cultural ideal set against the threatening forces of rapid industrialization, an "alien" immigrant population, and an insurgent literary realism that seemed to replicate the materialistic tendencies of the Gilded Age. This cultural project, which from the distance of a century appears almost hegemonic in scope, was largely the handiwork of Anglo-American authors who regarded themselves as cultural custodians, literary disciplinarians, curators of moral and aesthetic value. As Brodhead has suggested, our tendency to think of this era "by the historically dismissive term 'genteel'"[16] minimizes the extent to which such figures as Thomas Bailey Aldrich, Richard Watson Gilder, Edmund

Clarence Stedman, R. H. Stoddard, Bayard Taylor, George E. Wood-berry, and Barrett Wendell formulated a version of American literature that emphasized its special elevated quality and helped institutionalize that conception through editorships and contributions to the period's dominant magazines, including the *Century*, *Scribner's*, and the *Atlantic Monthly*. These figures may have deployed literature to articulate class identity, but they also acted on a faith that art might serve as a social uni-fier, providing an organic culture that in turn would form the basis for a more homogenous community. Literature, in this conception, was less an escape from a post-Darwinian world of harsh and impersonal ener-gies than a *solution* to it, an acculturating force with which to fashion a better nation and at the same time to provide a therapeutic haven for the individual fractured by the marketplace.[17]

One indication of the value attached to Emerson by these authors and critics is the number of times he appears in their lyric poetry—a poetry that in its dissociated aesthetics bears no resemblance to the now-canonical work of Whitman and Dickinson but that is characteristic of belletristic literature until roughly the First World War.[18] As William Crary Brownell explained in his 1909 essay on Emerson, "One feels in approaching any consideration of him, that his character is such as to implicate a lyric strain."[19] Edmund Clarence Stedman, who edited the immensely influential *Poets in America* (1885), speaks of Emerson in a lyrical apostrophe to the American sublime:

> High thoughts of thee brought near
> Unto our minstrel-seer
> The Antique calm, the Asian wisdom of old,
> Till in his verse we heard
> Of blossom, bee, and bird,
> Of mountain crag and pine, the manifold
> Rich song,—and on the world his eyes
> Dwelt penetrant with vision sweet and wise.[20]

George E. Woodberry, a successful teacher and critic who in 1907 wrote *Ralph Waldo Emerson* for the English Men of Letters series, recited an ode at Emerson's centenary services on 24 May 1903 that stressed the way in which Emerson as literary precursor had spurred genteel poets to become moral and aesthetic beacons for a nationally sanctioned human progress:

> So has our boyhood known,
> The heavenly glory felt in greatness gone
> . . . .

And him the first, whose early voice intoning
With pointing finger read God's primal truth.
From sire to son was stored the sacred seed;
Age piled on age to meet a nation's need . . . .[21]

And Richard Watson Gilder, whose poetry was given further authority by
his distinguished editorship of the *Century Illustrated Monthly Magazine*,
provides a distillation of genteel aesthetics, preoccupations, and anxieties surrounding the construction of Emerson as cultural icon in "To an
English Friend with Emerson's 'Poems'":

Edmund, in this book you'll find
Music from a prophetic mind.
Even when harsh the numbers be,
There's an inward melody;
And when the sound is one with sense,
`T is a bird's song, sweet, intense.
Chide me not the book is small,
For in it lies our all in all.
We who in El Dorado live
Have no better gift to give,
When no more is silver mill,
Golden stream, or iron hill—
Search the New World from pole to pole,
Here you'll find its singing soul.[22]

It is within this literary context that Holmes's celebration of Emerson's "light rhythmic" poetry and devaluation of the early essays is best
understood.[23]

Holmes was seventy-six when he wrote his biography of Emerson,
and much of the criticism he offers there, as it looks back on the enthusi-
asms of youth, can be attributed to the conservatism of age. To a man of
Holmes's generation, works such as "The American Scholar" had not, as
yet, come to be regarded as *literature* but seemed rather to belong to an
age of quaint juvenility, of hopeful, if somewhat amateurish, beginnings.
Certainly Holmes is not troubled by Emerson's incendiary sentiments
in *Nature* or "The Over-Soul." What *does* trouble him, however, is the
ease with which Emerson has been appropriated to authorize alternative canons of taste and values. Threatened with cultural superannuation,
Holmes's portrait of Emerson is an effort to memorialize, to inscribe his
Brahmin sensibility as a preferable order of things against the threat of
cultural oblivion posed by new forces at work in American life.

If Emerson is "a sweet-souled dealer in spiritual dynamite" (298) whose calling is "to supply impulses and not methods" (141), Holmes is careful to stress that the explosion he produced did not rattle beyond the crumbling walls of Calvinism. Unwilling to disrupt the established order of society, Holmes's Emerson repudiates not only the abolition movement but *all* reformatory causes. This rewriting of Emerson's actions makes sense when seen within the historical moment during which Holmes was writing. To many contemporary observers, the 1880s were characterized by numerous popular agitations that seemed harbingers of social cataclysm. Labor unrest attended efforts to institute an eight-hour day; populist movements increasingly entertained discussions of socialism; and the once (if always imagined) Anglo-American nation seemed increasingly diluted by waves of immigrants. Like other genteel critics, Holmes sought to counter what he perceived as the anarchic individualism of latter-day antinomians by claiming that Emerson's "largest and kindliest sympathy with their ideals and aims" (189) by no means represented an endorsement.

It is in this context that Holmes's chapter on Emerson's poetry must be read. As Len Gougeon has noted, the emphasis Holmes placed on that poetry is best understood as a conservative critique of an insurgent literary realism that violated conventional rules of social decorum and threatened to "reduce literary subject matter to a disgusting 'slop-pail' level."[24] Rescuing Emerson from those who would link the author's aesthetics to his celebration of "[t]he meal in the firkin; the milk in the pan; the ballad in the street" (*EL* 69), Holmes asserts that Emerson "was not often betrayed into the mistake of confounding the prosaic with the poetical, but his followers, so far as the 'realists' have taken their hint from him, have done it most thoroughly" (325). In so arguing, Holmes conveniently overlooks the Emerson of "The Poet," who proclaims that "distinctions . . . of low and high, honest and base, disappear when nature is used as a symbol" and who goes on to announce an aesthetics of the common: "Small and mean things serve as well as great symbols" (*EL* 454).

To some extent, Holmes's discomfort with insurgent realism is personal—the insecurity of an ambitious but aging author at a moment when American literary heritage seemed still very much up for grabs. His discussion of Emerson's poetry, then, was provoked by a barely discernible but still emergent countercanon of oppositional authors, who included Whitman, Thoreau, and Twain. This countercanon was making inroads significant enough to elicit Holmes's denunciation of Thoreau as "the nullifier of civilization, who insisted on nibbling his asparagus at the wrong end" (86) and of Whitman as an undiscriminating list-maker who "enumerates all objects he happens to be looking at as if they were equally suggestive to the poetic mind" (325). Mark Twain's infamous burlesque of Emerson (and Holmes) at Whittier's 1877 birthday party might be understood as the earliest example of the countercanonical effort to displace already cumbersome monuments of the immediate past—an effort that would soon explode in the fiery critical discourse inaugurated by Van Wyck Brooks within a generation. Conversely, Holmes's defensive claim that "Emerson is one of those authors whose popularity must diffuse itself from the above downwards" (315–6) is an effort to discredit the more earthbound texts of Thoreau, Whitman, and Twain.

Even more crucial to Holmes's discussion of Emerson's poetry is his sense that the American literary tradition—that American culture *itself*—is being assailed on all sides by forces capable of justifying themselves through willful misreadings and wrongheaded appropriations of Emerson. Announcing that it may be impossible to assign reasons for Emerson's fascination as a poet, Holmes proceeds to do so, albeit indirectly. Emerson's poetry may be guilty of "incompleteness" (339), of metrical simplicity, of "careless" versification and rhyme (329), but

> this we can say, that he lives in the highest atmosphere of thought; that he is always in the presence of the infinite, and ennobles the accidents of human existence so that they partake of the absolute and eternal while he is looking at them; . . . and that through all he sings as in all he says for us we recognize the same serene, high, pure intelligence and moral nature, infinitely precious to us, not only in themselves, but as a promise of what the transplanted life, the air and soil and breeding of this western world may yet educe from their potential virtues, shaping themselves, at length, in a literature as much its own as the Rocky Mountains and the Mississippi. (341–2)

In Holmes's analysis, the "serene" moral nature of his subject, most evident in his poetry, not only is separated from literary realism and the instrumental-materialistic world it represents but also is capable of ennobling "the accidents of human nature" and providing a teleology for both a native literature and that literature's cultural function. Yet if Emerson stands in Holmes's formulation for art's capacity to ameliorate a world diminished by the loss of faith and by political antinomianism, he does so primarily as a "serene, high pure intelligence and moral nature." This "moral nature" is of course a metonymic substitution for a once beloved idealism increasingly sublimated into a late-century sanctification of aesthetics—what George Santayana criticized in "The Genteel

Tradition and American Philosophy" when he asserted that a bland and idealized high-mindedness had hindered the ability of most Americans to confront or even recognize the conditions of their own modernity.[25] If Emerson failed as a writer to conform to contemporary and idealized aesthetic standards, his life was refashioned into an art object, an icon capable of transporting its devotee into a contemplative and anti-materialist realm. While the sanctification of Emerson's personality did not entirely replace his standing as a literary figure, it bleached out the hard conundrums of his prose, effectively eviscerating the extemporizing movement of his thought and writings. In a gesture that would become formulaic throughout the 1880s, Holmes conflates Emerson the writer with Emerson the man, subsuming aesthetic, philosophical, and political questions into exemplary biography and in the process illustrating the American literary tradition's efforts to blend its own halting creative efforts, "indestructible, with the enduring elements of civilization" (419).

II.

If we were looking for someone to stand opposite Holmes and his genteel portrait of Emerson, we could scarcely do better than Moncure D. Conway. Holmes was late-nineteenth-century America's embodiment of the genteel custodian of culture, one of its most prominent members in a brotherhood of taste and restraint. By contrast, Conway was one of the nineteenth century's notable (if now largely forgotten) nonconformists. His peripatetic career seems a veritable flow chart of the era's progressive preoccupations: a Methodist and then a Unitarian minister (Conway seldom remained still for long), he was also a prolific journalist and publisher, a historian whose *Life of Thomas Paine* (1892) is still a standard biography, an Ohio Hegelian, the leader of a free-thought congregation in London, a tireless advocate of women's rights and abolitionism, and an enthusiastic supporter of evolutionary theory.[26]

Conway's *Emerson At Home and Abroad* (1882), the earliest full-length study of Emerson after his death, is more personal recollection than objective reporting. If for Holmes *Nature* fell "like an aerolite, unasked for, unaccounted for, unexpected, almost unwelcome" (81), Conway's discovery of Emerson's essays during a crisis of vocation and religious belief at his Virginia home produced a "revelation." As Conway later confessed in his autobiography, the "glimpse of a vault beyond the familiar sky" provided by a passage of Emerson was a seminal moment that freed him from the social restrictions of his Southern childhood and led him to abandon the study of law for divinity.[27] Even as the more mature Conway came increasingly to distrust the "fog-bank of neo-Platonism" (his term for transcendentalism), Emerson remained his moral and intellectual pole star, not only an inspiration but a sometime collaborator. Conway's *Natural History of the Devil* (1859), which asserted that every animal is a human in arrested development, owed its central idea to a conversation with Emerson; his editorship of the reconstituted *Dial*, a successor to the earlier transcendentalist journal, was a tribute to his master. Even the role that lends Conway the most historical interest to contemporary scholars—his anomalous career as a Southern abolitionist—was by his own admission spurred by Emerson's faith in the unfettered self.

Conway's relationship to Emerson exemplifies the ways in which the author's influence extended well beyond the boundaries of the "literary" and helped to fashion individual lives. Henry Ford, in many ways the successor to the Gilded Age's robber barons, justified his role as a maverick capitalist by finding in Emerson a consoling image of the pragmatic realist who at heart was a transcendental dreamer. Frederick Jackson Turner, whose frontier thesis explained the progressive nature of American civilization, derived many of his ideas from the "perennially exciting" Emerson, whom he obsessively read and from whom he copied voluminous extracts (even as a professor at Harvard he was particularly fond of using Emerson's phrase, "the nervous, rocky West").[28] And Jane Addams, who as a young woman in Chicago fretted that Emerson might die before she could meet him, credited his faith in the "infinitude of the private man" as the source of her desire to open the progressive Hull House.[29]

Conway's response to Emerson is more closely associated with the idea of cultural change—more "radical" and dissenting—than in the cases just mentioned. Commemorating Emerson in his biography, Conway also presents him as a harbinger of things to come, a figure who not only discredits the ossified values and beliefs of the past, but promises the progressive fulfillment of egalitarian politics in the nation's future. The radical implication of Emerson's writings can be located in an aesthetics notable, Conway asserts, because "every word of Emerson began where authority ended."[30] To warrant such claims, Conway focuses on the early essays that had influenced him as a youth as well as the prefigurations of evolutionary theory discernible even earlier in *Nature*.

Relying upon the creative ethos of "The Poet," for instance, Conway asserts that American authors must eschew all tradition in order to apprehend nature authentically. Understanding Emerson's corpus as a repudiation of "all creators, whether scholars, preachers, politicians, or artists, who would borrow the oil of past ages or adjourn worthy work to the future" (223), he repeats Emerson's plea in "The American Scholar" for an art rooted in the everyday stuff of American experience and objects.

For Conway, Emerson's demand for a new aesthetic places him at the head of a poetic tradition to be more thoroughly exploited by Whitman, whose *Democratic Vistas* (1871) had provided a critique of the hierarchical conception of "culture" then being formulated by Holmes and the genteel tradition. It also installs Emerson as the founding spirit of a literature that "adheres strictly to the realms of actual knowledge and practical life, and sows its sound seed on real soil, and not on any cloudland of theory" (225). Unlike the poet described by Holmes, Conway's Emerson stands as a visionary precursor to a new kind of art founded on the radical similarity of all things and most closely aligned to America's insurgent literary realists: "The globule of blood and the rolling planet are one; a little heat more or less makes a bit of jelly a fish or a human brain" (109).

Still, for Conway, Emerson is ultimately less significant as a writer than as an example of a social catalyst. Emerson's role as cultural critic is not only amplified by Conway but transfused by his own requirements, which in turn are influenced by a broader historical context characterized by the ascendancy of empirical science and an intensified commercial and industrial environment that seemed to challenge a residual transcendental idealism. Despite his emphasis on the radical Emerson, Conway reflects the widespread yearning of postbellum American culture to reconcile traditional religious beliefs with inductive science: a trend that accounts for the immense popularity of the quasi-scientific theories of Herbert Spencer and John Fiske.

One of the most significant contributions Conway would make to subsequent Emerson studies was his linkage between the author's spiritual poetics and Darwin's theory of evolution; Emerson's far-reaching insights, Conway argued, made it "perfectly clear to him that the method of nature is evolution" (154). Conway rescued his subject from the backwaters of a prescientific past, at the same time freeing himself to imagine Emerson as a valid and relevant model for action and thought beyond the immediate historical context in which he wrote. Soon after encountering Darwin's ideas in the early 1860s, Conway enthusiastically incorporated evolutionary theory into a sermon as part of his efforts to rationalize religion, and he justified his claim by referring to the introductory poem found in the second edition of Emerson's *Nature*:

Now comes Darwin and establishes the fact that Nature is all miracle, without the special ones desired: that by perfect laws the lower species were trained to the next higher and the next to the next—until
Striving to be man the worm
Mounts through all the spires of form.[31]

Convinced that spirit rather than matter governs the upward progress of life, Conway asserts that "Emerson's view of evolution was a theory of Ascent" (158). Echoing Spencer's philosophy, which provided Americans with a description of reality in terms of process and progress rather than fixed classifications, Conway's Emerson conceives of man as a plant whose taproot might plunge down through the strata of natural history so that its flower and fruit would reach inexorably heavenward.

Conway deviates sharply from more traditional discussions of Emerson by claiming that his "theory of Ascent" explains and authorizes his role as social reformer and agent of cultural change. *Emerson at Home and Abroad* fits the pattern of many hagiographic memoirs to come, venerating Emerson's personality at the expense of more rigorous critical analysis, but it also accords its saintly subject the same position in American culture and history he had held in Conway's life: a catalyst of radical energy, a spokesperson for intellectual and spiritual freedom embattled against institutions that "prisoned the ideals of America in stoniest shrine" (95). The descendent of Puritans, Conway's Emerson redeems the old and rigidified religion by reanimating its spirit of democratic individualism. Moreover, historical patriarchs are deftly replaced in Conway's account by a spiritual mother: Anne Hutchinson, the antinomian Puritan banished for her religious heresy by John Winthrop.[32] In Conway's heated rhetoric, Hutchinson's "broken body and shed blood" provide "the sacrament of a New World covenant" capable of renovating the world (84). "She shares with Roger Williams the glory of having founded the first State on the planet organized on the principles of religious liberty" (82). While Oliver Wendell Holmes linked Emerson to his Puritan forefather, "the distinguished scholar and Christian" Peter Bulkeley, Conway rescues his subject from what he derides as "the frost of Calvinism" (22) in a passage that echoes Hawthorne's anxiety over his ancestry in "The Custom-House" section of *The Scarlet Letter*. "Peter Bulkeley, as we have seen, presided at the Synod which banished Anne Hutchinson. It is now visible as Bulkeley banishing Emerson" (82).

Connecting his subject's antinomianism with evolutionary theory, Conway describes Emerson's teaching as an injunction to social reform predicated on the indivisible unity and relatedness of humankind. As a result, "the essay on the Over-soul is the fullest expression which this central idea of his philosophy has reached." Emerson's democratic philosophy, which imagines "self-reliance to be self-surrender to the Over-soul" (108), leads to what Conway characterizes as his involvement in numerous social movements, including women's rights, associationism, and abolition. Describing his own politics as much as Emerson's, Conway is nonetheless original in his discussion of the influence on Emerson's

subsequent life and thought by his mother Ruth Haskins, his aunt Mary
Moody Emerson, and Sarah Bradford. Referring to Emerson's willingness
to lecture at the Second Annual New England Women's Rights Convention in Boston, Conway describes him as "among the earliest to demand
that the equality of woman with man should be represented in politics
and laws" (46). Indeed, equality is the keynote to Emerson's thought
throughout Conway's book. Brook Farm, the ill fated experiment in associative living, is portrayed by Conway as the inevitable outgrowth of
Emersonian transcendentalism. And Emerson's famous refusal to join the
experiment is softened by a sampling of journal entries from Hawthorne
and Margaret Fuller that reveal his frequent presence at the farm.

But the greatest cause to which Emerson lends his name and eloquence is that of abolition. "In every emergency during the anti-slavery
agitation," Conway writes, "and at each critical event in the national history, Emerson invariably spoke the right and serviceable word, as well
as the profoundest word" (309). Conway traces Emerson's anti-slavery
efforts to his willingness in 1831 to allow an abolitionist to lecture in his
church and discusses his important 1844 address on the "Emancipation
in the British West Indies." But his enthusiasm to prove Emerson's role as
an abolitionist leads to a stunningly inaccurate claim in which Emerson
is said to have convinced Lincoln of the practicability of emancipation
(313–4). In Conway's revisionary history, Emerson not only labors for the
cause of abolition but ultimately frees the nation's slaves. Commenting
on Emerson's poem about emancipation, the "Boston Hymn," Conway
notes, "Thus did the President of the literary, respond to the President of
the political Republic" (314).

III.

Conway's biography, like Holmes's, was widely praised in literary peri-
odicals. But its claims for Emerson as an agent of social, political, and
aesthetic change were largely overlooked. Instead, *Emerson at Home and
Abroad* received glowing reviews for its biographical interest and for its
authorization of New England's moral superiority concerning slavery.
Paradoxically, Conway's "radical" portrait of Emerson played a smaller
role in dethroning the genteel cultural ideal than what was arguably the
most restrained (and most perceptive) biography of Emerson written
in the decade following his death. James Elliot Cabot's 1887 *Memoir of
Ralph Waldo Emerson* focuses neither on Emerson's aesthetic accomplishments nor his social reforms, but on his philosophy. Incorporating

materials unavailable to other contemporary biographers, including private papers, journals, and letters to which he had access as Emerson's literary executor, Cabot examined the philosophical implications of the open-ended form in which Emerson chose to present his ideas. He embarked on this enormous project, he confessed in his preface, "to furnish materials for an estimate of [Emerson], without undertaking any estimate or interposing any comment beyond what seemed necessary for the better understanding of the facts presented."[33] If the result was an idealized portrait of "pure spirit"—a portrait, as Henry James remarked, that provided a "singular impression of paleness"—it was also the first intellectual history of Emerson, disclosing, as Horace Scudder wrote, "Emerson's conscious relation to his own thought."[34]

A fellow lecturer in philosophy with Emerson during Harvard's 1870 academic year, Cabot was a regular member of the Saturday Club and, more importantly, Emerson's literary executor. During the last six years of Emerson's life, Cabot not only organized the jumbled papers of more than four hundred lectures, but he also gathered that material for new "synthetic" lectures and essays, often completely reconstructing Emerson's manuscripts for an aphasic author whose declining mental faculties made such chores impossible. Before and after Emerson's death, Cabot collected and catalogued correspondence and more than 180 journals and notebooks, and he supervised publication of the 1883 Riverside Edition of the *Works*. Upon completing this task, he returned to the project that Emerson's children had requested and that he was by now more qualified for than anyone else: the writing of Emerson's biography.

A conscientious and meticulous editor, Cabot decided early on to "avoid all side-lights & exclude collateral figures."[35] The biography was to be less a formal portrait than a narrative of Emerson's intellectual development as told in his own words, a ghost-edited autobiography that lifted Emerson clear of his social context in order to emphasize his thought. Yet if Cabot's subject is the dignified seer of spiritual truths, he is also refracted through the lens of his biographer, who was philosophically committed to maintaining a balance between obdurate fact and the ideal. It is *this* Emerson, an exemplary figure of philosophical equipoise, that Cabot transmitted to the twentieth century in the most comprehensive biography prior to Ralph L. Rusk's *The Life of Ralph Waldo Emerson* (1949).

Cabot's emphasis on Emerson's philosophy was by no means anomalous or inappropriate for the time. As a number of contemporary scholars have made clear, Emerson stands as the figurehead of America's first important philosophical "school"—the pragmatist school of the late-nineteenth-century Harvard philosophers Josiah Royce, John Dewey, and William James.[36] What separated Cabot from others who grappled with

Emerson's philosophy was his intimate knowledge of Emerson's intellectual development as chronicled in the lectures and journals. In the *Memoir*, Emerson functions as a poetic thinker whose distrust of systematic reasoning is the source both of his aesthetic pleasure and his philosophical confusion. To those who would seek definitive answers from Emerson, Cabot asserts that his thought was less a solution to the problems posed by philosophy than an indication of them. In the precarious balancing act that is his book's *raison d'être*, Cabot offers nuanced readings of both his subject's philosophical idealism and his pragmatic strain, attending to Emerson's romantic faith in human capacity as well as his recognition of a mediate world entailing the shaping pressures of society and history. In the process, he accomplishes what no other critic to this point had: he offers a convincing hypothesis concerning Emerson's famously vexing contradictions. Maintaining that Emerson saw truth as conditional, Cabot notes that for Emerson "no definition is to be regarded as final, as if it described an ultimate essence whereby the thing is utterly discriminated from all other things, but only as the recognition of certain of its relations; to which, of course, no limit can be set" (2: 642–3).

In many ways, Cabot's Emerson looks forward to the vitalistic philosopher who would be valued by William James. A skeptical philosopher always in motion, this version of Emerson is neither complacent nor enthusiastic about the currents of history and social reform in which "truth" bobbed provisionally. "In principle, Emerson stood, of course, with the idealists, the reformers, the party of progress, or at least of aspiration and hope," Cabot explained. "But he could not help seeing that the existing order, since it is here, has the right to be here, and the right to all the force it can exert" (2: 390). Such passages have caused some critics to describe Cabot's memoir as "conservative."[37] Yet the skeptical philosopher Cabot describes, however quietistic in his attitude toward reform, is hardly the upholder of the establishment envisioned by Holmes. For Cabot, Emerson didn't defend the existing order as ideal so much as he believed it to be historically necessary. The earlier, revolutionary Emerson seemed simply to Cabot to represent a phase that was already outgrown by the 1844 lecture on "The Young American."

This effort to maintain a balance between Emerson's early idealism and later pragmatism can be understood in part as the genteel critic's effort to battle against anarchic individualism on two fronts: on the left, against latter-day antinomians who could point to Emerson's "Divinity School Address" as subordinating all tradition to intuition; on the right, and less obviously, against Social Darwinists, such as William Graham Sumner, who could legitimately claim to be the intellectual descendent of the Emerson of "Fate." Indeed, Emersonian language percolates throughout the writings of Sumner, whose popular "gospel of wealth" argued not only that "right" social policy conduced to the material wealth of society but also that a "good" man doggedly sought to promote his own well-being. Because "the human race has never had any ease which it did not earn, nor any freedom which it did not conquer," Sumner asserted in his 1881 essay on "Sociology," it was pointless to fritter away time on "those philosophies which are trying to find out how we may arrange things so as to satisfy any ideal of society."[38] Cabot, apparently discomfited by the implications of Sumner's philosophical laissez-faire, on the one hand, and anarchic radicalism, on the other, sought to produce a portrait of Emerson that stressed his balance and common sense. Emerson, he argued, never meant that the "rights of the soul" should lead to an insurgent antinomianism most commonly imaged in the 1880s in fearful descriptions of urban violence; nor did his insistence on the "might of established facts" endorse the equally dangerous behavior of robber barons (2: 391).

In his efforts to present an Emerson ever open to both sides of an argument, Cabot unearthed a version of the author still very much with us. The first person to identify Emerson's "First Philosophy," which contrasted the offices of Reason and Understanding (*JMN* 5: 270–6), Cabot found an author internally divided and incapable of constructing a systematic metaphysics. Emerson's admiration for science, and his oft-expressed desire to create a science that would explain the "original laws of the mind," never outweighed his deeper sense that scientific method limited the search for truth. Emerson's method, according to Cabot, was essentially poetic, involving the production of images based on belief rather than logic.

Cabot's analysis of Emerson, easily the most perceptive in the decade following his death, nevertheless sought to protect its subject from those who would appropriate his authority as founder either of a subversive intellectual tradition or an increasingly hegemonic "gospel of success." Three-quarters of the way through his book, Cabot ventures an interpretation of his subject's philosophical significance that deliberately subordinates the claim of Conway *and* of Sumner to a detached idealism: "What gave Emerson his position among those who influence thought was not so much what he said, or how he said it, as what made him say it,—the open vision of things spiritual across the disfigurements and contradictions of the actual" (2: 627).

If Cabot's *Memoir* is a revealing example of the personal and cultural politics that helped shape Emerson's reception during the Gilded Age, it is also a counterargument to assertions that canonicity tends to fix and rigidify the author—to circumscribe his or her interpretive possibilities by establishing "traditional" readings of the life and works.[39] Despite its careful balancing of Emerson's antinomies and its respectful presentation of Emerson's words, Cabot's biography redistributes the energies clustered around an increasingly canonized figure, generating in unexpected ways alternative "traditions." Receiving accolades by genteel critics for whom it was designed, Cabot's *Memoir* also served as the source for an interpretation that signaled his transformation from benign cultural ideal to the foremost figure in a second, oppositional canon of American literature that is still very much with us today.

IV.

John Jay Chapman wrote to Cabot in 1897 to say he had not "read any books or essays" about Emerson except Cabot's; "by Jove," he exclaimed, "I believe you had no shadow & are part of the light," and added, "I can't help regarding you as a part of Emerson and feeling as if he was not dead so long as you survive."[40] Indeed, resurrecting Emerson from the asphyxiating atmosphere of genteel literary culture was the task Chapman set for himself in "Emerson, Sixty Years Later," the two-part essay that appeared in the January and February 1897 issues of the *Atlantic Monthly*. From his vantage point just before the turn of the century, Chapman could view those forces at work in the initial construction of Emerson as solemn and stultifying, a monolithic appropriation:

> It is the irony of fate that his admirers should be more than usually sensitive about his fame. This prophet who desired not to have followers, lest he too should become a cult and a convention, and whose main theses throughout life was that piety is a crime, has been calmly canonized and embalmed in amber by the very forces he braved. He is become a tradition and a sacred relic. You must speak of him under your breath, and you may not laugh near his shrine.[41]

Chapman wrote at a time when Emerson's journals were not yet available; when the only major biography of Emerson (Cabot's) refrained from critical interpretation; when, moreover, the canonical Emerson celebrated by genteel authors and critics had so hardened into dogma that, as Holmes had noticed a decade earlier, "Emerson's life and writings have been so *darned over* by his biographers and critics that a new hand can hardly tell his own yarn from that of his predecessors."[42] Nevertheless, Chapman composed the first major reinterpretation of Emerson, one that challenged not only the cultural icon but the very grounds upon which Emerson's canonical status had been anchored.

Born a generation after Cabot but into the same aristocratic Boston milieu, Chapman, who referred to himself as a "belated abolitionist," nevertheless confessed in a letter that "I don't worship at the New England shrine."[43] (Only a year earlier the idea that New England's literary sites were in fact sacred places still populated by authorial ghosts had been reified in Theodore F. Wolfe's book on *Literary Shrines: The Haunts of Some Famous American Authors*, which offered readers a detailed description of "the abode of the princely man who was not only 'the Sage of Concord,' but, in the esteem of some contemporaries, 'was Concord itself.'"[44]) Chapman's apostasy enabled him to characterize Emerson as "the arch-radical of the world" ("Emerson" 202); his description was to a large extent the product of his own career, which in addition to forays in literary criticism also included the practice of law, political agitation (Chapman expended much effort attempting to reform New York's Tammany Hall), brief stints at writing poetry and drama, and incisive cultural criticism that argued that America's promise had been compromised by commerce and political corruption. His little-read *Causes and Consequences*, written a year after the essay on Emerson, opens with these lines: "Misgovernment in the United States is an incident in the history of commerce. It is part of the triumph of industrial progress." Sounding very much like the Emerson of 1837–42, the Emerson who still could entertain millennial hopes for what he called in "The American Scholar" "the conversion of the world" (*EL* 71), Chapman carefully details the process by which moneyed interests degraded political life and revealed how commerce bred intellectual dishonesty and the surrender of convictions both in public and in private life. The only adequate protest against the juggernaut of a brutal and mediocre capitalist society, he insisted, is the liberated individual.

To make sense of Chapman's now-classic interpretation of Emerson, it is useful to examine the chapter devoted to "Literature" in his *Practical Agitation* (1900). Always most perceptive when analyzing the world of commerce (William James once said about him, "He just looks at things and tells the truth about them—a strange thing even to *try* to do"),[45] Chapman was concerned in this essay with the transformation in the conditions of publishing and authorship during the 1880s and 1890s. Those conditions had arisen as the once-genteel publishing business gradually adapted itself to commerce; increasingly financed by venture capitalists who desired larger profits, editors and publishers found themselves pressed to exploit new, larger reading audiences. Discussion of these conditions was nothing new, of course, as is apparent in William

Dean Howells's *A Hazard of New Fortunes* (1890). But Chapman's analysis made particularly explicit the dangers both to authorship and an enlightened reading public whenever editors found themselves subsuming discriminating intelligence for the interest of finance or politics. The commercialization of literature, according to Chapman, carried the risk not only of conservatism but also the related risk of standardization and its inhibiting effects. In the most compelling portions of his essay, he revealed how mass-circulation magazines, far from producing works meant to palliate the "disfigurements of the actual" (as Cabot and other genteel authors had been claiming for years) in fact reinforced the very economic structure they opposed by standardizing their product: writing. As a mass-produced commodity subject to larger systems of distribution, literature had not only to "travel well" but also to normalize taste in order to secure its market against the depredations of other versions of the literary. The greatest economic enemy of literature as it was institutionalized by mass-market publishing, therefore, was aesthetic change: "The notable lack in our literature is this," Chapman wrote: "the prickles and irregularities of personal feeling have been pumice-stoned away."[46]

Anticipating the modernist poets by some fifteen years, Chapman would invest artistic innovation with social and political significance. Recalling Emerson's comment in "Art" that "[b]ecause the soul is progressive, it never quite repeats itself" (*EL* 431), Chapman in *Practical Agitation* challenged the assembly-line production of the expressive: "It is not because men stop growing that they repeat themselves, but they stop growing because they repeat themselves. They cease to experiment; they cease to search."[47] The economic setting of culture, then, produced a literature devoid of personality, a literature almost empty of thought, which in turn revealed the extent to which the culture had ceased to foster individuals. This constriction of the individual had political as well as literary results. "The sacrifice in political life is honesty, in literary life is intellect," Chapman noted; "but the closer you examine honesty and intellect the more closely they appear to be the same thing."[48]

Less an example of literary than cultural criticism, "Emerson, Sixty Years Later" sought to counter the numbing sameness created by late-century conditions of literary production as well as the larger impoverishments of social and political life created by American instrumentalism. But in order to claim Emerson as a countercultural icon, Chapman had first to clear away those aspects of Emerson and his writings still revered by genteel artists and critics. The faults he located in Emerson were therefore related to New England. Turning prior discussions of Emerson's Puritan heritage on their head, Chapman noted that for two hundred years "a dogmatic crucifixion of the natural instincts has been in progress"; although Emerson managed to extricate himself from the old creed in part, his insistence on the Moral Law and his assertion "*that the spiritual powers are sufficient to him if no other being existed*" revealed a "new form of old Calvinism as cruel as Calvinism, and not much different from its original" (178, 179; Chapman's emphasis). And while transcendentalism, like abolitionism, represented for Chapman a revolt against the emotional tepidness of a decayed Congregationalism or a rationalized Unitarianism, the old creed lingered nevertheless, evident in the "anaemic incompleteness" of Emerson's thought and writings. In a letter to his wife, Chapman identified Emerson's failing as that quality which had exalted him in the eyes of his genteel predecessors: "Strangely enough [Emerson] lacks body—avoirdupois. I cannot get over it. He would be as great as Milton if he had it. It's a most strange lack, this weakness of the sexual element. It makes a tin-pan effect like a weak old piano."[49]

It is the clamor of an out-of-tune piano that ultimately disqualifies Emerson's poetry from literary greatness; lacking "the fullness, the throb, the overflow of physical life," his verses stand in striking contrast to the prose, which Chapman claims as representative of his newly imagined hero and which enables him to call Emerson "a great artist, and as such . . . a complete being" (183). In many ways, Chapman's emphasis on Emerson's style reflects the late-century interest in aestheticism as an alternative to the crushing materialism of the period. But Chapman's analysis of Emerson's style was also erected on the foundations of Cabot's philosophical explication: "[A]ssured there was no such thing as literal truth, but only literal falsehood," Emerson "resorted to metaphors which could by no chance be taken literally" (151). As with Cabot, Emerson's recognition of the contingency of knowledge had for Chapman a political implication. Against the standardizing sameness of contemporary culture—a sameness Chapman blames on New England's "conservatism and timidity" (199)—Emerson left "a body of work which cannot be made to operate to any other end than that for which he designed it" (151).

Not only a revaluation of Emerson, Chapman's essay is also a revisionary study of American literary tradition that prefigures the more radical criticism of Van Wyck Brooks and the Young Americans. The Civil War, according to Chapman, had not created a heroic new literature but instead carried off a younger generation of men while stranding the old New England worthies "magnified beyond their natural size, like a grove of trees left by a fire" (198). Of this venerable group, only Emerson fought for original self-expression; his faith in the individual serves as a bludgeon for Chapman against antiquated literary ideals still embraced by public opinion. Declaring Emerson an "arch-radical" who revolted against "the evil whose roots were universal suffrage," Chapman's analysis looks forward to later modernists, particularly Ezra Pound, who found the writings of the genteel tradition symptomatic of the totalitarian direction in which America seemed to be heading. Emerson's writing reveals "the identity in essence of all tyranny," to which even democracy is prone (202).

Chapman's discussion of Emerson's thought and writing illustrates with particular clarity not only the tensions within Gilded Age literary culture—its complicity in the forces of material production from which it promised to deliver its readers—but also the manner in which an oppositional stance is capable of transforming and revitalizing a hegemonic conception of the existing literary tradition. "Emerson, Sixty Years Later," although rhetorically adopting a position outside mainstream literary culture, was in fact published in the *Atlantic Monthly*. If the essay appeared at a moment when the genteel conception of Emerson remained as sturdy as the busts of him that adorned the nation's halls of learning, it also signaled a growing understanding from within that genteel conception that the construction of a cultural ideal entailed the risk of converting Emerson into a figure capable of alienating many Americans: pretentious and effete, impractical and irrelevant.

Responding to Chapman after the first installment of the essay had been published, Cabot admitted that although he had approached "Emerson, Sixty Years Later" with reluctance, it nevertheless "seems to me you have come nearer the mark than anybody."[50] Within Gilded Age literary culture, which increasingly imagined canonicity as an institutional device to monitor the distribution of cultural capital, Emerson had become not only a sanctified author but also a focal point of various aesthetic and political interests. The differences between these interests may be seen to constitute his emergence within a newly imagined canon of American literature even as they reveal an internally divided effort at social reimagination whose most compelling question had to do with the meaning of America itself.

Chapman's essay participated in this effort and helps us to trace the direction a biography-centered approach to Emerson would continue to take, conflating Emerson the man with Emerson the writer. To Cabot he wrote:

Another idea has Occurred to me – that those original journals – ought almost to be printed Entire before they get lost – There may be points which your eyes or my eyes don't see which will be very important to some future biographer or historian[.] The records

of such a man have value forever. . . . You cant tell what fine point
may throw light on his whole epoch – A man of this completeness
seldom lives – He organically records his time.[51]

Indeed, for decades to come Emerson's most penetrating and influential critics would typically find him important less for his writing or his
thought than for his ability to provide an interpretive key capable of
unlocking the meaning of American "culture" and "civilization." If the
Gilded Age biographies of Emerson often exemplify "the chasm" Richard
Poirier claims "has always separated literary history or pedagogy from
the moment by moment experience of reading,"[52] they also provided the
groundwork for the academic institutionalization of American literature.
Unlike Hawthorne or even Thoreau, however, Emerson offered less a
model of realization for creative writers (there are few, if any, adherents
of an Emersonian "style") than he did a vocabulary for those who would
discuss, disagree, and otherwise interpret American life; that is, Emerson
enabled his critics to become *cultural* critics: Americanists. As we shall
soon see, the field of American Studies was virtually inconceivable without Emerson as ghostly precursor and model of enablement. Long before
the emergence of that field, however, Emerson's genteel critics, often both
critical and celebratory about the meaning of a conceptual space known
as America, would assume a detached position from the culture they critiqued, inoculating themselves against charges that American literature
was inferior to the Western tradition even as they advanced the meaning
of America as a viable field of discourse and study. Their example would
be followed by critics and public intellectuals as diverse as F. O. Matthiessen,
Perry Miller, and Van Wyck Brooks.

CHAPTER 3

How to Dismantle American Culture

Van Wyck Brooks and Oppositional Criticism

The young Van Wyck Brooks believed literature could change history, could serve as a cultural bomb, detonating inside the consciousness of readers and inciting them to revolt against a sick and constrictive society. Literature—Kafka's axe—could hack its way to the frozen sea within, releasing a restorative deluge upon the parched cultural landscape.

In a series of brash manifestos now considered staples of American intellectual history, the critic called for a literary revolution that would transform the social world by eliminating divisions between labor and capital, between "transcendent theory" and "catchpenny realities," and—in his most famous formulation—between highbrow and lowbrow culture.[1] In language astringent with scorn for the genteel generation and its Victorian ideals, Brooks argued for new figural modes to excite the perception and act upon the nation's fractured consciousness by replacing the "fastidious refinement and aloofness of the chief American writers" (*VWB* 84)—he referred chiefly to the Fireside Poets and other eminent Victorians like Thoreau and Emerson—with newer representations of fresh and authentic experience: "intimate feeling, intimate intellectual contact, even humor" (*VWB* 157).

Looking back on it, we sense in these early writings the febrile energies clustered around lower Manhattan in the years before and during World War I. From the period's social and sexual experimentation would emerge (in no particular order) Emma Goldman, the journal *Masses,* the 1913 Armory Show of modernist painting, and, somewhat more obliquely, the gradual radicalization of Italian anarchists Sacco and Vanzetti, who arrived in America, penniless and hopeful, the same year Brooks wrote his first polemic, *The Wine of the Puritans* (1908). That book instantly catapulted its author to fame, making him literary bohemia's most influential spokesperson—its Carlyle or Ruskin—a cultural visionary who discerned and articulated national ills under the supposition that by bringing "its beliefs and convictions . . . into play, the real evils that have been vaguely surmised spring into the light, the real strength of what is intelligent and sound becomes a measurable entity" (*VWB* 156).

More than any other figure of the era, Brooks was responsible for what has since become a twentieth-century intellectual parlor game: canon revision. In his case, this activity involved attacking the established pantheon of genteel poets and placing in their stead overlooked figures such as Melville, Dickinson, and the newly emerging naturalists. Much in the spirit of Wordsworth's preface to the second edition of *Lyrical Ballads,* Brooks announced a revolutionary literary ideal in such bracing works as *The Wine of the Puritans, America's Coming-of-Age* (1915), and "On Creating a Usable Past" (1918). He avowed nothing less than the razing of Victorianism's cloying influence, and on the basis of these breathtaking performances he stands as the protagonist in numerous breakthrough narratives that depict the emergence of an oppositional critical sensibility in America, an enduring inspiration to a long line of self-styled leftist scholars and critics to follow, including Newton Arvin, Vernon L. Parrington, F. O. Matthiessen, Perry Miller, and the New York intellectuals. To readers like these, his early essays activated a kind of criticism virtually unimagined to that point in the United States: a socially committed writing characterized by its unapologetic outsider status and its dedication to remaking society through literature.

Yet Brooks incurred enormous costs on behalf of his insurrectionary critical practice. Motivated by a longing to alter the bleak landscape of modernity's alienating industrial culture, he wrote within a tradition of romantically transgressive vision that at times seems to have aspired to nothing less than the wholesale undoing of Western civilization's rational order. He sought, at least rhetorically, to demolish a society of "blind, selfish, disorderly people" (*VWB* 113) and, in an apocalyptic reordering of experience, to transfigure its citizens into "a luminous people, dwelling in the light and sharing in the light" (*VWB* 113). He hoped to rattle and awaken America's complacent citizens—the same tepidly anxious and proudly anti-intellectual citizens Sinclair Lewis would deride in his 1930 Nobel speech entitled "The American Fear of Literature." We are perhaps overly familiar with these sorts of claims, with the celebration of resistance that has become literary criticism's axiomatic and aspirational motivation: its stated, if seldom fulfilled, *raison d'être*. What is remarkable about Brooks's career is the extent to which he actually succeeded. The rubble imaged by Eliot's fragmentary Waste Land as well as the affective disenchantment articulated by the Lost Generation are evidence of the genteel tradition's dissolution as it was thought to have been prompted by a Brooksian revolution.

Just at the moment of apparent triumph, however, Brooks began to experience a malaise every bit as pernicious as those he had previously diagnosed in the culture. His guerilla warfare against the genteel dispensation had succeeded *too* well; he now stood in the wan afterglow of a sustained and robust attack on a prior literature, an attack that had released energies whose consequences were unpredictable and unintended. Ransacking the cultural archive for a "usable past," Brooks had emphasized the role politics exerts in every act of writing and, in the process, had amplified (if not as much as he might have hoped) the canon. But he accomplished these things at the cost of his own sense of the literary: of its restorative generosity, its vivid particularity, its modes of meaning-making often experienced as a realm apart from more coercive rhetorics and discourses. Standing at the smoking crater of a literary and critical detonation, feeling divested of community, of selfhood, of authenticity, and of any understanding of how the literary might fund these ghostly projects, Brooks began the more difficult project of healing and reconstruction.

In 1920, the year Sacco and Vanzetti emerged from obscurity and into the forefront of a murder case involving the death of a Boston paymaster and his assistant, Brooks completed his last truly polemical work, a portrait of Twain. He embarked then upon a work of empathic identification, a study in which his own words and those of his new protagonist, Henry James, would become interwoven, indistinguishable from one another—almost as if he had so thoroughly internalized the plight of the American writer as to *become* him. Driven by a sense of guilt over the inadequacy of his earlier criticism to produce a viable communal and artistic alternative, driven to prove his worth as a critic, he became desperate, then delusional. By 1925—the year Sacco and Vanzetti, as well as the radical energies with which they are affiliated, were sentenced to death—Brooks himself felt increasingly haunted by failure, felt "the great luminous menacing eyes" of James following him about his new house in Westport, Connecticut, haunting him in what was supposed to be a pastoral retreat.[2] He began, in a sort of last-gasp effort, to attempt his "long-cherished idea of writing the paradise of the American man of letters,"[3] a biography of Emerson.

It was precisely at this juncture that he went mad.

If Brooks's effort at dismantling and reassembling American culture in some ways resembles recent critical engagements, it has its roots in a prior tradition, as well, one that runs backward through John Jay Chapman and Moncure Conway. His visionary attack on American culture in fact reenacted the program of a writer held in unparalleled esteem by his parents' generation. Put another way, Brooks's project—and the nervous breakdown this project exacted—was funded almost entirely by the visionary portrait of "The American Scholar" he received from Emerson, or rather, from a genteel refraction of Emerson he would alternately repudiate and adopt throughout his life.

Perhaps this was inevitable. Born in 1886, four years after the author's death, Brooks had the fortune, whether for good or ill, to have been saturated from a young age with what Oliver Wendell Holmes had called the "Emersonian atmosphere." His mother's closest friend, Eliza Kenyon, was not only romantically linked to Thoreau's literary executor but also ran a school for girls in the "Transcendental tone," where, as James Hoopes informs us, the young "Van Wyck first became acquainted with the lofty Emersonian idealism."[4] His high school essay, "The Mission of American Art"—with its pronouncement that "[w]e have a mighty slough of commercialism that only Art can reconcile with the Ideal"—might easily be mistaken for a watered-down and quasi-Arnoldian formulation of Emerson's "The Poet."[5] Soon after writing it, he chose to attend Harvard not only because it was "*the* school for writers,"[6] but because of its proximity to Concord, long understood by genteel men of letters as the mythical birthplace and *genii loci* of American literature. Visiting the small village, where shoddy souvenir busts of Emerson were sold (then as now) in shops along the main thoroughfare, the young Brooks could vicariously experience literary history by catching a glimpse of Emerson's "brightly lighted" house with "Miss Emerson [Ralph Waldo's daughter] at the window."[7] At Harvard itself, Brooks was instructed by Barrett Wendell, whose recently published *Literary History of America* had placed Emerson at the center of a "New England Renaissance," as well as by Bliss Perry, arguably the most influential Emerson scholar of the day.[8] Several times during his first semester at Harvard, Brooks made the obligatory pilgrimage to nearby

Concord, spending the night on one occasion in the Revolutionary-era Colonial Inn, he noted in his journal, "with the clock of Emerson's old church clanging . . . not five yard's from the window."[9]

Even if his personal experiences had been different, however, Brooks could hardly have escaped the Emersonian influence so thoroughly permeating American intellectual life at the dawn of the new century. Long a palpable and compelling imaginative presence for figures as diverse as Chapman and Oliver Wendell Holmes, Henry Ford and Jane Addams, Emerson's peak of posthumous popularity coincided almost exactly with Brooks's undergraduate years at Harvard (1904–8).[10] Emerson's centenary celebrations in Boston and Concord, occurring in 1903 and attracting many of the nation's intellectual heavyweights, were only the most obvious testaments to the author's cultural authority during this period, the inspiration for Brooks's own intensive program of reading the essays during the summer of that year. Charles William Eliot, president of Harvard at the time, described "the sweetness, fragrance, and loftiness" of Emerson's spirit and argued that the author's independent thought provided important clues to solving social, religious, and educational problems.[11] George Santayana, usually astringent in his response to the author, nevertheless understood Emerson as "a mystic, a moralist athirst for some superhuman and absolute good,"[12] while George Willis Cooke found in him "the spirit of democracy incarnated," a seer whose intuition of spiritual reality informed him that "all men are kin and have need for each other."[13] More idealizing yet was a lyric poem by Edith M. Thomas in a special issue of the *Critic* devoted to Emerson that eulogized "Thou of the vatic glance and orphic tone."[14] In the same issue, Gerald Stanley Lee (the Congregationalist minister and amateur social theorist Brooks would later savage in *America's Coming-of-Age*) admitted that "eleven of the volumes that wait just over my fireplace are by Ralph Waldo Emerson, and they are all about me."[15]

As Lee's remark makes clear, the image of Emerson early in the twentieth century had become not merely interpolated but in fact conflated with genteel identity. A commanding if somewhat diffuse presence in numerous biographies and academic literary histories, "Emerson" was a kind of shorthand for a range of associations and interests that included the devotion to an idealistic version of Culture; what Paul Elmer More called the academy's "outstanding figure of American letters"[16]; and an American saint whose aphorisms, collected in a popular 1905 calendar, were embraced by artists and business tycoons alike. Writing in 1907 (Brooks's junior year at Harvard), the genteel professor of literature George Woodberry articulated the dominant cultural response toward Emerson when he called him "the only great mind that America has produced in literature."[17]

The background of Brooks's youthful and fairly conventional reception of Emerson hardly prepares us for the vitriolic attack he would launch against the author in *The Wine of the Puritans*. Written a year after Woodberry's comment, Brooks's first work of criticism reads like the self-conscious desecration of an official literary monument. Composed shortly after its author graduated from Harvard, the work introduces a bracing topic with which a new generation of critics would soon occupy itself— what T. S. Eliot, in a review of the book, called "the failure of American life (at present)."[18] In Brooks's analysis, America's failure was not only the result of industrial incorporation and rampant materialism, but of an equally debilitating philosophical idealism that had long promised an escape from such materialism. Describing the polarization of the nation's character into practical intellect and an idealistic culture divorced from the life around it, the two fictional speakers in Brooks's polemic sum up America's appalling intellectual climate in a metaphor that simultaneously blames the historical Puritans and indicts the Emersonian idealism coursing through American culture with what felt like hegemonic inevitability: "You put the old wine [of Puritanism] into new bottles . . . and when the explosion results, one may say, the aroma passes into air and the wine spills on the floor. The aroma, or the ideal, turns into transcendentalism, and the wine, or the real, becomes commercialism. In any case, one doesn't preserve a great deal of well-tempered, genial wine" (*VWB* 6).[19]

Brooks's description of transcendentalism as a vaporous abstraction places him squarely within a well-established countertradition of Emerson criticism that begins with Carlyle's 1841 letter to the author complaining that "we find you a speaker indeed, but as it were a *Soliloquizer* on the eternal mountain-tops only, in vast solitudes where men and their affairs lie hushed in a very dim remoteness."[20] This critical tradition continues in Henry James's pronouncement about Emerson's thought that "we get the impression of a conscience gasping in the void, panting for sensations, with something of the movement of gills of a landed fish."[21] But if Carlyle and James serve as critical precursors to Brooks, the gleeful dismissal of Emerson in *The Wine of the Puritans* is more directly influenced by Brooks's experienced cultural moment in which "Emerson" was increasingly associated with a waning gentility that in hindsight appeared homogenous and stultifying. The polemic was an early salvo in a broader cultural contest waged against that gentility by a loosely confederated group of young literary radicals who included Brooks, John Macy, Randolph Bourne, Lewis Mumford, and Waldo Frank. The oppositional criticism of these radicals was in part an effort to capture the cultural space created and zealously guarded by those genteel men of letters discussed in the previous chapter. The stakes in this criticism of

America, however, were not primarily literary. Rather, the canonization of America's "standard" authors as lofty and unreachable seemed more widely symptomatic of an extinguishing of personal freedom, a contraction of opportunities, a tendency toward exclusion in an increasingly hierarchical society: precisely the problems Emerson himself identified and then denounced in "The American Scholar."

Raised in Plainfield, New Jersey, the son of a high-strung and cultured woman who had married a failure in business, Brooks felt all his life, according to Casey Nelson Blake, "the threat posed by commerce to the certainties of middle-class culture."[22] Lewis Mumford observed about his friend that if Brooks revolted "against his genteel moneyed background," he was nevertheless "fatally embrangled in it to the end of his days."[23] It was this "fatal" implication in gentility that infused the heated rhetoric of Brooks and his fellow literary insurgents, forging a criticism that renounced the past with Oedipal rage and envisioned a fresh beginning that would coincide with the discoveries of depth psychology, sociology, and modernist aesthetics. It was this renunciation of the past, furthermore, that initially precluded Brooks from finding in Emerson a cultural ancestor whose role in "The American Scholar"—as prophet of freedom, experimentation, and anti-institutionalism—might have been leveraged *against* the very genteel tradition with which the author had become posthumously associated.

Writing out of a sense of "national weakness" and cultural failure, Brooks brilliantly refashioned American history as a tale of repression, attacking what one critic calls a "carefully constructed symbol of [his] own making, the American Puritan. On [this Puritan's] shoulders was laid the blame for the spiritual failures of a moralistic and aesthetically numb America. He was the prohibitionist, the censor, the preacher, the member of the local PTA."[24] A founding text in an anti-Puritan movement that would soon reach its apogee in the denunciations of H. L. Mencken, *The Wine of the Puritans* lays the groundwork for later insurgent-critics determined to remake American culture by reimagining its literary history. In a sweep of the hand, Whittier, Holmes, and the other Fireside poets were in Brooks's account rendered invalid by "that preconception of the supreme virtues of thrift and industry" (*VWB* 5). But in Emerson there obtained the opposite problem: a flight from reality "inadequate for the expression of a great nation" (*VWB* 5). Along with horse-drawn carriages and sentimental three-volume novels, Emerson's tepid idealism was seen as an outmoded burden from the past—an "encumbrance," as T. S. Eliot noted[25]—no longer capable of confronting satisfactorily the problems of modernity facing Brooks and his generation.

Emerson would not have inspired such vitriol were he only a relic from the past. But he was for Brooks an obdurate presence, a malignant force that continued to exert a powerful, if outdated, influence on the way Americans thought and acted. As David Bromwich notes, Brooks felt that "the personal culture that Emerson invented" had become so deeply embedded in twentieth-century life that it had all but foreclosed any alternative vision, especially "the possibility of a common culture."[26] As an exponent of transcendental idealism wedded to an uncompromising individualism, Emerson was both the embodiment of America's cultural divisions and the central contributor to its current social impoverishment. Abdicating the American author's responsibility to fuse the concrete with the ideal, advocating an individualism easily appropriated by industrial capitalism, and perpetuating a philosophy that was nothing more than a heady "aroma," Brooks's Emerson was "a lofty and inspired sophist who begs the whole question of life" (VWB 6).

The publication of The Wine of the Puritans signaled a restructuring in the way American literature would be talked about and considered for decades to come, and in many ways it would prefigure the late-twentieth-century critical climate in which canonical decisions were made often on the basis of social and political criteria. Nowhere is this new allowance more evident than in America's Coming-of-Age, a work written six years after The Wine of the Puritans and extending Brooks's early thesis by dividing American culture into highbrow and lowbrow tendencies so as to mount a dialectical analysis of the nation's intellectual thought. "What emotions pass through an hereditary American," Brooks scoffs early in his book, "when he calls to mind the worthies who figured in that ubiquitous group of 'Our Poets' which occupied once so prominent a place in so many domestic interiors! Our Poets were commonly six in number, kindly, grey-bearded, or otherwise grizzled old men" (VWB 97). The national literary pantheon constructed in a previous generation by superannuated genteel critics like Oliver Wendell Holmes and still disseminated within college classrooms and "official" publications is understood by Brooks in 1915 as a factitious grouping of avuncular and irrelevant "Fireside" authors valued for their polite manners and conventional morality. Within this museum of cultural decrepitude, Emerson again occupies a central position, not only standing for a literature of high ideality but for the steadfast refusal to look critically, dialectically, at American society.

For Brooks, writing in America's Coming-of-Age, "The American Scholar" was a threadbare cultural inheritance, an artifact placed under glass in the 1890s because it contained "all the qualities of the typical baccalaureate sermon" (VWB 117). Emerson's address, once considered an inflammatory call to arms, now only revealed the "immense, vague cloud-canopy of idealism which hung over the American people during the nineteenth century" (*VWB* 99). As critics have noted, Emerson's address offered for Brooks neither rhetorical verve nor a prophetic strain of national destiny but exhibited just how much its author was "the very embodiment of the division between ideals and practice that rendered American literature so ineffective."[27] The draft manuscript of *America's Coming-of-Age,* which on the whole contains numerous revisions in Brooks's hand, is noteworthy for the utter absence of any such marks in the sections devoted to Emerson—as though his thoughts about the author had long been fixed in memory and rehearsed in private. Those thoughts, shaped by a cultural moment of frustration and unrest, ignore the radical energies of Emerson's address—particularly its call to intellectual action in times of crisis. Yet it is worth pointing out that in articulating a generational revolt, in calling for a form of action that would rewrite the past, Brooks reenacts the very cultural program of "The American Scholar" he publicly derides.

Brooks's critical devaluation of Emerson is extended yet further in "On Creating a Usable Past." Because it provides so apt an analog to later critical projects, this perennially quoted essay might be considered a founding document for the canonical revisionism of the 1980s and 1990s.[28] But the target of Brooks's polemic is not only a narrow and provincial cultural scene but that scene's reification by university professors responsible for an endless torrent of nearly identical American literary histories. Complaining that "[o]ur professors continue to pour out a stream of historical works repeating the same points of view to such an astonishing degree that they have placed a sort of Talmudic seal upon the American tradition" (*VWB* 219), Brooks argues that this inundation has walled off a vivifying past from contemporary creative artists who are in fact the only hope for creating a coherent national culture. "It is a peculiar twist in the academic mind to suppose that a writer belongs to literature only when he is dead," Brooks notes in a passage that remains relevant; "living he is, vaguely, something else; and an habitual remoteness from the creative mood has made American professors quite peculiarly academic" (*VWB* 82). For Brooks, America's professors of literature, entangled in institutional politics and complicitous with genteel culture, were practically required by their profession to circumscribe and deaden accounts of the nation's literary past, thereby "discouraging American writers from confronting the actualities of American life."[29] Himself among the first generation of American critics to be college-educated, Brooks alludes to the conception of higher education largely inherited from the German research model, with its devotion to specialization that kept students diligently working on tiny plots of knowledge, miniscule parcels that in turn resembled the splintered America he sought to reimagine into an organic whole.

Central to this project of reimagination was the attempt to discover a "middle plane between vaporous idealism and self-interested practicality" (*VWB* 95). Ransacking academic histories for his middle term, searching for a "poetry of life" that would "serve in harnessing thought and action together," Brooks discovered Whitman, whom he viewed as the "precipitant" of a "new tradition" who "effectively combines theory and action" (*VWB* 128). As Paul Jay notes, "Whitman's value as a poet lies [for Brooks] in the public, active nature of his engagement with America's social fabric."[30] Goaded by Emerson's call for a national poet, the cosmopolitan Walt was fortunate not to have been inhibited, literally or figuratively, by a frosty New England culture and could thus observe American life from ground level. Pioneering the rediscovery of a poet almost always regarded with discomfort by Holmes and other genteel critics, Brooks wrote that in Whitman "the hitherto incompatible extremes of the American temperament were fused. The refinement of the Puritan tradition, . . . able to make nothing of a life so rude in its actuality, turned for its outlet to a disembodied world, the shadow-world of Emerson . . . Whitman was the Antaeus of this tradition who touched earth with it and gave it hands and feet" (*VWB* 128). Whitman's fusion of America's opposing intellectual and cultural strains suggest for Brooks the possibility of a contemporary literature engaged with "actuality." By producing a social art that released "personality and . . . retriev[ed] for our civilization, originally deficient in the richer juices of human nature . . . the only sort of 'place in the sun' that is really worth having" (*VWB* 131), Whitman suggested an approach to modern life far more congenial and worthwhile than the detached idealism still served up by the nation's leading magazines and universities.

Against Whitman's ability to fuse America's highbrow and lowbrow cultures, Emerson stood largely as a cautionary antihero, a figure who no longer deserved to occupy space on culture's dusty bookshelves. Relying on an image of the author largely transmitted by genteel and academic critics—an image of the author concretized in the cheap white plaster busts he had encountered as a college student—Brooks did not rewrite the meaning of Emerson's life and work so much as he presented it within a new cultural paradigm that rendered all previous meanings obsolete. If he can sound at times like John Jay Chapman when he notes that Emerson "never lingers in the bodily world," or when he asserts "that Emerson was not interested in human life" (*VWB* 114), his most pointed insight is that Emerson, as well as "the superannuated boyishness of the Emersonian tradition" (*VWB* 118), "never dreamed of moulding society, and . . . was incapable of an effective social ideal" (*VWB* 116).

This lacerating depiction of Emerson and his institutional setting would prove remarkably influential. (Warner Berthoff noted long ago that the central achievement of the years after 1910 was "the consolidation of a *critical* context"; Brooks is more responsible for this consolidation than any other critic of the era.[31]) Waldo Frank—co-editor of *The Seven Arts* with Brooks, Bourne, and Paul Rosenfeld—similarly argued for modern literature's role in redirecting American society from material acquisitiveness. Named after Emerson, Frank nevertheless found in the author a particularly poor candidate for an enabling literary precursor committed to this goal. In *Our America* (1919), he condemned Emerson's retreat from the "actual world of men." Possessed of a style "vague and impalpable and abstract," Frank wrote, Emerson's prose reflected the fact that he "abhorred American affairs and was repugned by the traffic of reality."[32] For Brooks, this lack of social awareness had, paradoxically, resulted in a society foundered upon "unattached idealism" (*VWB* 120). For Brooks, then, dismantling American culture meant dismantling Emerson.

Given the stunning success of Brooks's early cultural criticism, its withering dismissal of an Emersonsian culture that would open the door for a wide range of aesthetic and social experimentation—given the subsequent influence this vision would have on an entire generation of writers, critics, and thinkers, it is surprising to encounter the following homage to the disavowed author written during the 1920s:

> "We paid you," [Emerson] had conceived men saying, "that you
> might not be a merchant. We bought and sold that you might
> not buy and sell, but reveal the reasons of trade. We did not want
> apes of us, but guides and commanders." And he was the incarna-
> tion of his own idea. He had reinstated, alone in the nineteenth
> century, the ancient figure of the sage, the giver of laws. . . . He
> had been the opener of doors for those who were to come after
> him. And every man had been to him for all men, the universe in
> a mask.[33]

More surprising is that the passage comes from Van Wyck Brooks's *Life of Emerson*, a biography that attempted to place Emerson at the center of what Charles E. Mitchell calls "a tradition of vibrant optimism and hope, a tradition [Brooks] felt America then needed to recapture."[34]

Brooks's about-face toward Emerson is one of the most remarkable critical reverses in American literary history. Rooted in the disappointments of the early 1920s, it would nevertheless inform the critic's subsequent work, beginning with *The Flowering of New England* and *Indian*

Summer and continuing throughout the rest of his life. Writing to his friend Lewis Mumford in 1925, the critic alludes to the profound psychological urgencies that reawakened his interest in Emerson when he confesses that everything he had written "so far has been a kind of exploration of the *dark* side of our moon, and this blessed Emerson has led me right out into the midst of the sunny side."[35] To the critic Joel Springarn he adopted the recently rediscovered work of Melville to describe what this "new" Emerson meant to him: "The monster I am trying to pull ashore is several diameters larger than any Emerson I have discovered in the history books, etc.—almost as big as Goethe. . . ." If this last remark suggests Brooks's desire to rewrite literary history once again, to discover in the past an enabling and generative present, the darkly eclipsed exploration he depicted for Mumford implies the more personal reasons he had for focusing particularly on Emerson. Long a victim of the erratic mood swings that were part of his manic-depression (also known as bipolar disorder), Brooks's interest in Emerson would coincide with an episode of desperately escalating mania, followed by a suicidal depression that resulted in almost continual hospitalization, both in England and America, for the next five years.

Brooks's celebratory portrait of Emerson has long occupied a central position in discussions that depict Brooks as a critic of "divided mind," an individual whose life was broken in half much as his perceptions were split by the oscillating moods of his illness.[36] As early as the mid-twenties, Waldo Frank and Paul Rosenfeld detected a "wavering or shifting" in Brooks's critical perspective;[37] on the margins of a 1924 letter from Brooks, Lewis Mumford wrote: "Important: The turning point in Van Wyck Brooks's development."[38] And Edmund Wilson, writing in 1940, noted that *The Life of Emerson* marked the beginning of Brooks's "second phase"—a stage in which dialectical criticism gave way to a strangely vernal rapture over "Our Poets." The conflict and tension once energizing Brooks's earlier work seemed magically to have disappeared.[39]

Not only has this "second stage" fared poorly with contemporary critics, its lingering reputation is largely responsible for Brooks's conspicuous absence from the critical canon. William Wasserstrom and James Hoopes, Brooks's most sensitive biographers, both lament his farewell to the "serious work of criticism"; Mark Roydon Winchell has described Brooks's later work as "the subjective babblings of a glorified journalist trying desperately to rewrite the history of this century and his own role in it";[40] and Peter Carafiol has depicted Brooks's later critical project, especially the Emerson biography, as a reflection of his inability to sustain the socially productive if personally damaging conception of America as a nation irremediably divided upon itself.[41]

What has gone unexplained in these accounts of Brooks's bifurcated development is how and why *Emerson*—and not, say, Whitman, or for that matter any number of "modern" writers such as Theodore Dreiser he had championed during the teens and twenties—reemerged as a moral and imaginative presence for him at precisely the moment he did. If Brooks's earlier radical protest can be situated during a brief period in which, as Richard Ruland and Malcolm Bradbury have noted, "the entire temper of the American arts altered,"[42] his biography of Emerson is a response to the cultural wreckage spawned in part by America's entry into World War I in April 1917. "The horrors of mechanical warfare and mass slaughter, the disintegration of European empires and the rise of Bolshevism in Russia, Wilson's failure to win American support for the League of Nations—everything conspired to alter the national temper irrevocably."[43] Having come of age *before* the war—unlike such authors as Hemingway, Fitzgerald, and Dos Passos—Brooks responded to the upheaval in the cultural landscape in part through a quasi-nostalgic recovery of the past funded by his own guilty sense of having contributed to a nihilistic new world order. Moreover, as postwar America witnessed a straitening of political possibilities, Brooks increasingly sought ways to imagine culture as wholly separate from politics. Though still critical of the acquisitiveness that had stifled imaginative work in industrial America, Brooks now encouraged writers to transcend their local circumstances and aspire to a form of artistic heroism detached from the conditioned aspects of history.

Intertwined in this saga of cultural decline was the lively literary politics of the time. During the early 1920s Brooks found himself increasingly attacked by young experimental writers he had largely encouraged into being, torn between a vestigial and somewhat Arnoldian vision of a socially committed art and the demands of an emerging modernist aesthetic that seemed to run counter to progressive thought.[44] At the same time, Brooks's longstanding preference for a distinctly *national* art, an art that would heal and even elevate the nation from within, was not without its pitfalls for a discerning critic, as he recognized himself in "A Question of Honesty":

> These nationalist critics answer with no uncertain voice. Cry up our native writers, they say, and without too scrupulous a regard for the actual merits of these writers. Boom them, boost them, praise them in season and out of season. What does it matter if one indulges a few exaggerations? At least it will focus the attention of the country on its own talent. We have been too humble; now is the time to be proud. Down with all these foreign mediocrities! Up with Messrs. Dreiser and Cabell! (*VWB* 234)

In a parodic "Imaginary Conversation" between Brooks and F. Scott Fitzgerald, Edmund Wilson presciently dramatized the older critic's quandary during the twenties. "Fitzgerald" expresses dismay at "Brooks's" apparent retreat into the nineteenth century just as a new crop of young authors "of precisely the kind you describe" were coming into prominence. These writers understandably felt as if "Brooks" had discovered "so many reasons why artistic achievement in America should be difficult that you seem finally to have become convinced it is completely impossible."[45]

Wilson's parodic critique referred specifically to Brooks's long-awaited biography of Henry James (1925). But his comments also encompassed Brooks's influential *Ordeal of Mark Twain* (1920), which had described the humorist, in what was by now a determined pattern of Brooks's thinking, as incurably divided by America's highbrow/lowbrow rift. Artist and businessman, satirist and entertainer, Twain ultimately disfigured his art in an effort to please his lowbrow American audience, while the more complex writing of Henry James suffered from the impoverished cultural situation of the American artist. Bedazzled by the social and cultural density of Europe (as Brooks himself had been during his numerous trips across the Atlantic), the sensitive James found himself repulsed by the desolate environment and crude energies of American life. Depriving himself of his "racial" heritage—and thus of a national point of view necessary for artistic success—James made a "pilgrimage" to Europe, becoming in the process "the magnificent highbrow," "the inevitable antithesis of Twain."[46]

Employing the empathic and paraphrasal style that would characterize his subsequent oeuvre, *The Pilgrimage of Henry James* cemented Brooks's reputation as what Wilson would call an "expert in American failure."[47] It also produced a backlash among young writers and critics, who asserted that Brooks's portrait failed to acknowledge the *aesthetic* power of James's accomplishment. If the older critic was still considered an oracle of "the newness" in established magazines, the burgeoning U.S. avant-garde increasingly charged him with cultural and social preoccupations that blinded him to what they believed were the separable and autonomous values of art. Reviewing the biography of James, Wilson admitted that it was of enduring value because it revealed for the first time the role played by James's social situation in his vast body of work. But Brooks's interest, "all social and never moral," made him incapable of penetrating the complex artistry of James. "[E]xpecting a really great writer to be a social prophet," wrote Wilson, Brooks was immune to James's tangible value for twentieth-century writers. Most damning of all, Brooks's recent criticism (and here Wilson's comments leap forward to Harold Bloom's scorn for the poststructuralist criticism of *ressentiment*) increasingly was "one of intense zeal at the service of intense resentment."[48]

Depressed after finishing a book that had given him so much trouble and that was then roundly criticized, Brooks returned to the author he had assiduously read twenty years earlier before entering Harvard: Emerson. The roots of the experience (the organic metaphor is apt) had begun at least as early as "On Creating a Usable Past" and *America's Coming-of-Age*, where Brooks could temper his critique of the author by praising "Emerson's position in the world of the spirit. There he truly lived and lives, and of American writers he alone appears to me to have proved the reality of that world and to have given some kind of basis to American idealism" (*VWB* 114). By the spring of 1924, Brooks would temporarily shelve his work on James in order to "go through a little Reconstruction Period of my own."[49] In a letter to Mumford, he complained of not having the heart "to write tracts any longer," feeling instead "all sorts of green shoots stirring again—oh, the blissful early morning sense of a new growth! I am going in for synthesis now, though it means fasting and prayers."[50] More than a year later, Brooks noted to his friend that "[f]or four months I have been living in a dream, writing a life of Emerson. It has been a sort of religious experience: I never before knew anything like it."[51] Having suffered a "breakdown" in the spring of 1925, Brooks now "felt as if I had expelled from my system the gathering poisons of years" and was deeply "conscious, deep down, of the value and meaning . . . the 'mission' . . . of literature."[52] What the experience of reading and writing about Emerson felt like for Brooks in 1925 is suggested by the manic excitement that soon accompanied his descriptions of the writer. To Springarn he noted that in discovering Emerson he was "on the road to carrying out my long-cherished idea of writing the paradise of the American man of letters, to follow the *Inferno* of Mark Twain and the *Purgatorio* of Henry James."[53] To Mumford he noted that work on the biography made him "feel ten years older and ten years younger at the same time, and so conscious . . . of the necessity of reasserting the idealistic point of view, with an energy and a faith our good country has not *known* for many years."[54] Within the cauldron of problems that included his own increasing mood swings, a more general postwar dysphoria, and the retrenchment of the progressive ideals he and other literary insurgents had advanced during the radical 1910s, Brooks found in Emerson the resolution to the centrifugal dialectics of highbrow and lowbrow, Twain and James, depression and euphoria. Emerson, determined neither by society nor psychology but instead by a triumphantly indigenous "wild will," seemed capable of rooting out "the hollow dilettantism of American culture [so] that generations to come might frame their own world with greater advantage!" (*Life* 212–3). In the wake of his era's "Spenglerian gloom and decadent anxiety,"[55] Brooks seemed to have found an example of inspiriting artistic courage capable of reshaping communal values and thereby the direction of American life. And in the process of writing about this figure, Brooks would find in Emerson a sketch of authentic action and identity for himself.

Midway through composing *The Life of Emerson*, however, Brooks suffered a nervous breakdown. For the five years of his hospitalization, the manuscript remained unfinished, "a kind of symbol," Robert Spiller noted, "of his failure to resolve . . . the dialectical crisis of his own personality—so much like Emerson himself."[56] If Emerson seemed to have become for Brooks a therapeutic agent, a biographical subject who could make him and his country "sane again," his example also served to call into question Brooks's entire critical project. James R. Vitelli notes that although Brooks experienced excitement in the twenties upon rereading Emerson, he must also have felt "doubts about his earlier reading of the Emersonian period," becoming "more and more uncertain about the whole course and tone which his work had assumed as a consequence."[57] More troubling, by the end of 1925 the healing figure of Emerson began to resist interpretation and to assume once again the ethereal characteristics of the genteel saint Brooks had once lashed out against in *America's Coming-of-Age*. To Newton Arvin, Brooks wrote, "I'm not sure it will come to anything. . . . the subject is so volatile that I have often felt I was trying to shape a mass of air."[58] And in 1926, in the midst of his illness, he told Springarn that the Emerson project "went up in the air several months ago."[59] Like Ahab, Brooks discovered that even when cornered, the leviathan of his imagination failed to yield its meaning.

The problem was personal, methodological, and philosophical. As a young cultural firebrand Brooks had examined literature through the lens of social *praxis*. But the merging of his personality with Emerson's prose—a form of critical *poiesis*—promised to immerse him in a richly contrastive language that might stand free, in Murray Krieger's description of aesthetic modes, "of all conceptual structures, all metanarratives, and thus, by implication, to function as a dissenting voice against them."[60] Brooks's aesthetic identification with his subject is evident in the style of the biography: not the biting critique employed so deftly in his earlier cultural criticism but instead a pastiche of quotes from Emerson's texts, letters, and journals that allowed the critic to efface his own voice and to obliterate intentionality while at the same time imputing moods to Emerson. It allowed him, in other words, to blur the lines of personality between biographer and subject.

This curious, experimental style—in part a function, Claire Sprague believes, of "Brooks's desire to have his works read like novels" (*VWB* 286)—had thematic importance as well. By merging his own identity with his subject's, Brooks enacted, at least rhetorically, Emerson's belief in the Over-Soul and the progressive democracy it could be seen to validate. He did so, it might be argued, while at the same time eliding America's complex social pluralism. Emerson's "mysticism," once considered by Brooks as that element of high ideality that rendered his thought and writing irrelevant to the realities of American life, now seemed to endorse the progressive democratic tendencies upon which an American canon could be founded. If this mysticism often blurred the boundaries between self and nature, it also implied the commonality of human beings and suggested a consensus about national destiny. Emerson, wrote the biographer in an especially self-revelatory passage that suggests the power of an immanent force resembling democratic consensus, "would suddenly lose the sense of his personality, and then this general life rose up within him. It was stronger and better than his own; and when he relaxed and gave it the freest passage, he felt an infinite force traversing his source" (*Life* 44). More important, to one experiencing a psychological crisis, this relinquishing of personality in the name of a higher cause exerted a powerful attraction, making Brooks's cultural interpretation almost a direct response to personal turmoil.

It is precisely his longing for a sense of "general life" that shapes much of Brooks's portrait. (Echoing Emerson's description of his sentences as "infinitely repellent particles," Brooks would describe the fractured condition of his own selfhood in a letter to Mumford: "The future is a bit vague. What isolated particles we all are!"[61]) The Emerson rediscovered by Brooks is by no means the airy highbrow of *America's Coming-of-Age* but instead a thinker intensely alive to the social environment surrounding him, "open at every pore to the common life" (*Life* 120). Firmly rooted in the rich soil of Concord, *this* Emerson rejected aesthetic and social withdrawal, surrounding himself instead with a menagerie of intellectuals.[62] And his travels as lyceum lecturer across an expanding America, in a typical Brooksian passage that incorporates a phrase from "The American Scholar" without attribution, distinguished him from more effete men of letters: "How could any writer, for the sake of his nerves and his nap, spare any action in which he might partake?" (*Life* 167).

Reviewing the biography in *The Symposium*, Morris U. Schappes noted that Brooks's Emerson was primarily a prose stylist, poet, and rebel—which is to say that Brooks had refashioned Emerson as a protomodernist whose aesthetic provided the grounds for resistance in its rootedness to experience.[63] Emerson "had gradually developed a style that was all his own. A nervous, intellectual style, swift, clear, and cold as a mountain stream. It was lean and spare as his own frame, quick as the steps of his feet as he swung along, lean and quick and thrilling as the wind . . ." (*Life* 232). But Brooks also presented Emerson as an antimodernist, describing him not as a social outsider but rather in terms more appropriate to Whitman; Emerson lived "[l]ike a poet, yes—no dainty, protected person, apart and odd. A traveler on the common highway, a frequenter of taverns, very naturally and heartily there" (*Life* 235). Within a democratic context, the poet-commoner was a kind of instinctual Orpheus; "One had only to sing . . ." Brooks remarks, again ventriloquizing his subject, "and the animal would be born!—and the god in man" (*Life* 162).

According to Brooks, it was the recognition of mankind's innate divinity that now inspired Emerson's protest against America's material acquisitiveness. Listening to "The American Scholar" (to which Brooks now devotes five pages of commendatory discussion), Emerson's audience experienced a remarkable transformation. "They could trust their instincts now, these rebels against the law of the commercial world—believe in their times, their country, believe that their dreams had meaning, believe that in them, and not in the gods of matter, lay their real hope of society" (*Life* 78). This description, which anticipates Perry Miller's reading of Emerson as a rebel "against commercialism,"[64] is less an objective account of the effects of Emerson's address on its audience than a subtle effort to control the reception and interpretation of Brooks's own work. To a young generation of socially disengaged modernists, Brooks hoped to offer aesthetic and social prescriptions by describing poetry as the product of a life expended "with intensity and faith" (*Life* 50) and remarking that "writers . . . must honour people's facts" (*Life* 167) in order to help signal "the dawn of a native genius" (*Life* 240).[65]

If Emerson was "one who in days to come was to call [his] faculties into the light and transform all of New England" (*Life* 38), Brooks also saw the author as radically subjective. It is the critic's emphasis on self-realization as the foundation of democracy that causes him to begin his work not with a Puritan genealogy nor description of Emerson's father—as had by now become common practice among Emerson's biographers—but with the idiosyncratic Mary Moody Emerson. Indeed, Emerson's aunt is Brooks's covert heroine, an example of social tradition *and* fully realized individualism. Brooks seems to suggest that the recovery of common values would, paradoxically, result in freedom from stultifying social conformity when he describes Mary Moody Emerson as both the product of "spiritual monarchs after the ancestral pattern" (*Life* 15) and, at the same time, "queerer than Dick's hatband. She was thought to have the power of uttering the most disagreeable things in twenty minutes than any other person living" (*Life* 8). For the Brooks of the 1920s, social renewal was increasingly predicated upon the release and cultivation of the personality; qualifying the implications of Emerson's radicalism, he conceded that the author "had little hope of modification by outward revolution. The change must come from within, through the richest growth of human personality" (*Life* 36).

Still, if Emerson illustrated the virtues of social engagement and self-realization, his usefulness to Brooks's critical project entailed several important omissions. Desperately needing to believe that great art might derive from a jubilant, fulfilling life, Brooks glossed over most of the contradictions and conflicts in Emerson's own biography. If forty pages are devoted to Emerson's happy childhood and career at Harvard (not until Ralph Rusk's 1949 biography would the more harrowing aspects of Emerson's childhood be recovered), only three brief pages chronicle the twelve often excruciating years of Emerson's life preceding his emergence as an essayist and lecturer. Hungering for a release from the psychological crisis that had steadily escalated during the early 1920s, Brooks downplayed the traumatic death of Emerson's son, Waldo ("But life had worn on, with its endless poetry, its short, dry prose of skepticism—like veins of cold air in the evening woods, quickly swallowed by the wide warmth of June" [*Life* 181]). It is Brooks's insistence on chronicling a fulfilled life—the *Paradiso* of the American writer—that ultimately disfigures his biography; it is his refusal to countenance any contradictions in his own Dantesque pilgrimage for salvation that makes readers of the book impatient. For if *The Life of Emerson* might be thought of as "the story of a man thinking, talking, and living in society,"[66] it is not a convincing account of a *writer* attempting to shape his thoughts and experience into formal constructions. Brooks's "synthesis," crucial to his Hegelian trilogy as well as to his emotional well-being, failed precisely because it presented a spiritual biography rather than the portrait of an artist whose example might be seriously considered and even emulated by a new generation.

In recasting Emerson to serve his own needs and those he perceived within the culture, Brooks in many ways repeated the practice of his genteel forbears. The Emerson who emerged in his biography, while a more robust fellow traveler on the dusty highway of American life than in earlier depictions, was nevertheless a cultural ideal whose personal example ultimately superseded anything his writings might have conveyed. By ignoring explicit analysis of Emerson's writings and by failing to present Emerson as a fulfilled *artist*, Brooks created an oddly immaterial figure no more substantial than the most grossly caricatured portraits of earlier critics and biographers. Ultimately, Emerson provided less an example for Brooks during the twenties than a refuge from a materialistic society that seemed increasingly to threaten the very existence of the artist. As Brooks became embroiled in the literary skirmishes of postwar America, as his manic-depressive illness came increasingly to parallel the boom-and-bust atmosphere of the nation just before the depression, Emerson seemed to offer a necessary flight into subjectivity even as he endorsed this flight in the pre–World War I language of populism and progressive democracy. Responding intensely to Emerson in the early twenties, Brooks drastically rewrote him in ways that suggest he was less important, as Blake notes, "for what [he] wrote, ultimately, than for how [he] had survived in a hostile environment."[67] With Emerson, Brooks's efforts to locate a usable past increasingly were transformed into something else: a quest for survival.

Driven by highly personal needs and psychic urgencies, Brooks's celebratory portrait of Emerson was by no means anomalous to those critics of the 1920s who would inspire the emergence of American Studies. *The Life of Emerson* might in fact serve as an index for a more widespread effort within and without the academy to reimagine Emerson as central to a fresh understanding of American culture. Brooks's image of Emerson bears a strong family resemblance, for instance, to that presented by Lewis Mumford in *The Golden Day* (1926), a revisionist literary history that influenced F. O. Matthiessen's *American Renaissance* in its vision of the antebellum period as an era "in which writers like Emerson, Thoreau, Whitman, Melville, and Hawthorne transformed the material facts of American life into higher expressions of artistic and spiritual truth."[68] For Mumford, America's history originated in Europe with the collapse of medieval organicism and the arrival of Renaissance and Reformation values to new shores. Borrowing Brooks's metaphors of biological growth and decay to express a cycle of cultural life—of "disintegration and fulfillment," as he called it—Mumford posited an America capable of endlessly renewing itself.[69] Guiding this cyclical vision of history was Mumford's sense that New England's antebellum literature furnished insights, as Blake has noted, "into American culture that challenged the 'pragmatic quiescence' of modern culture" and suggested a usable tradition for contemporary authors.[70] The Brooksian division of culture and experience was annealed during this period, according to Mumford, when "an imaginative New World came to birth" (*GD* 91). "The attempt to prefigure in the imagination a culture which should grow out of and refine the experiences the transplanted European encountered on the new soil, mingling social heritage of the past with the experience of the present," Mumford continued, "was the great activity of the Golden Day" (*GD* 278).

Central to Mumford's freshly invented canon was Emerson, recovered from the high ideality of the genteel tradition and remade as a philosopher who balanced the opposite poles of American experience and culture. "[I]t has been misconstrued," Mumford wrote in a refutation of Brooks's thesis in *America's Coming-of-Age*, "that [Emerson] lived in a perpetual cloud-world" (*GD* 100). Such misunderstandings were easily explained, however, for Emerson *had* withdrawn from society on occasion, sequestering himself from the encroachments of an incipient industrialism in the pastoral surroundings of Concord. But such withdrawals were strategic, Mumford argued, a conscious effort to step back from the hectic energies accompanying a "period of transition" in order to discern their larger patterns. By describing these patterns to readers and audiences around the country, Emerson had committed himself to a more noble action, making "possible a creative renovation" in frontier America (*GD* 101).

The most important aspect of Emerson's philosophy to Mumford was the emphasis he placed on the constructive quality of ideas. In a postwar era marked by the tightening of political possibilities and a wave of antisocialist sentiment, Mumford redefined modes of action through his Orpheus of a golden day: "Emerson rethought life," he wrote, "and in the mind he coined new shapes and images and institutions" (*GD* 99). Recalling Brooks's earlier dialectical analysis, Mumford portrayed Emerson's philosophy as a recoverable model for reconciling the divided streams of American life: "For Emerson, matter and spirit were not enemies in conflict: they were phases of man's experience: matter passed into spirit and became symbol: spirit passed into matter and gave it a form; and symbols and forms were the essence through which man lived and fulfilled his proper being. Who was there among Emerson's contemporaries in the Nineteenth Century that was gifted with such a complete vision?" (*GD* 104)

Working in a similar, if less celebratory vein, was Vernon L. Parrington, whose three-volume *Main Currents in American Thought* (1927–1930) was perhaps the most successful academic effort to apply political and social perspectives to the study of American literature during the 1920s. "[W]ho can forget the tingling sense of discovery with which we first read these lucid pages," Howard Mumford Jones recalled of Parrington's work, which was distinguished from previous literary histories by its "confident marshaling of masses of stubborn material into position. . . ."[71] And Lionel Trilling, in a later and more negative assessment of Parrington's work, nevertheless admitted that it had had "an influence on our conception of American culture which is not equaled by that of another writer of the last two decades."[72] Parrington's accomplishment was in effect the crowning achievement of the critical movement begun by Brooks (Richard Ruland notes that "Parrington succeeded in doing what Van Wyck Brooks never could: he provided a coherent usable past for the liberals").[73] Grounded on a leftist analysis that imagined American society as divided between humanitarian democracy and tough-minded economic realism, Parrington envisioned a progressive United States that seemed to synthesize both. In his efforts to balance the progressive, democratic values represented by Thomas Jefferson with a recognition of the less naive (if more aristocratic) response by Alexander Hamilton, Parrington's reordering of the United States' literary tradition stemmed less from aesthetic concerns than from his sense that, as a result of industrial culture, "the passion for liberty is lessening, and the individual, in the presence of creature comforts, is being dwarfed."[74] Like Brooks and Mumford, Parrington hoped to find in his recovered history a series of thinkers who might speak to the present situation. And like them, he viewed the artistic expression of these thinkers not as belletristic activity but as crucial documents produced by social processes: the "record [of] the spirit of a people," as Brooks had once stated in America's Coming-of-Age, "evidence of a material sort" (VWB 96).

David S. Shumway notes that Parrington's primary criteria in selecting authors for his discussion were their political significance; "literature became [in Main Currents] the record of [a] political struggle" between liberal democracy and conservative aristocracy.[75] Shumway's representation of Parrington's project is ultimately too simplistic, reducing his thesis on national trends in thought to a matter of good guys versus bad guys. But Parrington's vision of history as a struggle between opposing currents did provide the critic with a notion of literary movements as cyclical, enabling him, for instance, to divide the nineteenth century into two dominant periods, the Romantic Revolution and the Age of Realism, that would remain influential for decades to come. If Parrington's critical net was cast over a nearly unprecedented number of literary figures, including writers from the South and the West, he nevertheless devoted considerable attention and energy to the New England canon as it had been constructed decades earlier by critics of the Gilded Age.[76] Echoing Mumford, Parrington saw the Transcendentalists, with their mystic removal from a materialistic society, as "the father[s] of criticism" (MC 382) and asserted that "their very lives were a criticism and a judgment on New England and America" (MC 377).

Emerson played a particularly important role in this leftist interpretation of trancendentalism. Parrington's description of Emerson as a progressive political thinker not only stood in stark contradiction to conservative critics such as Oliver Wendell Holmes or Irving Babbitt, but it also answered the concerns of literary insurgents who distrusted Emerson's self-reliant individualism as encouraging a posture of detachment from social reform. Responding to liberal and conservative criticism, Parrington stressed Emerson's individualism as God-reliance, arguing that "[i]n accepting himself he accepted his fellows, and he accepted God" (*MC* 382). A direct conduit of the liberal-Jeffersonian ideal, Emerson's "transcendental theory of politics" provided a valuable counterweight to the Hamiltonian materialism then engulfing America; the transcendental perspective enabled Emerson to become an incisive cultural critic whose analysis of "the tragic gap between the real and the ideal" led him to conclude that America's failure to realize its potential stemmed from "pernicious social institutions which stifle the nobler impulses and encourage the baser" (*MC* 383). In recasting Emerson as "the man who was to become the most searching critic of America" (*MC* 386), however, Parrington wholly ignored Emerson the moralist or metaphysician, Emerson the poet, Emerson the prose stylist, and Emerson the mystic. Yet writing before the romantic enthusiasm of his age would be tempered by the grinding, quotidian realities of industrialism, Parrington's Emerson nevertheless saw evil as well as good, "the tragic gap" between the Jeffersonian ideal and the Hamiltonian reality. Out of this awareness he fashioned for himself a social role as lecturer and essayist that furthered the nineteenth century's "ebullient democratic faith" (*MC* 390) and led the way for future progressive fellow travelers.

That Parrington was able to cast Emerson in such a light during the 1920s is of course a reflection of the force and sustainability of Van Wyck Brooks's project of dismantling genteel culture in the United States. And that project suggests once again how a canonical figure may fill the personal and cultural needs of a reader or a critic in ways that may have little to do with that canonical figure's actual texts. Regardless of his reliance on an image of Emerson bequeathed by genteel critics, Brooks's version of the author was never simply a report of an irrelevant historical figure but rather a *recasting* of Emerson's cultural significance. The image thus transmitted—through the pages of *Seven Arts,* the *Dial,* the *Freeman,* and a host of other leftist intellectual magazines during the first two decades of the century—prefigured the versions of Emerson constructed by subsequent critics, including F. O. Matthiessen, Perry Miller, and Sacvan Bercovitch.

Brooks's reception of Emerson suggests, in other words, how a particular author may be marshaled in the service of an individual's own critical reputation, in turn transforming wider circles of readers. Growing out of a strong personal reaction to the context in which Emerson had been transmitted, Brooks's refashioning created a new interpretive paradigm that affected the practice of other likeminded critics. Waldo Frank's devaluation of Emerson, for instance, was accompanied by an acknowledgment that it would have been impossible without Brooks's "pioneering work" in "creating a consciousness of American life."[77] Mary M. Colum, writing in a 1924 issue of *Dial*, called Brooks "a pathfinder, a contributor of transforming ideas,"[78] while Paul Rosenfield in the same year ranked Brooks "second in pregnancy for the Nation" after Whitman.[79] This last comment illustrates with particular clarity the cultural politics of literary reputation—the way in which authors rise and fall not only according to the subtleties of the writer's aesthetic accomplishments but through the presentation and re-presentation of his or her work by critics and mass media. It also illustrates a larger, though now almost forgotten, cultural drama as well, one that features Emerson's brush with critical oblivion, his near disappearance into the void of literary forgetfulness, his nadir of repute during the first decades of the twentieth century and his improbable and meteoric return to critical acclaim. But most importantly, Brooks's reconfiguration of Emerson suggests how critical paradigms are forged within the tangled conflicts of personal dissatisfaction and cultural circumstances and how those paradigms take on a life of their own. Based upon residual interpretations of Emerson inherited from the genteel tradition, Brooks merged these with an increasingly dominant sense of cultural division in the United States, and in the process he created an emergent and soon-to-be-canonical figure.

Recalling those years when he and Brooks labored to reinvent personal canons of American literature, Lewis Mumford underscored the significance of Brooks's later work by describing it as an effort to "carry on and complete the great work Emerson opened in *The American Scholar*."[80] Mumford failed to specify exactly what he meant by this "great work," but we can gain some idea of it in *The Golden Day*, where Emerson's importance to a new generation is shown to be the way he "re-thought life, and in the mind . . . coined new shapes and images, ready to take the place of those he discarded" (*GD* 99). For Mumford, Emerson's cultural reign existed between two periods of materialism, the second of which continued to haunt American life and public policy well into the twentieth century. The work Mumford understood Brooks to have inherited from Emerson centered on a conviction that culture in general and literature in particular might function as a social force, might even "cure the ills of a stagnant culture."[81]

As a young critic, Brooks had replaced the perceived *absence* of a vital cultural and literary scene in America—a "beloved community" of art and friendship—with a nostalgic narrative of *loss* that in turn energized his critical and political projects. This fictive loss involved a circle of writers—*Emerson and Others,* as Brooks entitled one of his books—that eventually came to stand for a vanished yet representative group from the past. During his period of sustained psychosis, which was prompted in part by his fear that the heroically oppositional critic might prove incapable of effecting positive and meaningful change, Brooks substituted his profound sense of loss with an absence: a feeling that the literary-cultural realm had disappeared or lost its importance. Brooks's illness was prompted in part by a guilty sense that in trying to effect that change, his earlier and widely praised cultural critiques had killed literature as the treasured and separate realm promulgated by the genteel tradition. Having once announced in *America's Coming-of-Age* that "America is like a vast Sargasso Sea—a prodigious welter of unconscious life" (*VWB* 149), Brooks's manic-depressive psychosis included not only the delusional fantasy that the world would end with his death but that he was "a capsized ship at night with the passengers drowned underneath and the keel in the air."[82] Having overturned the ship of literature with which he identified, having failed in the megalomaniacal dream of redeeming America, and finally having *lost* the sense of literary possibility through the lacerating demystification of his own criticism, Brooks stepped, or rather fell, into the chasm of depression from which only the Emerson book could release him.[83]

Writing to Lewis Mumford in March 1929, Eleanor Stimson Brooks noted that her husband's "unreasonable and obsessional determination to die" was "based on the belief that he has failed and can never 'make good' again." This sense of failure, she added, stemmed directly from Brooks's sense that his book on Emerson was "unfinished and would make him ridiculous if it appeared. . . . all three doctor's [sic] agree that it may be this still-born book that is preventing his recovery."[84] As a result, Eleanor and Mumford arranged, against Brooks's wishes, the publication of the book. The tangled relationship between Emerson and Brooks is nowhere so poignantly suggested as in a long letter sent by Brooks's oldest son, Charles, soon after the book was published:

> At its bottom your *Emerson* appears to me less as a book, which
> I could for itself love or dislike, approve or disdain, than as a point
> of view. . . . What a relief to taste the flesh and blood of writing,
> after all the dried fish and boiled carrots peddled out by the . . .
> library mathematicians that beset us! . . . It is neither a work of
> art nor a mathematical formula. . . . you identify yourself with
> Emerson and make a hero of him. . . . Furthermore, I believe that
> if any book can bring a glimmer of light to this desperate land of
> ours, *Emerson* will do it![85]

Having conflated his father and Emerson much as genteel critics had once done in their own respective projects, Charles in many ways echoed not just his father but an entire generation dispirited by postwar apathy and the confiscation of meaningful dissent during the Jazz Age. For Brooks, Mumford, and other leftist critics during the 1920s, a single speech by Emerson—and increasingly the example of Emerson himself—attained new significance and fresh interpretive possibilities, becoming important enough to suggest the true origins of American cultural history. To carry on Emerson's work following the wreckage of the First World War not only described the intentions of many writers and critics, but also, and more profoundly, as we shall see, funded the emergent field of American Studies.

CHAPTER 4

F. O. Matthiessen and the Tragedy of the American Scholar

There seems to be something in an effort to understand the height and depths of life that makes for either faith and confidence or tragic despair. Emerson knew both; his followers often chose; and the toll has been heavy.

—Robert Spiller, "The Four Faces of Emerson"

I.

In the winter of 1938, while drafting the manuscript that would eventually become *American Renaissance,* the literary critic F. O. Matthiessen checked himself into McLean's psychiatric hospital, plagued "by the fantasy it would be better if I jumped out the window."[1] The immediate cause of his suicidal thoughts (which he would act upon nearly a dozen years later) was personal: he was convinced that Russell Cheney, the painter with whom he would share twenty years of his life, might soon die. Intimately connected to this fear, however, were grave concerns over his unfinished masterpiece. Matthiessen complained, for instance, of having "less satisfaction and less control" over the manuscript on which he'd already been engaged for nearly a decade. Unable to "turn off the pressure and relax" (*RD* 245), he admitted that he might have "gear[ed] my notion of this book too high" (*RD* 253) and now felt inadequate to the task of "writing the book I had wanted" (*RD* 245). Formerly energized by a project that had promised to place him "in contact with so many sides of American society," Matthiessen felt plagued by anxieties that left him enshrouded in a "film of unreality" (*RD* 248).

Given the scope and accomplishment of *American Renaissance,* such anxieties are understandable. The book's 1941 publication signaled the emergence of a new field that students and professors were particularly eager to engage and explore. Wilson O. Clough, a professor of litera-ture at the University of Wyoming, summed up the excitement when he wrote Matthiessen in December of that year and thanked him for having "indicated a new method for study of various periods of our literature."[2] For Clough and many others, *American Renaissance* suddenly meant the realization of a decades-long effort to insert American literature into a university setting. It meant the legitimization of an American writing fe-cund enough in craft and content to equal, if not surpass, other national literatures. It also represented the most nuanced effort to mobilize the American past so as to emancipate and instruct the politics of the pres-ent. And it meant the timely affirmation of democracy just as the United States entered World War II.[3]

That *American Renaissance* very nearly killed Matthiessen is a testa-ment to the toll the book exacted. *Why* his suicidal response to the work occurred when it did—after only a third of the book was complete—is suggested by the way in which his anxieties seem to coalesce around the figure of Emerson. Like a ghostly presence, Emerson's voice seeps into Matthiessen's account of his psychiatric malady, providing the vocabulary through which he articulates his anguish and sense of failure. Writing from the hospital about his concerns for the book, Matthiessen para-phrases Emerson's famous critique of American materialism—"Things are in the saddle, / And ride mankind"[4]—by describing how "instead of riding my work, it began without precedent to ride me" (*RD* 245). He laments—in words that recall Emerson's language in "The American Scholar"—that "[m]y great resource, books, has become meaningless." Despairing over the insufficiency of his manuscript, he frets that his par-ticipation is a ghastly charade, that rather than an "Aristotelian" critic he is merely "an enthusiast trying to be a critic, a Platonic rhapsode" (*RD* 246)—the very formulation he uses to describe that aspect of Emerson he finds least satisfactory. Finally, in a sentence that calls into question his ability to enact Emerson's *Man Thinking* as "the whole man" (*EL* 54) who might by his very completion transfigure the "state of mind" (*EL* 65) of his audience, Matthiessen wonders if "the self-knowledge which I have believed to be my sureness in making my life an integrated one" had in fact left him "shut off more than I am aware" (*RD* 247).

On the one hand, these Emersonian echoes suggest the extent to which Matthiessen had internalized the model of the American Scholar. If it is true, as Robert Spiller once noted, that in writing *American Renaissance* Matthiessen "accepted Emerson only because he couldn't escape him,"[5] it is equally accurate that no twentieth-century literary critic strove so self-consciously to enact Emerson's conception of the American Scholar as a unified sensibility vitally engaged in reshaping a failed or unrealized America through active cultural influence. This is not to say that Matthiessen took very seriously Emerson's writing *as writing*; far from it. His formalist reservations about the essayist would not only render Emerson a lamentable prefiguration of Thoreau and the other authors in his study, but it would also profoundly influence a subsequent generation of scholars who struggled to find an organic form in Emerson's aesthetic. Nevertheless, Emerson's essay on the scholar exemplified for Matthiessen a robust and compelling model of human agency and progressive action, and his deep identification with the figure is apparent in the testimony of many others. Bernard Bowron insisted that the critic's "commitment to scholarship as a special and indispensable kind of social action" made him *the* modern heir to Emerson's resonant archetype.[6] And for Leo Marx, Matthiessen's willingness to speak out on radical issues suggested his "mindful[ness] of Emerson's warning to the American Scholar not to defer to the popular cry" (*MR* 210). Such an image had been largely fostered by Matthiessen himself, instanced most famously in the introduction to *American Renaissance*. There he evoked the architect Louis Sullivan's "one fundamental test of citizenship, namely: Are you using such gifts as you possess for or against the people?" and concluded with the impossibly high-minded assertion that "[t]hese standards are the inevitable and right extension of Emerson's demands in The American Scholar. The ensuing volume has value only to the extent that it comes anywhere near measuring up to them."[7]

Still, Matthiessen's vocalization of Emerson while at McLean's also suggests a profound uneasiness with the writer and, at the same time, serves as a touchstone for exploring his psychological state as he struggled to become a twentieth-century American Scholar by writing *American Renaissance*. Here Emerson's shadowy presence in Matthiessen's depression recalls Freud's familiar insight that suicide never destroys just one person, that self-annihilation invariably wreaks vengeance on an internalized other felt to exercise malignant influence over its tortured subject.[8] While Matthiessen may have found in the American Scholar a vocational model that promised to unify culture and so rescue the intellectual from social isolation, he also discovered in Emerson's writing radical contradictions he believed were symptomatic of his own position as public intellectual—and private homosexual—in American society. Because Emerson's writing mirrored in so many ways the personal and intellectual conflicts Matthiessen himself hoped to resolve through the figure of the American Scholar, that writing proved more troublesome and threatening to him than any other in his canon. Indeed, Emerson's prose (with the exception of the journals) is almost entirely exorcised from *American Renaissance*. The result is not only a version of Emerson that is, as Richard Ruland once noted, "clearly the least successful portrait of *American Renaissance*,"[9] but a canonical author whose literary *presence* is mysteriously absent. Engaged in a deadly struggle with Emerson's writing, Matthiessen would expunge much of it from his book, restraining its more troubling imaginative energies and urgencies, but at the expense of the critical integrity he so desired.

There is a moment in Emerson's essay on "Experience" (1844) that captures precisely the dilemma Matthiessen would undergo as a reconstituted American Scholar in the first half of the twentieth century. Elegizing transcendental optimism while confronting its limitations, Emerson admits that if we once were "born to a whole," we now experience a "pain" that is "the plaint of tragedy," a recognition of the inevitable partiality of "persons . . . friendship and love" (*EL* 477)—and, by extension, of existence itself. Earlier, Emerson has confessed that "[g]hostlike we glide through nature, and should not know our place again" (*EL* 471), but now, following his revelation of the tragic insufficiency of a social world that can never be completely ordered or determined by the self and thus can never fully satisfy that self, he attempts to shed this spectral homelessness, to think his way back into some habitation of meaning. Abruptly dismissing the problems of disjunctive "friendship and love," he exclaims that "[o]f course it needs the whole society to give the symmetry we seek. The parti-colored wheel must revolve very fast to appear white" (*EL* 477).

Emerson's lapse into a nostalgia for primal wholeness, as well as his barely discernible discomfort with the ease and haste of his own meliorating explanation, looks back to the opening myth of the "The American Scholar." There, just seven years earlier, he had depicted contemporary life as fragmented and specialized, a "society . . . in which the members have suffered amputation from the trunk, and strut about so many walking monsters" (*EL* 54). Relief from social limitations occurred not from a distanced perspective—from spinning the wheel of society so quickly as to blur its divisions—but in returning to original splendor an integrated and fully quickened "*Man Thinking*." This harmonizing thinker, whose duty was "to cheer, to raise, and to guide men by showing them facts amidst appearances" (*EL* 63), would accomplish his task by employing the resources of Nature, books, and action. And he would accomplish it, more importantly, within a democratic context, thereby resolving the perennial tensions felt to accrue between self and society by positing, in Kenneth S. Sacks's words, "a naturally reciprocal arrangement between genius and populace."[10]

For much of his life, Matthiessen would yearn to achieve the serene wholeness whose intermittent presence and frequent departure Emerson mourns in "Experience." From his early twenties onward he would articulate a vision remarkably similar to the one evinced in "The American Scholar," insisting upon the need for a unified existence, an ontological wholeness that expressed itself politically (through democratic socialism), aesthetically (through a Coleridgean organic form), professionally (through a pedagogical practice that linked thought with action), and personally (through an effort to harmonize these competing approaches while at the same time living with Cheney in "the peace of absolute union" [*RD* 54]). "That's what I'm striving for, as you know," he wrote confidently to his lover in 1925, "the realization of a fully developed character, the realization that I am at the heart of life and no longer palavering at the fringes" (*RD* 86). If Matthiessen's yearning for integrity and wholeness expressed itself primarily in the vernacular of love early in his life, it soon exerted a pervasive influence in his approaches to the mutual tasks of criticism and social justice. In 1933 Matthiessen told a reporter for the *Harvard Crimson* that he believed "firmly in the possibilities of literature applied to life" and admitted his hope that the class divisions responsible for their respective estrangements might soon be eliminated.[11] Speaking only a few months before his death in 1950 (this time to the *Harvard Advocate*), he reiterated his abhorrence for "the life of the isolated scholar." As a "citizen first," he spoke now of his integrative goal as a "renewed sense of the responsibility of the intellectual . . . to be as true as possible to what his experience has taught him."[12]

Critics such as Jay Grossman and Henry Abelove have variously and persuasively linked Matthiessen's concern with the social division of "Man into men" (*EL* 53) to his homosexuality. Precisely how Matthiessen's gay identity led him at times to articulate an Emersonian vision of a meaningful universe conducing to the fundamental wholeness of human society can be traced back to the remarkable 1924 "Oxford Letter."[13] Written when Matthiessen was twenty-two and shortly after his arrival in England to begin a Rhodes scholarship, this fragment of autobiography attempts to take stock of its author's life and character as he begins a new life abroad. Admitting that in "temperament I have much of the feminine," his self-examination soon leads him to declare his ambition to become a professor of literature "because I think I can best express my abilities in it." He then describes recent developments in his religious and political thinking, confessing to himself that "I worship Christ although I do not believe the balance of the Christian dogma" and that he supports "the British Labour party, and am a Pacifist." To some extent, these personal investments are a reaction to his father, who had deserted the family when Matthiessen was a child, leaving him to feel abandoned: "His distinguishing characteristic is an almost absolute selfishness," he writes with evident bitterness. "He regards his own personal welfare, little else." Juxtaposing friendship against this portrait of paternal selfishness, he declares that in companions he invariably looks for "an appreciation of literature and art, a brilliant and fearless mind, and an idealism that finds in spiritual beauty and truth the end of life."

The majority of the letter, however, is filled with a searchingly frank discussion of his sexual orientation. While "absolutely convinced that there is no sexual inversion in any part of the family," Matthiessen traces his own homoerotic longings in detail from an early age. His first sexual experience, when twelve years old, occurs with an older boy and is the first of several infatuations that will increasingly trouble his young conscience. Eventually, as a student at Yale, he makes furtive trips to New York for anonymous sex in restrooms and movie theaters. Careful to hide such activities from his friends, he views his undergraduate sexual experiences as an isolating cycle of longing and shame, "the gratification of sheer animal desire." This severance from human community is briefly mitigated when he embraces, at the age of twenty, the Christian faith, finding there "a sublimation of many of my desires. I felt completely and fully happy for the first time."

In many ways, the letter provides unmistakable evidence of the "double-consciousness" Leo Marx viewed as the byproduct of Matthiessen's homosexuality at Harvard during the depression and war years—the aching division he experienced between a furtive private and an "official" public selfhood that ultimately informed his political and critical projects.[14] Edmund S. Morgan recently recalled that at Harvard, "Matty couldn't come out of the closet because *nobody* came out of the closet in those days," but that he nevertheless could be denied an administrative appointment at Harvard because it was "known that Matty was a homosexual and that was held against him."[15] Pearl Kazin Bell remembers a rare instance of Matthiessen's inner turmoil erupting to the surface when a group of students, giggling over the sexual content of O'Neill's *Strange Interlude*, were brought up short as Matthiessen slammed his book on the lectern and demanded, "Doesn't any of you know what it means to be neurotic, to have one's sexual being twisted with pain . . . ?"[16]

One thing the "Oxford Letter" reveals is that the social conundrum of homosexuality (exacerbated by the pain of his father's desertion)

influenced Matthiessen's politics as well as his equally passionate acceptance of Christianity, which in contrast to the Emersonian optimism
of "The American Scholar" would offer an epistemological explanation
of human frailty and suffering along with the possibility of redemption
through divine grace. The letter further provides valuable insight into another, if surprising, means by which Matthiessen would attempt to salve
his sense of dividedness. Confessing in the "Oxford Letter" that from
an early age he "began to admire intensely the physical vigor of older
men," he candidly asserts that as he became more sexually active he "always wanted to have the man as old as possible, naturally providing that
he was still vigorous." If Matthiessen recognizes that never having "had
any paternal affection may have something to do with" his preference in
partners, he soon attributes other meanings to his desire; admitting that
"what I delighted in most was . . . intercrural intercourse"—the ritualized
practice in ancient Greece by which mentors "penetrated" young men by
rubbing the penis between their thighs—Matthiessen consciously situates his sexual longings within a prior tradition of homoerotic pedagogy.
This dense associative context helps illuminate his passionate relationship
with Cheney, a taciturn New England painter who, exactly twenty years
older than Matthiessen, would serve as a cultural and intellectual mentor
in ways that have yet to be fully assessed.

Matthiessen's interest in American literature has traditionally been traced
to his reading of Lewis Mumford's *The Golden Day* (1926), described in the
introduction of *American Renaissance* as "a major event in my experience"
(*AR* xvii).[17] Unfamiliar with the American literary tradition before his trip
abroad in 1924, Matthiessen's reading of Mumford would soon lead him
to Van Wyck Brooks's thesis that American culture was divided between
"vaporous idealism" and the self-interested business class, which became a
foundational premise of his own criticism. But it was in fact Cheney who
introduced him to "classic" American literature—Cheney, who as a young
man had "nourished himself on Emerson, who prepared him to find, some
years later, Whitman as his poet,"[18] and who encouraged Matthiessen to
read *Leaves of Grass* almost as soon as the two men met on an ocean liner.
(As Grossman suggests, Whitman exists not only as intertext in the early
correspondence but as a covert role model, a symbol of the possibilities
latent in the two men's budding love.) Writing to Matthiessen in the winter
of 1924, several months after their meeting, the painter assumes the mock-
stentorian tone of tutor and baptizing spirit when describing Concord,
Massachusetts, as that "shrine of American literature in whose clean icy wa-
ter I have longed to duck your soiled soul."[19] And he would soon encourage
Matthiessen, trained as a scholar of Renaissance poetry, to write his first
book about the American local colorist, Sarah Orne Jewett.

More crucially, the relationship with Cheney provided early authority for what would become Matthiessen's ambivalent adherence to formal criticism. This critical approach—and especially the tensions created by its juxtaposition with his leftist politics—has become a central crux for critics of and apologists for Matthiessen's critical procedure. Unremarked upon to this point, however, is Cheney's role in providing an early and persuasive rationale for an aesthetic approach to art and life. Extolling "the richness of organic form" years before Matthiessen would read Eliot or the New Critics (*RC* 31), Cheney repeatedly critiques Matthiessen's early versions of himself as a socially engaged critic interested in "ethics" and "the study of the human spirit" (*RD* 102). Noting that "Tolstoi was only an artist and only of value to the world writing his novels," Cheney asserts that as soon as the Russian novelist "ran amuck as a Christian, his artistic life was ended; he was merely a moralist and reformer of value for, at the outside, a hundred years—while art is eternal" (36). This sentence—which argues against a purely instrumental approach to literature in much the same terms Matthiessen was later to do—is remarkable for the way it dismisses the young critic's commitments to socialism and Christianity. Writing even more explicitly of Matthiessen's political concerns, Cheney will lash out: "What the hell do I care for Davis or Coolidge or your pitiful La Follette [the Populist presidential candidate for whom Matthiessen voted in 1924] and his pricked bubble! They are gone tomorrow. Is Giotto gone tomorrow? You bet your life he isn't" (*RD* 54). Moreover, this strain of "aesthetic dissent"[20] in Cheney will occur undiminished as late as 1945, the year of his death, with his pronouncement that "the idea about painting carrying a social message" is merely a "phase. . . . Painting goes on and concerns itself with its own concerns. If those concerns are achieved it goes on living" (*RD* 344).

Despite such rebukes by his lover and mentor, Matthiessen never fully renounced a socially motivated criticism in favor of an ahistorical formalism. As his student J. C. Levenson recently remarked, "What makes it misleading to classify him as a New Critic is his always pressing beyond formalism . . . [to the] changes in moral, social, and political experience that helped explain changes in expression."[21] What Cheney *did* contribute to Matthiessen's developing critical perspective was a rationale for formalist criticism that not only spoke to Cheney's concerns as an artist but provided a conceptual imaginary in which the two men, both of whom felt painfully marginalized as homosexuals, could attain a sense of wholeness and of control within a privately constructed and aestheticized world. The editor of Cheney and Matthiessen's correspondence, Louis Hyde, focused his selection more on the two men's relationship and accordingly chose not to print their discussions about craft and aesthetics.[22] But the voluminous letters are in fact rich with details of Cheney's working method, which consistently emphasizes *poiesis*, or making, at the expense or diminution of *praxis*. Writing detailed and appreciative descriptions of media, composition, and intention, Cheney never makes claims for his art as morally enlightened, politically efficacious, or socially representative. The act of painting is consistently seen rather as a "struggle with myself" to achieve "a conception of style" (*RC* 45), to "get the motive impulse down in concrete form" (*RC* 58), and to locate a "frame-work of abstract form and color, good for its own sake" so that "it holds as real, irrespective of subject matter" (*RC* 80). More important, this processual method, "good for its own sake," ultimately provides the experiential ground on which Cheney can struggle to "be whole again" (*RD* 41).

Embedded in Cheney's aestheticism, then, is not just an alliance with artistic orthodoxies then becoming dominant via international modernism but rather a context-specific reaction to the socially excruciating conditions of homosexuality in the first third of the twentieth century—conditions invariably depicted by Cheney and Matthiessen as constrictive, limiting, and socially determinative. If Cheney is scarcely able at times to "face myself as I am," it is largely because "in society . . . as it is organized, [the homosexual is] outcast" (*RD* 80–1). Matthiessen registers his own painful awareness of the costs: "Can't you hear the hell-hounds of society baying, full pursuit behind us?" (*RD* 29). Within this social framework, Cheney's aesthetic formalism alleges that both the artist and critic can, however temporarily, transcend history-bound prejudices within the carefully delineated parameters of style. It further alleges that by approaching the work of art with empathic sensitivity, the reader or viewer can resist falling into prejudicial thinking and, in the process, participate in a kind of ethical self-formation potentially beneficial to the larger society. Admonishing the young Matthiessen for his use of cliché when writing about a Parisian prostitute, Cheney equates seeing—the foundation of his aesthetic—with ethical judgment. Insisting upon a form of perception unencumbered by ideology or orthodoxy, he belittles Matthiessen for describing the woman as a "painted whore"—"they are always painted"—and then advises, "Do everything possible to avoid the expected adjective in writing or speaking or thinking. . . . Trying to find the right word each time and trying to classify each time are the things that count" (*RD* 38). In a phrase that looks toward Lewis Mumford's observation that "Emerson's thought does not seal the world up into a few packets . . . and place them in a pigeonhole,"[23] Cheney reminds Matthiessen that "[e]verything that is pigeonholed as this or that is a dead thing" (*RD* 38).

Taken as a whole, Cheney's remarks clearly and thoroughly inform the critical principles evident fifteen years later in *American Renaissance* and can be seen as the governing ideas informing Matthiessen's bedrock conviction that the arts offer "the mind and spirit" an unprecedented opportunity "to preserve their health by the variety and scope of their action, by the free play, even the exuberance that only [they] can provide."[24] Moreover, they help illuminate Matthiessen's aesthetic formalism as his understanding, however sporadic, that politically instrumental readings of literature actually *threatened* rather than liberated a sense of autonomy already felt to be compromised by culturally determined attitudes toward his sexuality. In this, both Cheney and Matthiessen prefigure Murray Krieger's argument that the self-reflexive nature of the aesthetic provides a "subversive antidote to the political abuse of discursive power."[25]

Besides directing Matthiessen to American literature and laying the groundwork for his later formalist criticism, the relationship with Cheney allowed the critic to achieve an often tenuous but powerfully affective experience of "wholeness" and integration. To a friend Matthiessen confessed soon after meeting Cheney that he "had attained complete harmony with another spirit for the first time in my life" (*RD* 18), and to the painter he repeatedly summons the fusion of "mind, body, and soul in our perfect embracing love" (*RD* 86) as an ideal to be consecrated in their private lives. This sense of psychic completion—which Matthiessen clung to, often poignantly, for the next twenty years—would remain an important point of reference even while its enactment often precluded integration within a broader social setting. "My sex bothers me, feller," he would write to Cheney in a much-quoted letter from early in the Depression, "sometimes when it makes me aware of the falseness of my position in the world. . . . Have I any right in a community that would so utterly disapprove of me if it knew the facts?" (*RD* 200). Oscillating between rigidly demarcated public and private realms, between the seemingly conflicting roles of intellectual and lover, Matthiessen fell into depressive episodes whenever the demands of work and society caused him to spend whole semesters away from Cheney. Anticipating the crisis that occurred a decade later as he drafted *American Renaissance,* Matthiessen complains in a 1929 letter to Cheney of being lost "in loneliness. . . . There seems to be a film between me and everything. Nothing seems really vital: books are just a procession of words, and I can't find any real significance in my work. . . . I feel so pointless here away from the center of my life with you. I can't quite pull it off. I can't quite create the illusion" (*RD* 173). This admission prefigures many of the same complaints—a sense of "unreality," the desertion of pleasure in reading—that would eventually lead Matthiessen to contemplate suicide while drafting

American Renaissance. Significantly, the letter was written soon after Matthiessen had written a spirited call for "the history of American literature to be rewritten,"[26] a new history that would employ and integrate all known critical approaches. What the letter suggests, in other words, is a psychological pattern by which Matthiessen's hope to achieve wholeness (associated variously with Emerson's figure of the American Scholar, with an aesthetic and social criticism that emphasizes unity, and with his relationship with Cheney) is deflated by sobering disappointments (separation from Cheney and perceived sociopolitical failures, both of which he attempts to cushion by a compensatory Christian-tragic understanding). If this pattern in many ways echoes the pained pilgrimage described in Emerson's "Experience," it occurs for the first time in the critic's life almost immediately before W. W. Norton commissioned him to write a "new" literary history of America. *American Renaissance* can be seen as a work conceived at least in part within a psychic crucible of loneliness and depression triggered by the critic's closeted relationship. As we shall see, its conception also occurs at a historical moment when Matthiessen could hope that an American culture divided by the strains of economic crisis might be aesthetically unified within his critical program and then re-presented to the public. It reveals a moment when Matthiessen's self-identification coalesced with the larger identity of the nation, when the cultural opportunities created by the Depression seemed to offer him the chance to unify his own bipolarities—"the heights and depths of life," to use Spiller's phrase—and to do so in the name of a recovered literary past deployed in order to redirect the future.

II.

There are any number of passages in "The American Scholar" where Emerson must have made his audience uneasy, but none so dramatically as in the address's final paragraph. Having derided the nation's "sluggard intellect" and scorned his era's intellectuals as bookish and disengaged, he pronounced, "The scholar is decent, indolent, complaisant" (*EL* 70). In its inversion of the term "decency," the sentence predicts an entire tradition of Romantic-modernist cultural criticism that attacks social smugness and calls into question the valuation of such terms as "genteel," "respectable," and "elite." The sharpness of Emerson's attack, prompted in part by the economic collapse of 1837 and a corresponding anger at an apathetic intelligentsia, is palpable in the text more than a century later. Among other things, it proleptically calls into question the "professionalization" of literary and cultural studies, asking us to consider how

academic specialization might highlight, skew, and profit from the significance of a figure like Emerson. Although no contemporaneous account
of the speech notes the tone of Emerson's baritone when he delivered
the next line, it is tempting to imagine him, as Sacks asks us to, pausing
before he delivered the next sentence and peering out over the assembled
as he spoke: "See already the tragic consequences."[27]

No American literary critic of the twentieth century worked as tena-
ciously as Matthiessen to avoid the discordant consequences of a smugly
complacent academy. Eric Cheyfitz has recently noted that Emerson's
Phi Beta Kappa address defined "the function of the scholar" as acting
"in concert with the community in order to restore its members to 'self
trust,' that is, *integrity.*"[28] Given this definition, Matthiessen's work from
the 1930s onward is exemplary. If, as he wrote at the beginning of the
decade, "in the general disintegration of society since the war, we have
lost our faith in the possibilities of action,"[29] he would, like many writers
and critics of the era, come increasingly to work for social change during
the heyday of the Popular Front, encouraged at last that the radical intellectual might finally enter into fruitful communion with the larger society.[30] By the 1930s, Matthiessen was a stalwart socialist, one who repeatedly voiced Emerson's concern about a grotesque social fragmentation
in his own efforts to draw attention to the lamentable truth that "college professors lose sight of the central fact: that in a healthy democracy
there should be no wide separation between workers with their heads and
with their hands."[31] He joined and then became president of the leftist
Harvard Teachers Union, confiding to his friend and colleague Kenneth
Murdock that "[i]f academic freedom is simply the freedom not to voice
publicly the political and social convictions which you believe important
to the wellbeing of that society, I do not see much value in education."
Throughout the Depression he tirelessly crusaded for a wide spectrum of
social causes—reporting on labor conditions in New Mexico, canvassing
North End tenements in Boston on behalf of the Socialist ticket, and
serving on countless committees. These activities emerged from a broader
conviction, as he explained to Murdock, that "the most important function of the educator is to shape and direct contemporary thought."[32]

During this time Matthiessen became increasingly drawn to Emerson's
American Scholar. Much like Emerson, who during the Panic of 1837
privately lamented that "the land stinks with suicide" (*JMN* 5: 334) and
then delivered "The American Scholar" as an insurrectionary summons
to cultural renovation, Matthiessen, with countless artists and thinkers
of the period, experienced the era's economic devastation as a desperate
situation that provided a cultural opportunity for the committed intellectual previously ignored by a materialistic America. Harry Levin notes

that in the 1930s Matthiessen revealed "an ever-increasing determination to take seriously the ideals of Emerson,"[33] especially those calling for the scholar to act as a vital, integrated member of the community. Matthiessen's understanding of *how* the scholar was to contribute is suggested in a series of lecture notes on Emerson he delivered years later at the Seminar in American Studies at Salzburg. "What did it mean to be an American thinker and writer a century ago, in the early and mid 19th century?" Matthiessen asks. "[Emerson] set himself to the problem of articulating what it meant to be an American scholar, an American poet. He set himself to create an American consciousness."[34]

Matthiessen's own desire to create a new consciousness for his times is best expressed in the introduction to *American Renaissance*. A miniature manifesto written to bridge the gap between the scholar and the larger society, "Method and Scope" characterizes the critic's focus on just five authors as a verdict imposed by "the successive generations of common readers, who make the decisions, [and who] would seem finally to have agreed that the authors of the pre–Civil War era who bulk largest in stature are the five who are my subject" (*AR* xi). While admitting that other writers sold far more books during the antebellum period, Matthiessen remains committed to his five authors for two reasons: first, time has sifted what Thoreau called "the best books" (*AR* xi) from those less deserving, and second, that process of selection is further validated by each author's "devotion to the possibilities of democracy" (*AR* ix).

If Matthiessen's newly imagined canon would help provide an altar upon which the intellectual and his audience might come into fruitful communion, it is his formalist *method* that ensures such reintegration. Here he clears the ground of prior politically instrumental approaches by summoning and then rejecting the work of Granville Hicks and Vernon Parrington (and by implication, Van Wyck Brooks) as ultimately hindering "the understanding of our literature" (*AR* ix). While such approaches provide invaluable historical and social understanding of the production of works, Matthiessen ultimately condemns them for failing to live up to Louis Sullivan's assertion that a scholar's work must draw "him toward his people, not away from them," and that scholarship must be used "as a means for attaining their end, hence his" (*AR* xv). Aesthetic formalism, in other words, is not only the appropriate response to an exhausted and blindered historicism but is authorized by democracy itself—by the demands and requirements of the populace. Because "the main concern for the common reader" who "does not live by trends alone" is to read and enjoy texts that enliven human capacity, Matthiessen's primary task as a critic is to uncover the inner workings of those books felt to "have an immediate life of their own" (*AR* x).[35]

Given this understanding, by far the most surprising aspect of Mat-thiessen's opening section on Emerson is the almost complete absence of Emerson's actual *writing*. The chapter set aside for Emerson's prose, entitled "The Flowing," darts away from its topic almost as soon as it begins, enacting the practice of what Michael Lopez has called "that long line of critics who have elevated Emerson to unquestioned canonical sta-tus, all the while dismissing his work as unworthy of serious attention."[36] Instead, Matthiessen concentrates on Emerson's philosophy (largely to dismiss it) and examines with cursory disapproval Emerson's poetry (en-dorsing only "Days"). Evicted from his 125-page discussion of Emerson is any substantive or sustained analysis of the essays—the work long con-sidered Emerson's primary contribution to U.S. literature.

What Matthiessen *does* spend a great deal of time examining is Emer-son's interest in an organic form, especially as it was appropriated from Coleridge's *Biographia Literaria* and subsequently ratified by T. S. Eliot and the emerging critical hegemony of the New Critics. This narrowly conceived Emerson is notable primarily because "[o]rganic wholeness was what he admired most" (*AR* 28). Unable to appreciate the fragmentary, disjunctive, and elliptical style of Emerson's essays, Matthiessen is faced with the conundrum of having to begin his study with an author whose writing resists critical traction. To the extent that Coleridgean "whole-ness" can be discerned in *Nature*, Emerson's first book is given primacy in Matthiessen's analysis. But although he never explicitly acknowledges it, the critic's selective focus on Emerson's earliest work presents a prob-lem best illustrated by his abrupt swerve from the author and toward the sculptor Horatio Greenough. Employing Greenough as a surrogate mouthpiece for Emerson's early aesthetic theory, Matthiessen repeats the artist's observation that in a healthy society "everything is generative and everything connected" (*AR* 147). The sculptor allows Matthiessen once again to express his central concern that an American culture divided by class and capitalism has led to fatal social isolation for the artist and a more general social turbulence, as evidenced when Greenough is approv-ingly shown to have asserted that "social and economic equality [are] the only right foundation for art" (*AR* 148).

Matthiessen's hastily diverted focus to Greenough suggests in part his discomfort with Emersonian individualism and his unwillingness to take into account what John Michael has called the "structural and historical difficulties [for Emerson] of mounting a political appeal in a liberal de-mocracy without appealing to individualism and to the individual's judg-ment, allegiances, actions and identity."[37] But Matthiessen's discomfort differs from that of many previous critics in the way it conflates Em-erson's insistence upon the individual as simultaneously a political *and* an aesthetic failing. "The problem of Emerson's prose," he writes in a sentence remarkable for its implications, "was the same as that of his philosophy, how to reconcile the individual with society, how to join his sentences into a paragraph" (*AR* 66). Matthiessen's fusion of Emerson's fragmentary aesthetic with his advocacy of the unfettered self suggests, on the one hand, a straining to locate a direct correlation between art and social concerns. But underlying the gesture is a much larger presumption bolstering Matthiessen's project, the notion inherited from Van Wyck Brooks that literature was symptomatic of cultural health and that organic style therefore implied social coherence. Matthiessen's effort to recuperate from the past such a literature was made in the hopes of healing a splintered America while at the same time providing himself—as critic, as political activist, as homosexual—a self-integrating social role. In this single sentence he suggests both the ambitious scope of his critical project—to redirect American culture and, in the process, to heal his own inner divisions—and his anxiety that this project, which relied on analogy instead of causal evidence, was doomed to failure.

In hindsight we can see that by suppressing from *American Renaissance* all but the early "organic" Emerson, Matthiessen leaves out a writer who refuses to stay put, a writer whose prickly aesthetic suggests his profound interest in a spontaneous unbinding from the past and a dismissal of those structures of affiliation that would impinge upon the intuitive and the improvisational. "Life only avails," this Emerson famously states in "Self-Reliance," "not the having lived. Power . . . resides in the moment of transition from a past to a new state, in the shooting of the gulf, in the darting of an aim" (*EL* 271). Mark Edmundson is mostly correct when he notes that "[t]he textual equivalent of [Emerson's] inspired movement is the passage from one sentence to the next, so that Emerson's antagonist is not only everything he has received from culture and from others, but his own previous utterance and in fact everything he has thought and said before."[38] What makes this self-creating Emerson even more compelling is the way his readers so often sense, just below the surface of heroic aphorisms, a more representative anxiety about the practicability of his dynamic and protean project. "*If* we live truly, we shall truly see," Emerson notes in a characteristic hypothetical. "*When* we have a new perception, we shall gladly disburden the memory of its hoarded treasures as old rubbish" (*EL* 271; my emphasis). Such doubt, a tonal undercurrent to many of Emerson's most orphic statements, bespeaks not only a Yankee skepticism grounded in flinty factuality but a greater awareness of those social pressures besetting the individual in a democratic polity as well as a pained recognition of the transience and unsustainability of the very moods that allow one to consider such imperious social detachment in the first place.

This restless, questing, extemporizing prose style—the stylistic performance of self-creation through constant self-revision that at times seems
to verge on psychic suicide—rejects the relatively static cosmology of *Nature* in favor of a radically disjunctive vision. And this vision, in turn, was
provoked by Emerson's awareness of the historical givenness of language,
self, and society. An entire critical tradition, beginning with Stephen E.
Whicher's *Freedom and Fate* (1953), has located this epistemological division in biographical terms that link the less transcendent aspects of Emerson's thinking to the death of his oldest son, the attenuation of his visionary powers, and the consequent writing of "Experience." It in fact can be
discerned earlier—much earlier in the case of the journals, and certainly
as early as the mid-1830s in the essays and lectures. In "The American
Scholar," for instance, Emerson recognizes that no writer can "entirely exclude the conventional, the local, the perishable from his book, or write a
book of pure thought" (*EL* 56). By "Experience" (1844)—the essay that
Whicher uses as a key piece of evidence and that Matthiessen reacts to
with particular antipathy—he can wearily confess, "I know better than to
claim any completeness for my picture," admitting that the fault derives
from "the discovery we have made, that we exist" (*EL* 491, 487). Though
recent critics have found in the later Emerson a reformer committed to
the abolition of slavery and other laudable progressive causes, this socially
engaged figure is perhaps best understood within a larger vocational trajectory by which the young transcendental visionary ceded to a conditioned skepticism that, striving to countenance all refractory limitations,
increasingly chose to focus on more local issues.

At times in his analysis, Matthiessen seems to take as a personal affront
what he regards as Emerson's failure to consistently endorse an organic,
whole, democratic community, repeatedly accusing him of "losing himself in his vaguely luminous doctrine of divine inspiration" (*AR* 135).
If the "early" author had been useful to the critic—authorizing the pre-
rogatives of the American Scholar as one who might inspire both "the
whole society" *and* "the whole man" (*EL* 54)—the process of anxious
self-becoming Emerson eventually performs undermines Matthiessen's
own ambitious efforts at cultural critique. And it undermines those efforts precisely because the conditions out of which it arose bear a strong
resemblance to the historical context in which Matthiessen began writing *American Renaissance*.[39] If Matthiessen conceived of his role during
the early 1930s as a corollary to the American Scholar, if he set his sights
"high" for his massive literary history because he had perceived an historic opportunity for sociocultural change, by the time he actually began
drafting the book, history had already, perhaps inevitably, begun to tres-
pass on his sense of those possibilities.

Indeed, by the time Matthiessen checked himself into McLean's Hospital in 1939, he had just been involved in a bruising and unsuccessful battle with Harvard's administration to reinstate two professors fired for their leftist political beliefs. The Walsh-Sweezy case, as it came to be known in journals such as the *New Republic* and the *Nation*, had provoked a national outcry by those who viewed it as an egregious abridgement of academic freedom.[40] Led by Matthiessen, a group of 131 faculty members signed a document protesting President James Conant's decision against the ousted professors, forcing the administration to form a committee to investigate charges of unfairness. Despite the committee's recommendation to rehire the dismissed professors, Conant refused to budge, leaving Matthiessen bitter toward what he called, in an undated letter to Daniel Aaron, the president's "slide-rule autocracy."[41] Writing an open letter to the committee, Matthiessen attacked the administration for falling short of "any conception of democratic justice or wise educational policy" (*RD* 229–30).

Even more distressing was the late-summer trip to the Soviet Union that Matthiessen took with Cheney. Marred by the gathering German threat on the borders of Czechoslovakia and an impending sense of doom throughout Europe, the trip is remarkable in that it goes entirely without discussion in Matthiessen's correspondence—a rare and arguably significant lacuna. While impossible to know for sure, it seems likely that during his trip—a typical pilgrimage for the leftist intellectual in the 1930s—Matthiessen encountered evidence of repression and violence impossible to ignore but that he needed to suppress. (More than a year later, he was still capable of writing a broadsheet declaring that "[t]he magnificent stand of the Red armies against the Nazi invaders means even more than a heroic defense of the Russian homeland and the Russian people. . . .[it means] the only basis for lasting peace is to be found in international socialism.")[42]

More certain is the alcoholic spree Cheney succumbed to soon after their return. In general Matthiessen seems to have regarded Cheney's alcoholism with a mixture of tolerance and anxiety. An unpublished letter from 1935 has him calling Cheney's "perfectly reckless uncontrolled" behavior a desecration of "the extraordinary blessing of our union, . . . like spitting on a crucifix."[43] But three years later, following a binge soon after their Soviet trip, Cheney miserably confessed that "he wanted to die" and thereby paralyzed Matthiessen with fear of "being alone again" (*RD* 247).

All of these events occurred against a broader backdrop of political acquiescence, the widespread perception of failed hopes and lost causes. "[T]he period after 1935 was not," as Richard H. Pells notes, "a fulfillment of but a retreat from the creative ferment and radical possibilities of the early 1930s."[44] In the wake of a European crisis that produced a paradigm shift in U.S. political discussion from socialism-versus-capitalism to democracy-versus-fascism, Matthiessen's focus in *American Renaissance* on each writer's devotion to democracy reveals a similar shift in priorities: a newfound willingness to harmonize with rather than to challenge the nation's dominant ideals. The sudden efflorescence of the language of democracy just prior to World War II undoubtedly exerted a gravitational pull on Matthiessen's yearning for social purpose, allowing him to feel, however ambivalently and briefly, like an integral member of society rather than society's critical conscience.[45]

If Matthiessen's historical context provided him with an increased appreciation for chastening circumstances, it also contributed to the full-fledged consideration of tragedy that immediately follows his discussion of Emerson and Thoreau. Matthiessen had briefly touched upon the topic in his earlier book on Eliot, and his interest in Elizabethan drama surely contributed as well. But *American Renaissance* provides the most extended and searching exploration in his work of tragedy's meaning and significance, elevating the mode to a preeminent position in his canon of taste. Matthiessen finished his chapter on tragedy—which opens his study of Hawthorne and Melville and would eventually be titled "The Vision of Evil"—just before entering McLean's. Read side by side with the section on Emerson, it redefines the American Scholar as "the hero of tragedy," a "man in action" perpetually "in conflict with other individuals in a definite social order" (*AR* 179). Registering the aesthetic and political problems he had encountered in Emerson, as well as the assault on his hopes for an organic community, Matthiessen's introduction to tragedy announces a shift in his hierarchy of values, from authors with a commitment to democratic possibilities to those whose tragic art issues from the realization that such commitments were likely to be only partially fulfilled in a fallen world. If tragedy was "built on the experienced realization that man is radically imperfect," it also "contain[ed] a recognition that man, pitiful as he may be in his finite weakness, is still capable of apprehending perfection, and of becoming transfigured by that vision." In a passage written after his hospitalization and slow recovery to mental equilibrium, Matthiessen extols the author of tragedy as one who "must be as far from the chaos of despair as he is from ill-founded optimism" (*AR* 180).

Matthiessen's focus on the tragic might be seen as a therapeutic effort to think his way out of a depressive isolation, to will himself from "being immobilized by darkness to being sustained by it," as Jonathan Franzen recently portrayed his own plight as a novelist isolated by the values of

American society.[46] But the lasting influence of this effort is evident in Gerald Graff's statement that "[t]he 'tragic vision' of American writing [would bespeak] a sense of innocence betrayed, of pastoral hopes disappointed, a conviction, as Leo Marx summarized it at the end of *The Machine in the Garden*, that 'the aspirations once represented by the symbol of an ideal landscape have not, and probably cannot, be embodied in our traditional institutions.'"[47] Indeed, after World War II, the "tragic" would increasingly serve as an organizing principle for the emerging field of American Studies, helping to order such perennial issues as democracy and the artist, self and society, God and man. Moreover, while contributing to a symbolic-romance theory of American literature that enabled midcentury critics to value works that seemed to focus on the individual separated from society, it also highlighted its own failure to resolve conflicts within a social setting. The tragic, that is, seemed to mirror the context in which many American Studies scholars would come of age, the "tragic vision" that followed the exuberant involvement by many of them in the Popular Front now providing them with a critical vocabulary to express, among other things, personal disappointments that arose from a sense that the country had failed to achieve its ideal through organized social action—and that, in the Cold War era, such failure was inevitable.

Given Matthiessen's interest in the topic, one might reasonably expect him to locate in the disjunction between Emerson's thought and action the tragic dimension he felt to be so important to American literature. After all, as Henry Nash Smith has insightfully remarked, Matthiessen's desire to respond to "the complexities of experience"—coupled with his ambition to embody the role of *Man Thinking*—produced two abiding interests: the meaning of tragedy and the meaning of democracy. These two concerns, "which were respectively the highest values . . . [Matthiessen] perceived in art and politics" (*MR* 228), seem to have marked what Giles Gunn calls the "determining boundaries" of Matthiessen's thought.[48] They would also seem to coalesce in Emerson, to inscribe his thoughts on the relationship of the artist and society as well as his tough-minded recognition, in Whicher's terms, of "fate" as well as "freedom."

But Matthiessen fails to see anything tragic about Emerson, finding instead an optimistic philosopher blandly oblivious to the vision of evil. This inability to discern the tragic in a figure whose very consciousness seems irremediably divided between a vision of the ideal and a recognition of the fleetingness of human ability to realize even a *portion* of that ideal can in part be explained by Matthiessen's peculiar conception of tragedy. Attempting to blend his dual commitments to democracy and Christianity, Matthiessen required the tragedian to imagine her hero as a representative of individuals in society (the same impulse, for instance, that spurred Arthur Miller to conceive Willy Loman) while at the same time portraying a world in which good and evil were intermixed. In a crucial passage of *American Renaissance*, Matthiessen explains that "not only must the author of tragedy have accepted the inevitable co-existence of good and evil in man's nature, he must also possess the power to envisage some reconciliation between such opposites, and the control to hold an inexorable balance. He must be as far from the chaos of despair as he is from ill-founded optimism" (*AR* 180). Emerson fails to achieve a mature tragic vision, in Matthiessen's view, because he is unable to sustain the balance—either philosophically or stylistically—between despair and optimism, incapable of reconciling the simultaneous existence of good and evil. In many ways echoing a long tradition by which Emerson was thought to have escaped to the ideal whenever experience failed to measure up, Matthiessen's portrait of Emerson is of the blithely confident transcendentalist, a familiar picture that prevents him from reading seriously a work such as "Experience," which would soon come to be seen as *the* tragic work by Emerson.[49] Matthiessen asserts that Emerson's relationship to grief, "in spite of his ample experience of it in the cumulating deaths of his first wife, his two most talented brothers, and his oldest boy . . . dissolved in the wistful flow of his 'Threnody'; only rarely, most notably in his essay on 'Fate,' did he stick to his observation that 'no picture of life can have any veracity that does not admit the odious facts,' that 'great men have always been perceivers of the terror of life'" (*AR* 181–2).

Had Matthiessen been more inclined to examine the later Emerson whose work betrayed a profound skepticism in all totalizing theories of art or society, he might have discerned an even more "tragic" author suitable for his new criteria. Had he analyzed, say, *The Conduct of Life* (1860), completed like his own work on the brink of war, he might have discovered a "usable" Emerson painfully aware of the circumstanced present and of the tragic realities that underlie history-bound cultures.[50] Instead, renewing his criticism of Emerson as a prelude to his more favorable study of Hawthorne and Melville, Matthiessen accuses Emerson of having "conceived the heart in such pure isolation that his speculations now seem remote from violent actuality." Admitting that the early Emerson "was not unconscious that evil existed," Matthiessen declares that the "limitations of his temperament" nevertheless insured that he inevitably understood "ugly facts [as] merely partial and [to] be transcended" (*AR* 181–2). Unable to find a compensatory tragic component to Emerson's thought that might have redeemed him from the abandonment of his earlier ideals, Matthiessen dismisses a writer who remained hopeful of democratic possibility even while countenancing the tragic, a writer whose very aesthetic might be seen as the attempt to reconcile the competing urgencies so obvious in Matthiessen's own work.

III.

That task is left instead for one of the most remarkable close readings in *American Renaissance,* an analysis, both rhetorical and social, of the concluding episode of Melville's *White-Jacket.* I take my cue here from Donald E. Pease's brilliantly intuitive linking of White-Jacket's harrowing fall from the mast of his frigate with Matthiessen's own obsessional desire to leap to his death from a great height.[51] Displacing his recent suicidal compulsion onto a work of fiction, Matthiessen devotes more interpretive energy and sheer verbiage in his discussion of White-Jacket's fall than in his entire discussion of Emerson's prose. Significantly, if ironically, entitled "Autobiography and Art," this chapter details what Matthiessen describes as Melville's "first extended instance when the two halves of his experience, his outer and inner life, are fused in expression" (*AR* 390).

Matthiessen's pyrotechnic interpretation is significant for several reasons. White-Jacket is often seen as a reformist narrator who, as Richard Chase noted, "denounced the American navy to the American people in the name of humanity and democratic principles."[52] As such, he seems to recover Matthiessen's reformist purpose as the author of *American Renaissance.* Furthermore, White-Jacket's narration is generally thought to recount "the psychological growth from innocence to experience by means of a confrontation with evil."[53] Projectively identifying with this characterization, Matthiessen locates in the jacket from which the narrator takes his name the evil of "bad luck and isolation" that in turn nearly causes his death. Climbing aloft to reef the ship's halyard, White-Jacket mistakes this jacket for a sail and in pulling it down loses his balance and falls "—down, down, with lungs collapsed as in death."[54] Prefiguring Matthiessen's own complaint at McLean's that he felt blinded by the "film of unreality," Melville's narrator describes his descent in excruciating detail meant to prolong our anxiety in much the same way that Poe can shorten our breath with excruciating details of suffocation: "With the bloody, blind film before my eyes, . . . I thought to myself, Great God! This is Death! . . . Time seemed to stand still, and all the worlds seemed poised on their poles. . . . As I gushed into the sea, a thunder-boom sounded in my ear; my soul seemed flying from my mouth" (*WJ* 393).

Terrifying as this fall is, it is accompanied by a redemptive baptism that puts the narrator back into vital communion with life. "The feeling of death flooded over me with the billows," he says of his immersion: "Purple and pathless was the deep calm now around me, flecked by summer lightnings in an azure afar. The horrible nausea was gone; the bloody, blind film turned pale green; I wondered whether I was yet dead or still dying. But of a sudden some fathomless form brushed my side . . . the thrill of being alive again tingled in my nerves, and the strong shunning of death shocked me through" (*WJ* 393). Matthiessen's fascination with this passage may suggest the extent to which he read it as an allegory of his own vertiginous plunge into depression. If so, it also suggests the precarious ascent into health he associated with social integration, the "thrill of being alive" always connected in his experience to contact with others.[55] In pointing out Melville's "extraordinary mastery of material" as evidence of his "integrity of sensibility and expert command of language" (*AR* 393), the critic also discerns an organic form woefully absent in Emerson. Of particular importance to Matthiessen is the fact that Melville's breathtaking description is not the result of autobiographical experience but rather the sympathetic reimagining of a passage in Nathan Ames's *A Mariner's Sketches* (1830). Not bound by Emerson's individualistic desire to speak only original utterances, Melville paradoxically becomes for Matthiessen the fulfillment of the American Scholar: proof "that there should be no artificial separation between the life of the mind and of the body, that reading, to a quickened imagination, could be as much a part of assimilated experience as adventures" (*AR* 395). Moreover, Melville's ability to enter into sympathetic communion with others, forged by "the maturing of thought and emotion that comes from intense living," has significant political ramifications. By dispensing with radical individualism and "projecting himself into others' actions," the author not only enables his narrator to cast off the stigma of isolation—White-Jacket finally sheds his garment while swimming to the surface—but to enter into an "imaginative fellow-feeling" upon which democratic community might be grounded (*AR* 395).

Matthiessen's close reading of *White-Jacket* in many ways stands as the apogee of *American Renaissance*, a moment of poise and equilibrium unattained throughout much of the book. Melville will eventually prove disappointing, his vision of tragedy too detached for comfort from a sense of Christian ethics. And the author for whom he had most held out the hope of synthesizing America's diverse strains—the poet of his young love, Whitman—will prove upon mature reexamination to resemble all too clearly the sentimental optimist William James derided for his "indiscriminate hurrahing for the Universe."[56] But if his analysis of *White-Jacket* remains a stirring and technically dazzling performance, for those aware of his 1950 suicide from the twelfth floor of the Hotel Manger (a hotel he picked, with typical consideration for his friends, on account of its distance from their homes), the organic fusion of aesthetic and political ideals in a passage that echoed his suicidal fantasy is both troubling and poignant. The reading of White-Jacket's fall suggests Matthiessen's yearning to accomplish in his writing what he could not in life: a satisfying confrontation with "the experienced realization that man is radically imperfect" and, at the same time, a marshaling of the resources necessary to "possess the power to envisage some reconciliation between" a vision of perfection and the recognition of its impossibility (*AR* 180).

For some recent commentators, Matthiessen's suicide is ultimately the result of his conflicted attempt to fix and define the canon of an American "renaissance" while at the same time stifling those aspects of himself (his socialism and particularly his homosexuality) he could not comfortably fit into his critical revisioning. "Matthiessen's Popular Front figure of 'America' suffered a sobering fate," Jonathan Arac notes, adding that the cultural renaissance Matthiessen described would become "a postwar myth of empire. A mobilization intended as oppositional became incorporated hegemonically; American studies gained power by nationalistically appropriating Matthiessen."[57] For Arac and other contemporary critics, *American Renaissance* seems less an act of emancipatory scholarship than the culmination of earlier efforts to consolidate and legitimate a homogenous grouping of writers that excluded women, diverse ethnicities, and variant points of view into a white, Protestant academy's "classically corporate or consensual project."[58] Matthiessen's eventual suicide and the note he left behind maintaining that while he no longer believed himself to be "of use to my profession," he remained "a Christian and a socialist" are viewed as the inevitable consequences of such inner divisions—a variation of Bowron's remark soon after the news of Matthiessen's death that it was his "unshielded sensibilities" that ultimately killed him (*MR* 222).

While these comments are accurate as far as they go, they tend to flatten and caricature Matthiessen, gesturing toward the historical importance and influence of his work while dismissing its actual content (much as had genteel critics in their encounters with Emerson). In response to these readings, this chapter contends that we might do better to see *American Renaissance*—conceived by Matthiessen as an enactment of the twentieth-century American Scholar on the stage of cultural opportunity—as eventually becoming its author's "Experience." To the extent this contention is accurate, it is particularly revealing that the "tragic" Melville who comes to stand for a revised American Scholar in *American Renaissance* is shown by Matthiessen to voice a "mixture of attraction and repulsion at his . . . contact with Emerson" (*AR* 185). Attracted to a vocational model that seemed to promise the redirection of material existence by imagining an immanent unity suffusing those particulars, Matthiessen himself would eventually be repelled by an Emersonian aesthetic that implied a world not unified by any single purpose, a pluralistic and radically contingent universe that threatened his precarious sense of self as well as his political commitments. In arriving at a tragic American Scholar, Matthiessen would ultimately be forced to expel the complex Emerson, to deny the value of an American literary form that sought to record the twists and turns of the ever developing consciousness as it confronted obdurate fact. This expulsion did not occur unwittingly; like the Emerson seen by Richard Poirier as having "already anticipated any degree of sophistication that might be brought to him,"[59] Matthiessen was painfully aware of his inability to fulfill his aspirations as a critic. This awareness caused him to anxiously wonder whether he—rather than Emerson—had become a mere "Platonic rhapsode," a cheerleader for American literature who in the final analysis had read the literary evidence no less instrumentally than Granville Hicks and V. F. Calverton before him.

In her study of suicide, psychiatrist Kay Redfield Jamison cautions those wishing to "assign meaning to the logistics" of suicide to be wary of "entering an inaccessible state of mind."[60] While self-annihilation may be triggered by any number of stresses—including the loss of a loved one and situations perceived to cause great shame—it almost invariably can be traced back, according to Jamison, to an underlying predisposition, particularly to depression and other mental illnesses.[61] Matthiessen's suicide has been variously attributed to the death in 1945 of Cheney; his disappointment in his book on Henry James;[62] the vitriol to which he was increasingly subjected in the local and national press as an unrepentant leftist intellectual during the Cold War; and, lurking just below the surface of these attacks, the insinuation of his homosexuality.[63] While these factors no doubt contributed to his death, there almost certainly existed in his personality a tendency toward dark despair about whose intermingled sources—hereditary, social, situational—we can finally only speculate. What *is* certain is that such despair not only led him to question the efficacy of his work but at times provoked him to search for healthful contact, to strive in his work to effect meaningful transformation in the lives of his audience that would in turn render experience more secure, more enduring. In this way, Matthiessen enacted the tragic role of the American Scholar.

CHAPTER 5

Perry Miller's Errand into the Wilderness

*It may be, if we carefully guard ourselves
against self-deception, that the most valuable
product we have to export is our self-distrust.*
　　　—Perry Miller, "The American Humanities
　　　　　　in an Industrial Civilization"

Few topics in American Studies have proved so irresolvable as that of the public intellectual.[1] The problem dates back at least as far as "The American Scholar," in which Emerson challenged the self-conception of his Harvard audience by suggesting that "[t]he scholar is decent, indolent, complaisant" (*EL* 70) and then proposed a relationship, tenuously formulated, between intellectual work and social activism. The question of how intellectuals—most of whom now reside in the academy—may best effect social change persists with unabated urgency in our present moment; as David Farber notes, "democratic publics and purveyors of elite knowledge are not and, virtually by definition, should not be easily mated."[2] While Emerson may continue to challenge readers to imagine "precisely how intellectual work [might] constitute . . . political intervention,"[3] Lawrence Buell writes, the verdict is still out on how precisely to harness the often baffling, if symbiotic, relationship between the social, cultural, and political realms.

It is fitting that Perry Miller struggled with the problem that continues to vex the discipline he helped bring into being.[4] While Miller is largely remembered for his still-influential scholarship on Puritan thought and theology, he in fact struggled for much of his professional life with Emerson's call for intellectual activism as well as with the contradictions engendered by that call. "There are at least two things you have to keep in mind about Perry," his former student Edmund S. Morgan recalls: "The first was that he was brilliant, the smartest person I've ever known. The second was that he hated to be thought of as bookish. He wanted to be Ernest Hemingway, to go where the action was. To *do* things with his intelligence. And the tricky part is that he tried to combine both these sides of himself."[5] J. C. Levenson, another student, recalls the active life of the mind Miller strove to achieve: "At the height of his career, he bespoke an intellectual vitality that relished the prospect of working through great jungles of fact and idea and finding what would connect a possibly very minor incident to major histories that mattered deeply to us all."[6] And to David Levin, Miller "seemed to express the hunger to achieve and reconcile" a wide range of contradictory roles: "The scholar and the creative artist, the scholar and the man of the world, the scholar and the hearty democrat, the historian and the original philosopher influencing his own time."[7]

However skeptical Miller was of transcendental optimism—however restless, contradictory, and voracious he was as a thinker—Emerson's performative and urgent mandate that the intellectual act in times of crisis would remain a potent challenge and model for him, shaping his understanding of literary history as, at the very least, a sometime social activity. His lifelong desire to fuse thought and action is most memorably described in what might be taken as the opening chapter of American Studies' Genesis—the preface to *Errand into the Wilderness*—when in an "epiphany" on the Congo River Miller experienced the "pressing necessity for expounding my America to the twentieth century."[8] Thus began a career of historicizing the American past in a manner that served both as cathartic self-explanation and as a call to national destiny. This project, predicated on ideals of American exceptionalism and a fictive historical integrity that have since come under substantial scrutiny and revision by a subsequent generation of critics, initially led him to the spiritual origins of the American past. He chose the Puritans, he tells us in a characteristically evasive tautology, because "I wanted . . . a coherence with which I could coherently begin" (*EW* vii). But the inner logic of his project eventually led him to reconceive his work within the rubric of public intellectual as outlined in Emerson's "American Scholar" and enacted during his lifetime by such diverse figures as Van Wyck Brooks, F. O. Matthiessen, and Edmund Wilson.

Like most American literary historians during the mid-twentieth century, Miller came to view Emerson as the molten center in the Ptolemaic universe of American literary history; similarly, he believed that, in the words of T. S. McMillin, "the definition of America is tied to the definition of Emerson."[9] Accordingly, some of his most important utterances about American culture gather around Emerson and seek to establish a "usable" version of the author as someone who wished above all else to make ideas a force in a world hopelessly immured in an inert materialism. This is not to say that Miller's various remarks on Emerson are thinly veiled attempts at sociopolitical suasion. The complexity of his rhetoric and ideas, the irony with which he always viewed the romantic naiveté of Emersonian transcendentalism, as well as his insistence that history be taken on its own terms, prevents him from ever simply mobilizing Emerson for topical intervention. Moreover, Miller's eclectic and iconoclastic thought, consistent only in its antagonism toward a priorism of any kind, reveal him to be the sort of intellectual Edward Said praised more than a decade ago, one of "those figures whose public performances can neither be predicted nor compelled into some slogan, orthodox party line, or fixed dogma."[10] Still, what his essays and lectures on Emerson *do* throw into relief are historical moments when the plight of the public intellectual seemed particularly to impinge upon his own life and work—moments when he sought to summon and then to speak to a public in what amounted to a secular jeremiad, moments when he asked literary history to perform deliberative, if oblique, action on matters of public consequence.

In 1939–40, for instance, as the Harvard campus erupted in a bitterly politicized debate over U.S. intervention in World War II, Miller wrote "From Edwards to Emerson," a dazzling piece of scholarly synthesis that covertly rebuked campus communists and isolationists while at the same time suggesting the basis for more effective intellectual activism. Returning from service in the Office of Strategic Services to find America steeped in a postwar complacency that touted the hegemony of democracy, he meditated on the promises and dangers of the American gospel in "Emersonian Genius and American Democracy." And as Cold War anxiety coalesced with his own sense that the study of America had been co-opted by an imperial project that in turn led to intellectual repression, he found himself describing with increasing frequency the Emersonian scholar as a "lone wolf," an outsider fiercely protective of independent thought while at the same time fated to obscurity, misappropriation, and bitter alienation.

If Miller's greatest contribution to American Studies is his unprecedented excavation of Puritan thought, he would also bequeath a portrait of Emerson as a religious radical, a "dangerous man" capable of upsetting the status quo, that has proven remarkably influential for the past half century. This portrait was fashioned during a specific point in cultural and political history and, as such, should be regarded as an enabling concept, a projective wish-fulfillment achieved during a fleeting moment of cultural opportunity and professional confidence. "At times," historian Charles McLaughlin recalls, "and especially later in his life, I had the feeling Perry was trapped. By his material, by personal divisions, by the times. I believe he wanted to escape the Puritans, to strike out in new directions, to talk to larger audiences the way Edmund Wilson had, for instance. But he didn't know how to do it. He didn't know how to escape."[11] In a lecture delivered toward the end of his life, Miller confessed that while he didn't "have great sympathy with transcendentalism . . . I was brought up in it. My father belonged to it and for some time it will have a special appeal to Americans."[12]

The brand of transcendentalism Miller's father subscribed to specifically was that of George D. Herron, the Chicago-based Christian socialist and author of *The Christian State: A Political Vision of Christ* and *The New Redemption: A Call to the Church to Reconstruct Society According to the Gospel of Christ*.[13] A vocal proponent of the late-nineteenth-century social gospel, Herron emphasized progressive change through moral suasion and a liberal appeal to human rationality during the late nineteenth and early twentieth centuries. "History and prophecy have always pointed toward a time of industrial peace and social brotherhood," he preaches with typical certitude in his 1890 "The Message of Jesus to Men of Wealth."[14] A quarter century later he would describe World War I in florid transcendentalese as a cosmic battle for the "self-governing Divine Presence in man."[15]

Miller's response to his parents' beliefs was emblematic of a larger generational revolt against genteel optimism and the reigning orthodoxies of his age. As a young man, he had dropped out of the University of Chicago, lived among transients in Colorado, moved to Greenwich Village to write "true-confession" stories for pulp magazines, performed a walk-on role in Eugene O'Neill's *Desire Under the Elms* and, finally, set off for two years as a merchant seaman.[16] Yet his bohemian revolt, however representative of the Lost Generation, took on a distinctly personal and conflicted form. If he liked to proclaim himself a "goddamned atheist,"[17] there nevertheless existed within his personality an inherited and compensatory fascination with soul-ravishing experience. As Walter J. Ong remarked, "Perry was given to epiphanies, or at least interested in them. He had enough of the Protestant search for conversion in him to look for things that would suddenly change his life."[18] Despite his fervent disavowals, Miller's spiritual hungers are palpable throughout his descriptions of the New England theology as a response to "man's plight in a universe God created" (*EW* 50) and his identification of the dominant Puritan emotion as the "sense of the overwhelming anguish to which man is always subject" when, "standing alone in the universe," he feels "not only minute and insignificant, but completely out of touch with both justice and beauty."[19] Even if we concede Miller's repeated claim that his research was empirical and fashioned without preconceived theories, the Puritans he describes throughout the 1930s are largely a product of the existential crisis and resulting sense of alienation he, like many of his generation, experienced upon encountering the strident and disjunctive social forces following the First World War.[20]

Much of Miller's contribution to American Studies, as well as his efforts to perform the role of public intellectual, can be understood as a conflicted response to his parents' fetishized New England heritage. This response manifested itself most typically in a magisterial irony that comprises much of his critical tone and temperament. Seeking to tear down and then re-write their genteelly idealized past as well as their uncritical enthusiasm for the "transcendental" Herron, Miller's project, on a personal level, seems designed in part to recapture "the happiness" Nietzsche describes as that experienced by the historian upon discovering "he is not wholly accidental and arbitrary but grown out of a past as its heir, flower and fruit, and that his existence is thus excused and indeed justified."[21] This happiness could only be accomplished for Miller, however, if the inherited past was rei-magined as "usable" to a generation that envisioned itself in oppositional terms. As a result, his study of Puritan intellectual history positions him in rebellion against both the genteel past as well as a number of domi-nant ideas in early-twentieth-century American historiography—in par-ticular the economic determinism that had underwritten Charles Beard's interpretations of America and Frederick Jackson Turner's frontier thesis.[22] A New Deal Democrat, Miller bristled at crudely reductive economic in-terpretations of American life as well as at the progressive optimism that guided much contemporary leftist politics, as he makes clear in the for-ward to *Orthodoxy in Massachusetts* (1933): "[I was] so very naïve as to believe that the way men think has some influence upon their actions, of not remembering that these ways of thinking have been officially decid-ed by modern psychologists to be generally just so many rationalizations constructed by the subconscious to disguise the pursuits of more tangible ends."[23] As he would admit twenty years later in the reissue of that book, his initial decision to focus on the Puritans also occurred within a larger social context exemplified by Van Wyck Brooks and H. L. Mencken's broad-brush condemnation of American society as shallow, materialistic, and anti-intellectual. "My contemporaries and I came of age in a time when the word 'Puritan' served as a comprehensive sneer against every tendency in American civilization which we held reprehensible."[24]

The first volume of *The New England Mind*, which sought to rehabilitate the Puritans from this Brooksian stereotype, emphatically proclaimed Miller's underlying assumption that ideas construct reality, that a society's way of knowing is framed more by its system of beliefs than its material reality. This assumption echoes Emerson's belief in "Circles" that "[o]ur culture is the predominance of an idea which draws after it this train of cities and institutions" (*EL* 403). Ultimately, Miller is less interested in the political and social praxis of the Puritans than in describing the belief system that structured their political and social reality. In a remark still bracing for its modernity—even postmodernity—Miller notes that ideas are "born in time and place, that they spring from specific environments, that they express the force of societies and classes, that they are generated by power relations."[25] But if Miller's Puritans were notable for their intellectual rigor and heroic spirituality, if they were a people whose ideas had been formed in adversarial relationship to the impious complacency of a commercial class that spawned an optimistic materialism, they also were destined to bitter disappointment in the outcome of their project. Witnessing and enunciating the existential spectacle of the isolated individual adrift in a world that had clearly failed to measure up to an ecstatic vision of piety, purpose, and intellectual leadership, the Puritans in Miller's work would prefigure his own efforts to engage and shape the issues of his times. "From Edwards to Emerson" may be, as David M. Robinson writes, "one of the great acts of synthesis in American literary history,"[26] but it is also a work vitally engaged with the prewar moment in which it was written. Miller's effort to discern a coherent intellectual strain from Puritanism to transcendentalism is not only a classic example of cultural nationalism during a time of international crisis but also, if less obviously from our historical position, a focused polemic against the orthodox leftist response to the impending threat of fascism.[27] The essay grew in part out of specific conditions at Harvard where, prior to the Hitler-Stalin pact, many left-leaning students and faculty remained vehemently opposed to American intervention in the European conflict. Socialists, communists, and even some New Deal Democrats—still suspicious of the propaganda, militarism, and false patriotism that had emerged during the First World War and viewing the Nazi emergence as further evidence of the collapse of capitalism—spoke out against U.S. involvement in the war. To many campus intellectuals, the Soviet Union still remained the best defense against fascism, and despite recent revelations about Stalinist atrocities, it still seemed to hold out to activists like F. O. Matthiessen the greatest promise for worldwide reform. Recalling the heated political discussion at Harvard during the late 1930s, John Lydenburg asserts that the principle question at the time was whether liberal democracy could solve the Depression-era crisis of capitalism, or whether totalitarianism—of either the communist or fascist variety—was an inescapable, perhaps even desirable, fact.[28]

While Miller wasn't "as explicitly political as F. O. Matthiessen or some of the other professors at Harvard during that time," Morgan recalls, he nevertheless was deeply immersed in the debate concerning U.S. intervention in the European conflict. Leo Marx remembers that Miller was an "ardent interventionist," which "in the language of the day" meant "vociferously anti-Soviet."[29] Miller's position is further underscored by the controversy created by his close friend and fellow Harvard instructor Archibald MacLeish, who argued in the *Nation* early in 1940 that scholars and writers, too complacent and inactive during the preceding decade, now bore responsibility for the wave of totalitarian oppression afflicting Europe.[30]

The contemporaneous importance of MacLeish's now-forgotten statement cannot be overestimated. Subsequent issues of the *Nation*, the *Partisan Review*, and other journals devoted themselves to rejoinders. MacLeish's term for complacent intellectuals, "the irresponsibles," which inverted a longstanding discourse about the "responsibility of the intellectual," quickly became a code word for ivory-tower political dithering. And his condemnation of leftist intellectuals hinged in part on shifting the terms of debate—from economics, in which the Western powers and Nazi Germany were lumped together as capitalist nations against the superior example of the Soviet Union—to politics. In this analysis, democratic Western powers stood in self-evident opposition to the totalitarianism of the Soviet Union and Germany, both of which were culpable for "the destruction of the whole system of ideas, the whole respect for truths, the whole authority of excellence which places law above force, beauty above cruelty, singleness above numbers"[31]

But neither the Stalinist regime nor the Third Reich was MacLeish's primary target. At the heart of his article was an attack on those American intellectuals who had allied themselves with a collective theory of social action that exonerated them from personal responsibility and even allowed them to condone totalitarian atrocities. "[S]cholars and writers of our generation in this country" were to blame for the destruction of law and the life of the mind because they had not fought for "the common inherited culture of the West, by which alone our scholars and writers lived."[32]

The reaction to MacLeish's jeremiad was almost unanimous condemnation. The editors of the *Partisan Review*, for instance, solicited reactions from twenty prominent writers, including Henry Miller and Edmund Wilson, all of which were negative. Yet in the flurry of responses and counter-responses that included unanimous derision by the New York Intellectuals, Miller publicly sided with MacLeish, arguing in a subsequent issue of the *Nation* that ivory-tower materialists were in fact naïve isolationists who posed as left-wing radicals while contributing nothing to the practical action necessary for improving the world. Even worse, Miller continued, "the few [academics] with broader vision," by which he presumably meant MacLeish and himself, were inevitably "met by their colleagues with spoken or implied rebukes for having deserted the citadel of the fraternity, their precious freedom from partisanship."[33]

Miller's comparatively unpopular support of MacLeish grew out of his sense that Soviet totalitarianism and German fascism posed a threat to intellectual inquiry around the world. This position emerged largely within the local circumstances at Harvard, especially in Miller's disagreement with F. O. Matthiessen over the issue of U.S. intervention. As many former students recall, Matthiessen was the "virtual personification" of engaged activism, a gifted teacher whose "radicalism was the response of a whole human being."[34] While Miller and Matthiessen together created Harvard's American Civilization program during the 1930s—a collaboration that founded American Studies as an academic discipline—their relationship was, according to Marx, always "intense and, finally, rivalrous."[35] As the president of the socialistic Harvard Teachers' Union, an organization of more than one hundred faculty and graduate students, Matthiessen oversaw what at the time seemed a momentous political debate: whether or not to give a token five-dollar donation to the antiwar Student Union. Miller, who viewed himself as less politically naïve and more mindful of history than Matthiessen, vehemently disagreed. When the organization voted to contribute to the antiwar movement, a rift developed between Miller and Matthiessen that never entirely healed.

If "From Edwards to Emerson" is both a work of scholarly bravura announcing Miller's ambition to extend his reach beyond the seventeenth century and an effort to reconstruct American history in order to redirect the culture's understanding of itself, a concurrent reading is possible: the essay can be seen as an oblique assault on then-predominant leftist pacifism Miller saw as unwittingly aligned with conservative isolationism. By interrupting his work on the Puritans in order to examine Emerson, Miller discovered a historical analogy between the 1830s and the 1930s that enabled him to explain America to itself and, he hoped, to exert intellectual and moral leadership over a segment of the population he and MacLeish both felt had been woefully complacent.

He did so in the essay's opening paragraphs, referring to the "depressions of 1837" and the "American blitzkrieg against Mexico" as crises that had activated Emerson and Thoreau's most vigorous expression

(*EW* 187). Because Miller perceived in Emerson's transcendental revolt against the Unitarian establishment an analogue for his own disagreement with Harvard's political left and because he would always retain ironic sympathy for generational revolt carried out by the young, it was important to bracket the early Emerson from the later author whose seeming complacency Miller derided.[36] (Like Matthiessen, he would express contempt toward Emerson for lacking the Puritan's tragic sense of sin.) Miller dismisses the older author while referring to the impending catastrophe in Europe by noting, "I am as guilty as Emerson himself if I treat ideas as a self-contained rhetoric, forgetting that they are, as we are now discovering, weapons, the weapons of classes and interests, a masquerade of power relations" (*EW* 198). Disavowing the influence of German romanticism in Emerson's "mysticism and pantheism," Miller argues instead that they were indigenous products of seventeenth-century Puritanism. This native pietistic tradition, however, is marked by a tragic legacy that grew out of its "dual heritage" (*EW* 193). Reminiscent of Van Wyck Brooks's division of American culture into high- and lowbrow, Miller finds Puritan ideology split by its ideal of the ardent soul, on the one hand, and by its propensity for groupthink and conformity, on the other. The germ for this thesis had been planted in the first volume of *The New England Mind*, and it forecasts the "declensionary" narrative Miller would further elaborate in the second. But in dramatizing the conflict between the "heritage of the troubled spirit and the heritage of worldly caution and social conservatism" (*EW* 193), Miller was also echoing his own conflict with Harvard's liberal consensus, which opposed intervention because, in Harry Levin's recollection, it believed "that in the long run British imperialism and American capitalism were an even more serious menace to the world than Hitler."[37]

Within this recovered history, Jonathan Edwards was a noteworthy example of a saving remnant in the divided old theology, an extension of its inherent, if often suppressed, mysticism. Describing Edwards's discovery of a "dynamic world, filled with the presence of God, quickened with divine life, pervaded with joy and ecstasy" (*EW* 194), Miller conveyed his deeply felt sense of Puritanism's emotional content, which only later became systematized into an elaborate logical framework of thought. This pietism, as Miller had already suggested in *The New England Mind*, was the animating principle of American intellectual history, illustrated now by Edwards's doomed cry of defiance against the narrow orthodoxy of Charles Chauncy, whose Enlightenment rationalism and efforts to "reeducate the New England taste" had resulted in the gradual "rejection of the Westminster Confession, indeed of all theology, [so that] at last [there] emerged the Unitarian churches" (*EW* 196). In conceiving of Edwards as a solitary, impassioned rebel quixotically battling the monolithic and essentially conservative forces of society, Miller discovered a vital link to Emerson, who not only challenged Unitarian orthodoxy but who now seemed suddenly a worthy model of intellectual activity during times of conflict.

Here Miller participated in an already established tradition of foregrounding the "radical" possibilities of Emerson.[38] What is new about Miller's portrait is his insistence that "certain basic continuities persist in a culture" (*EW* 184–5), a claim that would not only enable him to link Edwards and Emerson but would eventually direct subsequent work in American Studies by the likes of Leo Marx, Henry Nash Smith, and others. Still, for Miller in 1939, a more immediate context informs his innovative approach to Emerson: "It is hardly surprising that the present generation, those who are called upon to serve . . . , greet the serene pronouncements of Brahma with cries of dissent" (*EW* 186), he suggests early in the essay. Indeed, Miller was anxious to scrape away the veneer of wispy transcendentalism that had accumulated on Emerson's likeness over the years in order to reveal a writer who had inherited a radical impulse from Edwards and "could see in his own ideas a certain relation to society" (*EW* 198). If Edwards was guilty of "inciting the populace" (*EW* 194), Emerson's "latest form of infidelity" would be similarly viewed as an oppositional stance toward the combined forces of "rationalism in New England and . . . capitalism" (*EW* 198).[39]

The power of Miller's interpretation is evident in the recollection of former student David Levin, who remarked that

> For me and several of my friends, the greatest revelation in Miller's
> lectures on Emerson was his proof that in the 1830s Emerson was
> a dangerous man, a magnetic proponent of what Andrews Norton
> called the latest form of infidelity. When Miller intoned Emerson's
> stirring command to call a popgun a popgun even if the ancient
> and honorable of the earth affirm it to be the crack of doom, or
> Emerson's defiant "If I am the devil's child, let me speak as the
> devil's child," everyone in the lecture hall (Emerson D) must have
> felt the electricity.[40]

As Levin's comments suggest, the radical intellectual heritage outlined by Miller was translatable to other historical moments. The wellspring of Puritan conviction that courses through the early Emerson's writing was the vehement reaction, Miller asserts, to a "code of caution and sobriety, nourished on oyster suppers" and still guarded by the status quo (*EW* 197). Far from being "at fundamental odds with . . . social reforms,"[41] as John Carlos Rowe has recently described it, Emerson's transcendentalism was to be understood not as an ideal construed in the isolation of nature but as a weapon picked up in "reaction against Unitarianism and . . . in . . . revulsion against commercialism" (*EW* 198). Transcendental fervor was a resource employed against the era's tepid morality and the economic interests that supported it.

Miller's target wasn't just the hegemony of Boston's State Street and its intractable relationship to Unitarianism. Emerson's dynamic transcendentalism is understood within Miller's analysis as an antithesis to and an antidote for the entangled interests of business and politics, an indigenous attitude to be mobilized against static institutions that would elevate certitude and orthodoxy at the expense of active judgment. Put another way, one of Miller's subtexts is the conditions at Harvard described above. The unholy alliance between conservative and communist isolationists enabled Miller to understand in a new way the ground from which Emerson wrote; as he notes, "One does not have to be too prone to economic interpretation in order to perceive that there was a connection between the Unitarian insistence that matter is substance and not shadow, that men are self-determining agents and not passive recipients of Infinite Power, and the practical interests of the society in which Unitarianism flourished" (*EW* 199). The examination of Emerson's response to this alliance enabled Miller to suggest a way in which the intellectual might productively confront an almost monolithic resistance to the mobilization of heroic ideas. To sharpen his point, Miller deemphasizes Emerson's pragmatic Self-Reliance, which had long served as an apologia for a business culture with a vested interest in the status quo. In doing so, he also thwarts leftist intellectuals who see in Emerson's praise of the unfettered self a threat to communal values. By rediscovering a pietistic (and even antinomian) Emerson and by focusing on the vision of the upwelling spirit that enabled one to reject vested authority, Miller suggests the possibility of transformative social practice. Led by this "dangerous radical" (*EW* 186), a younger generation, "who by all the laws of economic determinism ought to have been the white-headed children of Unitarianism," had instead "elected to become transcendental black sheep." While admitting it was still necessary to know "more about the nature of social change in general" (*EW* 200), Miller implied that such change *had* occurred when subsequent generations "came under the spell of Emerson's transcendentalist tuition," uttering "new heresies" (*EW* 202) designed to dismantle progressive rationalism and economic interests that had coalesced into an oppressive social orthodoxy.

Miller's first essay on Emerson prefigures the redirection of his own energies as an intellectual during wartime. "Dashing off rather romantically to war," as Morgan recalls, he enlisted in the O.S.S., where he became a Propaganda Analysis Officer serving in Europe in 1942. After attending Psychological Warfare School in Washington, he soon attempted to transform ideas into weapons by editing *Frontpost*, a German-language newspaper dropped behind enemy lines to lower enemy morale. Almost concurrently, MacLeish would publish another article in the *Nation* on the very kind of work in which Miller was engaged. "Psychological warfare," MacLeish wrote, " . . . is nothing more and nothing less than that brand of warfare of which the field of battle is men's minds, the objective men's opinions."[42]

Miller's own developing thoughts on the role of the scholar during this time are vividly revealed in a series of contentious letters to his friend and colleague, Kenneth Murdock. Responding to "The Irresponsibles" himself, Murdock had articulated his belief that the scholar's primary responsibility was to train students in the humane values of the past in order to produce a generation of accountable citizens.[43] Now, between graphic epistolary descriptions of "haphazard bombing" by the Germans, Miller took Murdock to task, belittling his decision to remain in Cambridge with his family and to continue teaching at Harvard. His own relish for the vital work of the Office of Strategic Services no doubt exhibited just "the sort of vulgar assertiveness which Kenneth has so often quietly deplored." Replying to Murdock's description of household concerns, he airily quips, "you will surely understand me when I say such problems seem to pertain to a very remote world—and that I was ever concerned in such a world seems an implausible and gossamer dream." And in his most scathing reiteration of Emerson's attack on intellectual complacency, Miller lashes out at his friend: "If you believe in the life of the mind," he writes, "now is the time to go into libraries and write the book that the world may, perhaps, come to respect in the future. But for Heaven's sake, don't confuse the book with what *this* war is about!!"[44]

The above passage has been interpreted as the historian's effort to compartmentalize his intellectual activity from war service.[45] Miller's hyperbole is in fact an effort to redefine intellectual work as vitally engaged in the world outside libraries, at least during times of crisis—a reiteration of Emerson's belief that "[i]t is a shame to [the scholar] if his tranquility, *amid dangerous times*, arise from the presumption, that, like children and women, his is a protected class" (*EL* 65; emphasis added). For Miller, Murdock's claim of intellectual autonomy masked disengagement. In dangerous times the responsible intellectual must abandon the distanced knowledge normally his or her métier and apply thought to particular problems on the experiential terrain. If this resulted in short-term professional self-sacrifice, not to mention the very real possibility of finding one's self in harm's way, it provided its own compensatory benefits. In a passage reminiscent of Emerson's pronouncement that without action, the scholar "is not yet man . . . . [w]ithout it, thought can never ripen to truth" (*EL* 60), Miller reports toward the end of the war to both his wife and Murdock: "I have not been under any very heavy fire and probably won't be, but I have had the experience I needed and wanted, and I feel born out in my belief that for speaking with conviction to this generation, it is an invaluable experience."[46]

And yet, if Miller hoped to return to Harvard and speak with conviction, it comes as something of a surprise that while he appeared in the classroom still wearing his uniform and boasting of his exploits on the field of battle, he almost immediately became more tentative about the role of the public intellectual. In doing so, he echoed uncannily what some critics see as Emerson's own retrenchment from his more "radical" statements of the 1830s, a time when it had seemed as if the scholar might come forth within a narrow historical moment and help create a new cultural and social order.[47] While the late 1930s had seemed to Miller an era of crisis during which "The American Scholar" was the most pertinent Emersonian text, the postwar years of 1945–50 would redirect Miller's focus to those seemingly more tempered writings from 1844 onward. Miller's postwar version of Emerson would no longer be of a passionate and socially engaged critic but rather a thinker now distrustful of the social self, given more to contemplation than to direct public engagement.

On the surface, nothing would seem farther from Miller's own situation. The conclusion of the war in many ways marked the solidification of his career as scholar and intellectual; his return to Harvard in 1945 was not only celebrated with a new chair in American Literature, but his status as a public intellectual was confirmed by friendships with the Arthur Schlesingers, Adlai Stevenson, and J. Robert Oppenheimer, as well as by State Department-sponsored trips to Japan and Europe during the early fifties.[48] Yet as his writings on Emerson reveal, Miller was increasingly ambivalent about his earlier faith in the efficacy of thought in American culture. Perhaps this has to do with experiencing the Second World War, in Bruce Robbins terms, "as a sort of Golden Age of significant collective action, in relations to which the self-seeking routine and compromises of postwar work seem mean and meaningless."[49] Perhaps the horrors of wartime also contributed. In a letter to F. O. Matthiessen, Miller described the conflict not as a heroic adventure but rather as "a phantasmagoria of fighting . . . and drinking." Admitting that "behind the Quai Dorsay I managed to shoot and kill . . . one German," he concludes with an uncharacteristic affective flatness, "I haven't yet been able to make out what I feel about that, or whether I feel anything."[50] Charles McLaughlin recalls that "Perry changed after the war. There was the womanizing and the legendary drinking, which really started to become a problem when he returned."

As editor of *Frontpost*, Miller had labored to put into practice MacLeish's ideas about intellectual warfare. But as Nicholas Guyatt points out, the newspaper appears not to have been "an especially successful venture."[51] Miller himself conceded as much to the *Boston Globe*, noting that "it takes a hell of a lot of shelling to knock [the Germans] out of their holes, and it takes just as concentrated a beating to get at their minds."[52] In a marked turnaround from his earlier comments to Murdock, Miller wrote in a chastened tone to Matthiessen that following his rush to action he now had "a very poignant sense that it is I who have fallen away and that you there who keep the faith are the norm by which I measure my declension."[53] If Miller had previously imagined spirit and materiality as warlike opposites, his wartime experience promoted a renewed respect for the latter's obdurate nature that can be seen, among other places, in his second volume of *The New England Mind*.

An even bigger source of Miller's ambivalence was the altered and nearly unrecognizable landscape of postwar American society. Having once stood against his communist colleagues and the Popular Front in the late 1930s, he soon found the project of democratic renovation advanced by MacLeish and others now nearly destroyed by its own success. Postwar affluence coupled with Cold War polarization resulted in a narrowing of ideological discussion and a waning interest in the experimental climate of the immediate past. Literature students of the mid-forties and fifties, as one commentator has noted, were "the traditional professor's ideal student, the industrious bookworm, serious and mature and motivated, but the bookworm nonetheless."[54] Far more troubling, the work these students were engaged in often seemed more overtly driven by the ideological climate than by the "objective" investigation valued by Miller. Yale's description of its new American Studies program in 1952, "designed as a positive and affirmative method of meeting the threat of Communism,"[55] hints at the felt need for cultural persuasion after the Iron Curtain descended. Harvard's own American Civilization program, created by Miller and Matthiessen, was soon widely regarded as a blueprint for the expansion of American Studies both domestically and abroad. To the extent that such programs were driven by cultural nationalism, as Donald E. Pease notes, "the Cold War scenario silence[d] dissent [among American literary scholars in the 1950s] as effectively as did Ahab in the quarterdeck scene."[56]

Pease overstates the case—failing to account for the contestatory values discovered in American Renaissance texts by a new generation of scholars or the critical, even denunciatory work of historians such as Richard Hofstadter—but he does accurately convey an academic climate less politically charged and active than before the war. Miller's return to academe, in other words, was accompanied by a diminution of political debate and, in the field of history, at least, an increasingly instrumentalist view of the profession. As Guyatt remarks, many approaches to American history after the war deliberately reflect National Security Council planning documents that suggested the United States seek "to win the ideological war not by declaring the superiority of American ideas but by presenting American democracy as basically non-ideological, an incidence of nature rather than man."[57] Such a view can be found in the hundreds of books and articles on the topic of democracy published during and especially after the war,[58] but nowhere so conspicuously as in Daniel Boorstin's *The Genius of American Politics*, which argues that "the genius of American democracy" arose neither from particular individuals nor institutions but "from the unprecedented opportunities of this continent."[59] As a result of those opportunities, "we do not need American philosophers because we already have an American philosophy, implicit in the American Way of Life."[60] Boorstin's book, which despite its ideological imperatives ultimately argues against exporting American-style democracy on the grounds that it can't be duplicated, nevertheless reflects the challenges to American historiography during the Cold War. Its reading of American history often seems shaped to fit an emerging consensus scholarship that imagined American democracy as organic, natural, and objective. As a prophetic utterance of the American Way of Life, Boorstin notes in his conclusion, "Emerson's 'American Scholar' . . . still speaks to us."[61]

The Genius of American Politics suggests just how dominant had become what Philip Gleason calls the "democratic revival" as an explanatory myth in the Cold War battle of ideas. But the book is especially emblematic of a particular moment, its publication coinciding almost exactly with the author's testimony before the House Committee on Un-American Activities' investigation into communist subversion on college campuses, especially Harvard.[62] Ellen W. Schrecker has chronicled in detail the way in which the Communist Party in the university was transformed "from an unpopular political movement into a threat to national security" following the war, culminating in the infamous HUAC investigations of 1953.[63] In that year, she notes, "the main congressional investigators called up more than one hundred college teachers" in the hopes of purging higher education of radical elements.[64] Among the first to testify in the high-profile hearings (along with Granville Hicks and Robert Gorham Davis), Boorstin, a former student of Miller's, admitted his earlier membership in the Communist Party. He also identified three fellow Harvard historians as former communists and described his present opposition to communism as an "attempt to discover and explain to students, in my teaching and in my writing, the unique virtues of American democracy. I have done this . . . in my forthcoming book called *The Genius of American Politics.*"[65]

Miller's view of transcendentalism had already been consolidated in 1950 with the appearance of the highly influential anthology *The Transcendentalists,* a work that reveals the critic's simultaneous interest in and condescension toward youth movements. Appearing almost contemporaneously with the HUAC proceedings, however, is his "Emersonian Genius and the American Democracy," which appropriates the central terms of Boorstin's title and then sets them in opposition. Indeed, Emerson's idea of genius is revealed by Miller as fundamentally endangered by a democratic public seldom interested in the nuances of thought. The target of this essay is no longer the communists and other leftists Miller had once believed were too complacent in the face of European fascism, but rather an American political climate so intolerant that a Senate subcommittee designed to ferret out communists had received national approbation. Within this particular context, Emerson no longer appears as "dangerous" as he had in Miller's earlier essay. In fact, the truly dangerous figure from the past is Andrew Jackson, a dismantler of privilege whose laissez-faire philosophy opens the door to the nation's preoccupation with material wealth and its complacency toward retrograde politics. If Miller's wartime Emerson successfully rebelled against Unitarianism, his postwar version reacts far less assuredly toward a Jacksonian ideology that increasingly seemed inevitable. Countering statements by historians such as Boorstin, Miller claims that his subject's intermittent but lifelong belief in an intellectual *aristoi* set over and against the vulgarity of an emerging Democratic party "poses difficult problems for those who would see in him America's classic sage."[66]

Embedded in this observation, of course, is Miller's keen awareness that Emerson and democracy were terms currently being marshaled into service by the ideological requirements of the Cold War. Also evident is his sense that because such terms were being used in the adversarial cause of a new war, they enabled intellectuals to maintain a rhetoric of opposition even as they accommodated themselves to the nation's anticommunist temperament. To counter this tendency, Miller first reveals democracy to be above all else a contestable value. If "[t]here was a great temptation [for Emerson] to identify this upsurging of democracy with nature" (*NN* 168), his idealist theorizing is thwarted by a practical problem: "democracy in the abstract could not be dissociated from the gang of hoodlums" then running the country (*NN* 169). Writing about conditions in many ways analogous or parallel to his own, Miller describes an Emerson whose self-conception as a scholar is confronted by a sociopolitical movement that seems to ratify his faith in the Over-Soul while at the same time politically empowering a "democratic rabble." In one of his most penetrating passages, informed by his new familiarity with Emerson's private writings, Miller notes that "[t]he soliloquy—the endless debate with himself—runs throughout the *Journals;* it turns upon a triangle of counterstatement; democracy raises the problem of genius; genius the problem of Napoleon and the American politician; they in turn raise the problem of democracy and America" (*NN* 168). Miller's own context seeps into the essay as he declares that "Emerson was frequently on the point of making democratic naturalism signify an open, irreconcilable war between genius and democracy. . . . Had he let himself go in this direction, we could summarize him in a sentence: America's philosopher condemned America's democracy as something unnatural" (*NN* 169).

If the interplay of Cold War culture and Miller's complex personality is apparent in this essay, no sentence better illuminates the difficulty of his larger project to reconceive America than the question he poses upon Emerson's behalf: "[H]ow then ought an American intellectual act toward the Democratic party?" (*NN* 170). The danger Miller perceives isn't so much critical capitulation or scholarly complacency—as in the case of Boorstin—but rather a crippling sense of despair and alienation confronting the American intellectual as he or she struggled to cope with the fact that the best cause was all too often led by the worst people. Miller's considered response to this conundrum acknowledges the historical weight and seeming inevitability of democratic ideology while refusing at the same to minimize the dangers of cultural and social bankruptcy posed by an uncritical acceptance of that ideology. For Emerson, he writes, it was "the play of his mind [that] kept hope alive and vigorous by circling round and round, by drawing sustenance from, the inexhaustible power of genius" (*NN* 171).

In many ways, Miller's defense of the "play of mind" is a consistent statement of his earlier protohumanist opposition between ideas and material reality. It is also an acknowledgment of the visionary—rather than the programmatic—nature of Emerson's words in "The American Scholar." But in his shift of emphasis from a "religious radical" capable of upsetting the old order to an intermittently disenchanted thinker who "define[d] the genius as one who has access to the universal mind and who receives its influx in wise passivity" (*NN* 172), Miller registers the widespread academic withdrawal from overt politics and social activism typical of postwar culture. Trying to resolve the tensions of the public intellectual, he discovers compensatory relief in the free play of the scholar's mind, in the possibility of that free play to still make a difference. In a refrain of Emerson's idea that the democratic genius "apprises us not so much of his wealth as of the commonwealth," Miller is able to find in unfettered thought a national duty: "A sort of higher patriotism warms us, as if one should say, 'That's the way they do things in my country'" (*NN* 172).

Such a statement reveals the ideological constraints of the intellectual during the Cold War even as it suggests the oppositional strategy adopted by many American Studies scholars. Indeed, Miller's evocation of a "higher democracy" may be taken as an axiomatic statement by many disaffected intellectuals during the 1950s. These intellectuals argued that the "real" America was not to be found in the *vox populi* but in the countertradition of artists and thinkers who embodied the ideal America precisely because they opposed the actual America. Though it is true that many American Studies programs were created to perform the ideological work of anticommunism, those within such programs tended to understand their work as jeremiadic: an assertion of American exceptionalism that was celebratory, to be certain, but celebratory of an ideal all too obviously betrayed by the dominant culture. "Perry has often been tarred with the brush-off of succumbing to 'American Exceptionalism,'" notes a former student, Cushing Strout, who maintains that Miller's approach was "not provincial or chauvinistic" but rather a critical effort to "question American identity."[67]

For Miller in 1953, the "quandary" of the intellectual in a democracy "we now confront as terribly as did Emerson" (*NN* 172). His apparent solution—an Emerson whose thought ultimately redounds to a higher form of democracy—in some ways anticipates Sacvan Bercovitch's later assertion that even the reformatory Emerson "reaffirmed the basic tenets of [middle class] culture."[68] While admitting that democracy is "a serious, real, and terrifying power in modern western civilization," Miller urges his readers that "something more should be required of the scholar, the poet, the man of religion, than timid antipathy to a blatant democracy" (*NN* 173). That "something more," found in Emerson's journals, not only offers a description of "how an intelligent and sensitive man lives, or must learn to live, in a democratic society and era" (*NN* 172), but of how one can work "toward making genius democratic" (*NN* 173). If these statements look forward to Miller's increasing interest in the role of education in a democratic society, they also reveal his understanding that democratic ideology was inextricably tangled with the "property, . . . fences, . . . [and] exclusiveness" of capitalist materialism. Given such conditions, it was left to the American Scholar to inspire "some Bonaparte" who would revolt against a civilization that "is essentially one of property" (*NN* 173).

By accepting Jacksonian democracy as underwriting a larger historical tendency toward individual freedom, Emerson "could criticize his country without committing treason" (*NN* 173). Here Miller comes close to suggesting that the transcendentalist might effect social transformation by grounding such transformation, as Robert Milder would have it, in "a reinscription of perceived reality to be accomplished by some new paradigm giver, himself an instrument of historical design."[69] But if Miller's essay opens the door to such a possibility, it does so just barely. The conclusion of "Emersonian Genius and the American Democracy" shows a figure less confident in his ability to change perceptions than a deeply conflicted thinker trying to make sense of his own situation. Repeating Emerson's assertion that all democratic movements have a deep cause because they come from the great mass of citizens, Miller concludes:

> This was written by no flag-waving, tub-thumping patriot shouting "My country right or wrong." This is no campaign orator mouthing the word "democracy" even while desecrating it by his deeds. It was written by a great American, a serious man who could finally run down the devil of politics and declare that his name was levity, who understood as well as any in what the difficult ordeal consists, that magnificent but agonizing experience of what it is to be, or to try to be, an American. (*NN* 174)

This analysis would soon be extended by Miller in a lecture on "Foundations of American Democracy," given shortly after the HUAC hearings in 1953. Escalating the rhetoric of his jeremiad, he claims that Emerson "always reserved the right to ask whether democracy really promised the fulfillment to those ambitions of the spirit which he was most concerned to preach and to protect."[70] When the spirit was constrained by those who pretended to espouse democracy while in truth merely looking after their own self-interests, Emerson "scolded" the nation "for not being democratic enough."[71]

Miller's 1953 portrait of the Emersonian scholar reflects his belief that "in times of public crisis we are not to submit or sit apart, we are to become active critics of our society" and that "[t]he best patriotism in such emergencies is not conformity, it is speaking out against those abuses which have brought us into a dire predicament."[72] But this revised Emerson also suggests a retrenchment from an earlier confidence in the intellectual's ability to shape and influence policy or social thought. Like

Emerson, who from the mid-1840s onward would become more involved in immediate practical issues like abolition, Miller would focus increasingly on more particular causes, including the Oppenheimer trial and the issue of education. The reasons for this retrenchment, necessary in light of new historical limitations, are many: the way in which "democracy" had been appropriated not as an ideal but as a tool of demagoguery; the increasingly science-based way in which education was viewed during the Cold War; the distrust in the search for truth felt by many intellectuals after the atomic bomb; and Miller's ambivalence at not reaching a supra-academic audience. Jesper Rosenmeier recalls that Miller's lecture style, "which would have made him a terrific seventeenth-century divine" was in part aligned with his ambition to be "a very public intellectual."[73] During the last decade of his life his speeches and articles would contain more references to Emerson and "The American Scholar" than in any other period of his career. But increasingly that Emerson would be neither the 1939 provocateur of social efficacy nor the 1953 thinker cautiously optimistic that his ideas might one day invigorate the democratic polity. The Emerson who occupied Miller for the rest of his life not only became increasingly marginal to the larger culture, but he would eventually undermine Miller's project of "expounding my America to the twentieth century" (*EW* vii).

On the face of it, Miller's preoccupation with Emerson during the 1950s and early 1960s suggests his increasing belief that the scholar was one of the most subversive forces in American society. Speaking to audiences of earnest young students throughout the country, he boasted that "the pursuit of knowledge, far from being an obedient servant, may find itself at odds with the society that has supported it."[74] He claimed furthermore that because "the human mind is the most unsettling force, and the most uncontrollable, that afflicts humanity," it had the capacity to disrupt the lives and beliefs of those who "conform to the compulsive ethic of this society."[75] In a 1955 lecture on Emerson's address, he lamented that "because the really creative mind of the nation [has always been] entirely preoccupied with business," the scholar must ever "stand in a state of virtual hostility to society."[76] And three years later, at the height of the Cold War, he defiantly claimed that the scholar, unwilling to harness his work to the demands of ideology or national service, accordingly stood "convicted, by the nature of his act, of being un-American."[77]

Set against this confident portrait of the scholar, however, is Miller's increasing willingness to minimize the historic importance of Emerson and other transcendentalists. They were, he notes in a posthumously published essay on "New England's Transcendentalism: Native or Imported?" a "small band and had little or no effect upon American politics and economy," their real importance being "that they were the first (and in many ways the most eloquent) protests of the American sensibility against what in their day was rapidly becoming and in ours has implacably remained a 'business' civilization."[78] In his 1955 lecture on "Emerson's 'American Scholar' Today," Miller confessed, "I think it a complete misreading of 'The American Scholar' . . . to try interpreting it as a genuine program of action."[79] And in 1960, Miller would again define the movement headed by Emerson as "essentially a protest against this material culture" while at the same time insisting that transcendentalism "really doesn't have a major effect on American thinking."[80]

By the late 1950s and early 1960s, Miller's Emerson had become the double victim of American culture, fated to cynical appropriation by the institutions he sought to reform while at the same time entirely ignored by the democratic polity he hoped to direct and vivify. If this Emerson emerges to some extent from empirical history, he also suggests Miller's own frustration with the increasing specialization of the academy and its audience; the smug and widely held version of an "America" whose imperial aspirations were ultimately exemplified by the threat of worldwide extinction; and Miller's own disappointment in trying to present a nuanced account of history as national destiny to an audience more interested in material success. In a 1955 lecture delivered at Goddard College and devoted to revealing the contemporary relevance of Emerson's scholar, Miller mockingly identifies himself with the author by confessing that the principal difference between himself and his subject is that Emerson's audience of students had actually *wanted* to hear him speak. Whereas the historical Emerson had wondered in his address "what light new days and events have thrown on [the scholar's] character and his hopes," Miller claims to have had the good fortune of devoting "his life to the biography of the American scholar." But he adds that "as for his hopes—well, has he any?"[81]

Miller's question illustrates the tangle of personal and professional urgencies, the demands of ideology and culture that necessarily influence any interpretation of literary history. For the first time in his career, his vision of the scholar had become apocalyptic, colored by the language of anxiety and extinction that would occur in his other addresses about the atomic age. Presenting democracy as a double-edged sword—useful in throwing off the shackles of privilege and convention, dangerous when appropriated by the "energies of business"—his picture of Emerson now reveals more intractably than ever a thinker acceptable neither to liberal nor conservative ideologies and painfully aware "of all the forces which hemmed him in."[82] Much of Miller's 1955 address is concerned with condemning the way in which Marxist *and* neoconservative thinkers had misunderstood and mistakenly disavowed Emerson. Both factions displayed "their own obtuseness" by insisting he be read literally.[83] Re-grounding Emerson's conception of the scholar on the "poetic vision" of Self-Reliance, Miller now sees Emerson's famous address as "a romantic vision of human possibilities, of human freedom behind the iron lid—and as such 'The American Scholar' is preeminently valuable to us."[84]

Given the tendency for the scholar's pronouncements to be appropriated by reductive polemics, given also the disenfranchisement of the scholar in a world dominated by material interests, Miller announces that "Emerson is not preaching either liberalism or conservatism; he is not a radical and he is not a reactionary. He knows wherein consists the essential freedom of the mind, no matter how heavily it be born down by lids of iron. Out of such knowledge—in his case painfully and arduously acquired—he brings forth his romance of a scholar's trust in himself."[85] This unaffiliated Emerson to some extent can be seen as an extension of Miller's earlier praise for the free play of thought and as a reflection of his own career as a thinker who critiqued both the left and the right. But it also can be understood as an effort to separate Emerson, if not from social context, then at least from any perception of self-interest, to free him from the constraints of historicity in order to be more adversarial, more truly critical. In seeking to free Emerson from the political contests of his time, Miller threatens to make his subject less vital to the culture he is meant to represent, and to the present culture as well.

The strategy can be understood, at least in part, as a very early variation of what Bruce Robbins calls the "end-of-the-intellectual story."[86] This narrative—which became something of a professional pastime during the culture wars of the 1980s and 1990s and continues in Richard Posner's recent *Public Intellectuals*—writes the obituary of previous intellectuals in order to "retrieve a public voice or position that was once preeminent and unquestioned, but is so no longer."[87] As McLaughlin remembers of this time, "I had the feeling Perry was haunted by the specter of [Edmund] Wilson, that more than anything he wanted to be someone like Lionel Trilling: a presence in the cultural landscape and not simply a professor." More poignantly, Miller's 1955 version of Emerson hints at his dawning awareness that his complicating mind, his refusal to engage historiography with a priori theories, made the role of public intellectual nearly unattainable and a vision of the future unimaginable. Perhaps it is for this reason that Miller increasingly comes to refer to the later Emerson, a benign figure celebrated by the college he'd once scandalized and destined to be misunderstood by the Gilded Age professoriate.

The evidence for this disenchantment can be found in Miller's last public statements about Emerson. In "New England Transcendentalism: Native or Imported?" he is still able to locate an "incendiary" and original thinker combating an "American order" "which pawed men into confor-mity."[88] But Emerson's voice of dissent is now seen as a kind of "moral innocence," a feeble blow "against the corruptions of civilization" be-cause it refuses to sufficiently take into account the lived realities of that civilization.[89] Emersonian utterance, in Miller's last discussion of it, has become a futile strategy by which the speaker strives to deny any influ-ence upon himself of the context he wishes to critique. As a result, the Emersonian scholar "is a student but all the while a rebel against study,"[90] an intellectual fractured by the recognition that things *are* in the saddle, that thought *is* more often used to justify material interests than it is to transform those interests. Ultimately, the recognition of his own difficult position within American society—as a public intellectual whose secu-lar jeremiads were as misunderstood and misappropriated as Emerson's "American Scholar"—would lead to a retreat from his earlier claims. In a rambling 1960 address on "Transcendentalism," Miller interrupts him-self to make clear the toll exacted on the midcentury intellectual hemmed in by the various forces of political quiescence, professional expectations, and democratic leveling: "I don't come here as an apostle of any cause. I'm a historian. I don't believe in anything myself."[91]

Having stood on the banks of the Congo nearly forty years earlier, Miller had glimpsed a portent of American empire, "its appalling power" (*EW* ix), and had found in that moment a vocation to reconceive the imperial project in terms of thought and spirit. If there is much in our contemporary moment to provoke skepticism about this idealistic and nationalistic project, it was nevertheless undertaken with an insistence that the literary historian view America not as an embodiment of hu-manity's highest aspirations, but with the "self-distrust" Miller insisted on throughout his life.[92] Standing before college audiences during the late 1950s and early 1960s, hoping to invoke the self-distrust imperative for the American Scholar, Miller seems to have encountered a vision as terrifying and "tawdry" (*EW* vii) as the one he had glimpsed in Africa: an American public that, despite his best efforts to expound its historical meaning and thereby reconceptualize its sense of possible futures, had remained unaccountably decent, indolent, and complaisant.

CHAPTER 6

Sacvan Bercovitch as "American" Scholar

Sacvan Bercovitch's American Jeremiad
should make it impossible for anyone to use
easily the word America.

—Jonathan Arac, quoted in
Paul Bové, *In the Wake of Theory*

No contemporary U.S. literary critic has more embraced the contradictions emerging from Emerson's opposition to American modernity than Sacvan Bercovitch.[1] That opposition, as we have seen, extends and ramifies through the genteel response to industrialization, immigration, and the literary realism felt to be their corollary; through Van Wyck Brooks's disavowal of that genteel response and his scorched-earth search for a history that might correct and even redeem it. It is an opposition coiled tightly in the conflict suggested by F. O. Matthiessen's pained and faintly sarcastic inscription to his friend-antagonist Perry Miller: "For Perry and Betty [Miller] with much gratitude, though the former has latterly indicated that he finds little value in the method employed in these pages."[2] If Matthiessen and Miller each confronted American literature "not only as an academic field but as a problem of cultural destiny,"[3] Matthiessen's fraught dedication belies a deep disagreement over the best way to employ the study of literature so as to redirect the national imaginary. Miller felt that *American Renaissance,* while admirably sensitive to aesthetic concerns, lacked a historical consciousness concerning the contexts from which its five canonical authors emerged. Matthiessen, as we know, regarded any literary history that blithely dispensed with formal considerations as reductive and dangerously instrumental.

The conflict between these competing modes of interpretation released a creative groundswell within the emergent discipline of American Studies: a ferment during the early Cold War years that included such important works as Henry Nash Smith's *Virgin Land* (1950), R. W. B. Lewis's *The American Adam* (1955), Richard Chase's *The American Novel and Its Tradition* (1957), and Leo Marx's *The Machine in the Garden* (1964). In hindsight, what these studies share is a critical exploration of what was described as the distinctive nature of American thought and writing: its "Americanness." In the process, they often blended historical and aesthetic concerns in ways that strengthened and consolidated a set of themes and myths, authors and canons, which had emerged nearly half a century earlier with the radical criticism of Van Wyck Brooks and the Young Americans. And much as the genteel critics of a previous century had understood themselves as the self-appointed guardians of taste and culture, the first generation of Americanists identified themselves as explicators—and therefore as *makers*—of what they considered the "true America." Harsh critics of the nation's tragic failure to achieve its ideals, the Americanists of the 1950s and early 1960s, often radical students and activists before World War II, renovated the jeremiadic tone of the depression-era Popular Front to denounce the social and political constraints imposed by the Cold War.

What authorized this particular conception of critical activism was a sense that the problems afflicting the nation—problems exemplified by the House Un-American Committee hearings, by an increasing social conformity that silenced difference, and by the Manichean view of the world divided between Us (or the U.S.) and Them (the U.S.S.R.)—were primarily political and economic. For Perry Miller, the lamentable American reality could be located in the consolidation of business and democracy. For F. O. Matthiessen, it was class and social divisions masked by liberal mainstream Democrat-Republican politics. What these conceptual frameworks held in common was an understanding that culture offered a delimited space wherein counterexamples to American instrumentalism might be discovered, reformulated, and deployed to renovate the nation *before* entering the fields of social and political power.

The abiding power of American Studies' initial collective effort to formulate and establish this space is nowhere so palpable as in the critical backlash it inspired from the mid-1970s through our present moment: a wholesale demystification of the nationalist premises of American Studies that recalls the attack against gentility led by Van Wyck Brooks. This time the role of Brooks was played by Sacvan Bercovitch, whose two major works from the period—*The Puritan Origins of the American Self* (1975) and *The American Jeremiad* (1978)—initiated the task of revision by situating the roots of an American mythos not in the American Renaissance but within Puritan rhetoric. By directing his critique toward the expressive and imaginative forms of the Puritan past, Bercovitch's audacious writings signaled an important shift in the understanding of culture that has remained remarkably influential. After Bercovitch, culture no longer seems to many critics the disinterested location for abstract reflection or political opposition but rather the place in which American power most pervasively resides. In this vision, power permeates and therefore shapes individuals, coercing compliance not through the crude energies of force but rather through those media previously thought to be the very grounds of resistance: language, the aesthetic, literature.[4]

Two things are important about this development as it applies to American literary criticism and American Studies. First, the immediate and ardent adoption of these ideas in the U.S. academy suggests the explanatory force they carried when applied to the conditions of twentieth-century American modernity. Just as Matthiessen's focus on the tragic was the result of disappointed hopes for social reconfiguration during the Depression, so, too, can Bercovitch's subversion/containment model be understood as the response to a historical moment: a moment when the radical energies of the sixties dissipated and were absorbed by mainstream interests. Conjoined with this de-radicalization was the increasing dominance of televisual and advertising cultures, which in turn produced the blurring of distinctions between fiction and reality described so presciently by Philip Roth[5] and which yielded themselves particularly well to the kind of analysis offered by cultural criticism.

Second, such analysis posed serious problems for those seeking ways to imagine alternatives to the dominant culture. For if power was suddenly imagined as immanent in culture, culture increasingly would be understood as that which inscribed and therefore limited not only the actions of the individual but his or her thoughts, feelings, even psyche. In other words, the shift to culture would shrink the imaginable grounds of oppositional criticism to smaller and smaller increments, eventually endangering the concept of agency altogether.

This critical shift and its perilous results are embedded in Bercovitch's sweeping reexamination of American literature and culture, a revisionist project invigorated during a moment, as Lawrence Buell remarks, when "the first and perhaps only 'school' ever to dominate American studies—the so-called myth-symbol approach—began to come under serious attack both methodologically (for liberties taken in selection and interpretation of historical evidence) and theoretically (for its consensus approach to American history, its tendency to posit a 'mainstream' of American thought)."[6] While an entire generation of American Studies scholars had followed the lead of F. O. Matthiessen and Perry Miller in describing the emergence of a national literary tradition defined by its aversion to conformity and its celebration of the unfettered self, Bercovitch discerned in such emancipatory narratives something else entirely: the rhetoric of an "exceptional" national mission designed to foreclose competing figures as well as competing possibilities of the self and of society.[7] Animated by this insight, Bercovitch transformed the "classic" writers celebrated by Brooks and enshrined by American Studies as irascible individuals revolting against convention into a collection of cultural spokespersons whose demands for social change, however charged with the fire of prophecy, were made nevertheless on behalf of the dominant culture of liberal democracy, that "poem in our eyes" (*EL* 465) imaged by Emerson as the nation.

The force of this new reading, however bracing and suggestive of new interpretive energies, however likely to compel revisions of categories and assumptions, contained within it the seeds of a despairing loss. For Bercovitch's analysis of America's rhetoric and ideology seemed to portend that all efforts to critique the United States were *already* prefigured and inscribed by that power—that opposition was inevitably absorbed into a larger, seemingly inexhaustible and airtight consensus in the manifestly exceptional destiny of the nation. Within this context, Bercovitch's work might be seen not only as a sustained involvement with the legacies of Matthiessen and Miller but also, at times, as the sorrowful requiem for those legacies experienced as no longer available. This engagement with critical precursors—figures he simultaneously emulates and repudiates—is mediated most clearly through his revision of Emerson, whose thought and writing is always seen as the test case for resistance to American consensus.

"It was the Emerson connection that spurred my interest in the Puritans," Bercovitch recalls, "and the influence of Emerson, as I see it, casts a long shadow forward in American culture, even unto our own times."[8] Much like Matthiessen and Miller before him, Bercovitch has been inexorably drawn to Emerson's example when reflecting on his own cultural project—haunted by the ambiguities of Emerson's rhetoric, its latent capacities for dissent and consent (for consent *through* dissent), its blithe naturalizing of existing American realities, on the one hand, and, on the other, its reckless and exhilaratingly modern proposal to transform the world through an uninhibited troping of that world.[9] Particularly suggestive are Bercovitch's earliest scholarship, in the 1960s, on "The American Scholar" and his subsequent and frequent return to Emerson's figure of *Man Thinking*. For if he suspects that the intellectual's trajectory from theory to praxis might be fatally severed by ideology, and if the conception of social change and its enactment seems permanently dissolved in the hegemonizing field of American culture, Emerson's myth of the integrated intellectual resonates with particular force. At times Emerson is understood by Bercovitch as "the locus classicus of American dissent" and the author who most strikingly "labored against the myth [of American exceptionalism] as well as within it"[10]; but he is also a preeminent example of ideological co-optation, his early writing an effort to "make Romantic natural theology an expression of the national dream"[11]—"The American Scholar," in particular, an address in which "*individualism, the people,* and *revolution,* considered in their highest aspect, political and spiritual, correspond to America."[12] Emerson (or rather, a particular *version* of Emerson) presides over Bercovitch's corpus like a doppelganger, the Americanized self that he, an impoverished Jewish-Canadian immigrant who came of age in an Israeli kibbutz, is perpetually in danger of becoming.[13]

The irony is that while he ultimately finds Emerson incapable of effecting meaningful social change or escaping the entanglements of power, Bercovitch himself enacts a form of resistance that can be traced directly back to Emerson. I refer to that aspect of the author discussed in the first chapter: his refusal to commit for long to any stance, a refusal that always foregrounds his realization that to choose action is to invoke affiliation. This Emerson repeatedly writes, thinks, and performs the *absence* of position, a centerless imaginative power that can only be domesticated at the expense of misreading. Emerson's absence of position is made possible by the aesthetic generation of multiple positions, multiple perspectives, none of which are allowed to remain choate or fixed for long.

This restless figure can be seen in Emerson's self-exile from the carefully delineated social position of minister at Boston's Second Church. It acquires symbolic figuration through the lintel onto which he would inscribe the word *Whim* and is made further legible by the exasperation with which Margaret Fuller complained of his "inhospitality of the soul"[14] or with which George Ripley received his refusal to participate in the Brook Farm enterprise. It is evident in the way he so often has been received throughout American literary history, whether as a philosopher, poet, author, or prophet. It is there in Perry Miller's triangulation of Emerson's journal entries to discern a proleptic dissenter against Cold War hegemony, or in F. O. Matthiessen's tensely unresolved portrait of Emersonian action and aesthetics. Most clearly it can be discerned in

Emerson's prose, in the injunction that "[b]ecause the soul is progressive, it never quite repeats itself" (*EL* 431), or, in "Circles," the vision of the open and indeterminate nature of the universe.

Even as he denies its possibility for radical change in the context of Emerson's own life and times, Bercovitch consistently performs a version of this mode of Emersonian resistance and a-positionality in his own work. A potentially radical prophet, Emerson nevertheless "completes [the work of] the fathers," in Bercovitch's reading, so as to articulate and thereby solidify a national myth that justifies its emerging imperial power. Yet in *The Puritan Origins of the Self* and *The American Jeremiad*, Bercovitch repeatedly (and subtly) shifts his own perspectives and foci when discussing Emerson, revealing his efforts to work around what he understands as the limitations for dissent and opposition imposed by the national imaginary. These efforts are most clearly thematized in his essay on Emerson for *The Rites of Assent*, the last essay he wrote for the book, which he has recalled as "my effort—the biggest effort I've ever made—to compromise with actually calling myself something of an Emersonian. It's the essay in which I do the most to try to Americanize myself in a conscious way."[15] "Emerson, Liberalism, and Liberal Dissent" is the culmination of Bercovitch's thinking on the writer as well as upon what the critic himself views as the totalizing force of a mythologized "American Way." It describes an Emerson suspended in ideological equipoise at precisely the moment when the words "individualism" and "individuality" competed for cultural endorsement in the wake of Jacksonian democracy. If both terms are seen to resonate with Emerson's primary belief in "the infinitude of the private man" (*JMN* 7: 342), *individualism* connoted the grasping materialism associated with the democratic dispensation while *individuality* bespoke the self-enrichment promised by continental associationism and other quasi-socialist schemes.

Here Bercovitch's influential portrait of Emerson—as an almost-radical who ultimately, if grudgingly, adopts the Jacksonian concept rather than accept a belief system detached from "America"—not only contradicts the unrepentant radical described by Perry Miller. It also suggests a covert portrait of Bercovitch himself, as immigrant, "wandering Jew" (his words),[16] and American Studies professional—a figure whose own maverick efforts to promote a disciplinary leveling that would dismantle the political ideologies underwriting the United States eventually threatened to subsume the very discipline which had allowed him to arrive at his insights. "People seem to see me as a carper, or demeaner, or reductionist," he wrote in a 1995 letter, "—and whether or not I am so *in effect* I do it all as a would-be believer—in this case, a disappointed would-be Emersonian."[17]

Bercovitch's "discovery of America"—his career as a "disappointed would-be Emersonian"—is the result, as he reminds us early in *The Rites of Assent*, of circumstances "interchangeably personal and professional" (*RA* 1). One of the first major American literary scholars *not* to be born in America, the critic grew up Yiddishist of Ukrainian parents in a French Catholic slum of Montreal. "We were poor," remembers one neighbor, "but the Bercovitch poverty was special. . . . The atmosphere was emotionally charged, and [Alexander] Bercovitch and his wife seemed at daggers drawn."[18] Bercovitch's father, a gifted if somewhat unstable artist, did not share the radical beliefs of his wife, Bryna, who had joined the Red Army in 1917 and continued for many years to believe in the utopia of a worker's paradise, bequeathing her son's unusual middle name by conflating those of the recently martyred Sacco and Vanzetti.[19] Bercovitch's professional oscillation between art and politics, between aesthetic form and an interest in literature's social engagement, might be taken as the negotiation, however displaced or unconscious, between competing parental emphases. Bercovitch's father, a "very isolated person" "[w]ithout any political commitment himself," separated from the family soon after Sacvan was born and abandoned it for good when his son was nine.[20] Like F. O. Matthiessen, whose reaction to his missing father would manifest itself in a criticism that stressed communion, Bercovitch's response to the departed Alexander Bercovitch is buried in his understanding that American writers always struggle to "'complete' their fathers."[21]

Bercovitch's mother remained committed to what her son referred to as the "big words like Truth and Beauty and the Future of the Working Class,"[22] words that resonated with the affective and compensatory urgencies of a religion whose eschatology implied an end to the hardships of poverty and cultural isolation. In response to his mother's version of ideological struggle, Bercovitch developed an ambivalent skepticism toward rigid systems of belief while remaining always a person who wanted "to believe," who felt "that people are lucky who are able to believe," who anguished over his own inability to "get hold of any definite belief."[23] Like the Emerson of "Experience," who grieves because grief has nothing to teach, or the Melville about whom Nathaniel Hawthorne observed, "he can neither believe, nor be comfortable in his unbelief,"[24] Bercovitch's critical consciousness is defined by an almost nostalgic longing for a vanished belief system that is always accompanied by a lacerating derision for such nostalgia.

From the age of nine Bercovitch lived with a series of foster families, an experience that intensified his sense of marginalization and loneliness. After high school he migrated to Kibbutz Nachshon, near what was then the Jordanian border and the Old Road to Jerusalem, "partly because I had no prospects, partly because the kibbutz seemed to me a socialist utopia," partly because it held out the promise of community and connectedness.[25] "It was a way of life I wanted to believe in. I wanted to believe that people could change. I tried very hard."[26] But though he found he could empathize with particular injustices, with local causes, Bercovitch learned that "to believe a party, or a line, or an individual, I could not do."[27]

Neither his early upbringing nor his experience at the kibbutz put him in immediate contact with the rhetoric of an "exceptional" America. But they are submerged touchstones to what would become his scholarly migration, first toward the Puritan Way and later to the "classic authors" of the antebellum period. His mother's abiding if unrequited attachment to the socialist cause as well as the kibbutz's adherence to a Zionist orthodoxy deeply inform his insights into the self-justifying rhetoric necessary to sustain an idealized settlement of a "hostile" land, a wilderness. These experiences also account for his competing and often unresolved efforts to appreciate the shaping force of that rhetoric. Bercovitch's thinking on the regulating teleology of social or national ideals was powerfully enhanced by his immigration in his late twenties to the United States. There he pursued a belated if meteoric academic career that emerged, moreover, within a historical moment when the apparent decline of a national consensus provoked by the Vietnam War prefigured a similar dissensus in the academic field that had blossomed out of the contradictory legacies of Matthiessen and Miller. The "reciprocity between the personal and professional" partially originating within these circumstances enabled Bercovitch "to channel my resistance to the culture into a way of interpreting it" (*RA* 1).

If this movement from resistance to interpretation in many ways mirrors a larger trend whereby the counterculture would become commodified and absorbed by corporate interests, for Bercovitch it resulted in *The Puritan Origins of the American Self*, easily the most audacious work of Americanist criticism to follow the "myth-symbol" school. Describing how the rhetoric of American identity enabled Puritan writers to yoke the sacred and secular into a teleological narrative of national destiny, the tone of the book most resembles the work of Perry Miller in its assumption of a presiding and magisterial authority, a mastering assimilation and ordering of the vast graphomanic exertions of the Puritan divines. But this authoritative stance is counterbalanced by an almost breathless interpretive excitement, an impassioned querrulousness energized through its encounter with a wealth of noncanonical primary material. Rael Meyerowitz may be correct to suggest that *Puritan Origins* is Bercovitch's effort to gain "a modicum of acceptance within the rhetorical system whose logic he lays bare"[28]—a suggestion bolstered by the critic's repeated references to "*our* tradition" and "*our* classic writers." But acculturation into American society seems finally of less consequence to Bercovitch than does fulfilling an intellectual (and professional) ambition that manifests itself in an ambivalent preoccupation with critical forbearers. That preoccupation runs unabated throughout Bercovitch's career, evident in the dedication "To the memory of F. O. Matthiessen and Perry Miller" that begins *Reconstructing American Literary History*; in the title of one of his most characteristic chapters, "The Puritan Errand Reassessed"; as well as in his influential discussion of "The Problem of Ideology in American Literary History" delivered at the Salzburg Seminar cofounded by Matthiessen. *The Puritan Origins of the American Self* begins the pattern of conflating and revising the masterworks of Miller and Matthiessen. It reinterprets Miller's study of the Puritans, traces cultural continuities much in the manner of "From Edwards to Emerson," and concludes with a compressed examination of the authors Matthiessen had canonized in *American Renaissance*.[29]

Ultimately, the book's impressive revisionary march through the textualized worlds of the Massachusetts Bay Colony and the Revolutionary period finds Emerson as its telos.[30] Emerson's centrality to Bercovitch's thinking had already been signaled the same year in an anthology of essays on the writer. "Emerson the Prophet: Romanticism, Puritanism, and Auto-American-Biography" begins by citing Harold Bloom's assertion that while English Romantic poets inevitably swerve from their literary precursors, "American poets labor to 'complete' their fathers." Bercovitch goes on to say: "The contrast seems to me a compelling cultural as well as literary insight. It directs us to Emerson as the central figure of the American Renaissance; it recalls the strong prophetic strain in Emerson's thought; and for my present purpose most importantly, it suggests that the long foreground to Emerson the prophet is the legacy of the colonial Puritan fathers."[31] Emphasizing the cultural continuation between Emerson and the colonial past secured for Bercovitch a coherent field not unlike the one Perry Miller discerned on the eve of World War II when, in "From Edwards to Emerson," he discovered a pietistic strain running between Jonathan Edwards and Emerson that produced a unified cultural inheritance that might, in a "war of ideas," be capable of resisting the assaults of European fascism and totalitarianism. Yet Bercovitch's depiction of cultural continuity, written three years after the United States' withdrawal from Vietnam, was freighted with far more ambivalent implications. Its preoccupation with the redemptive narrative of "America"—a narrative founded on a self-exalting myth of a saving remnant—could be understood in this cultural context as the skeptical response to an eroding national consensus and a sense of imperial disarray. Even so, the resistance and suspicion one might expect in Bercovitch's first book is by no means obvious; its subversive thesis is balanced, almost softened, by the author's admission that the American myth was sustained "by positive factors," including the facts "that America actually turned out to be a land flowing with milk and honey, and in an age of emergent nations it became something of a light to the world" (*PO* 185).

This national candescence achieves its greatest illumination for Bercovitch in the writings of Emerson, "the most influential thinker of the [antebellum] period and the crucial figure in the continuity of culture. Through him the distinctively American modes of expression matured" (*PO* 163). Emerson exemplifies, in Bercovitch's analysis, the processual forging of a representative selfhood that might combine the sacred and secular meanings of "America," so that ultimately, "[t]o be an American is to assume a prophetic identity; to have been an American is to offer a completed action that makes destiny manifest" (*PO* 121).[32] Bercovitch calls this distinctive structure of identity formation "auto-American-biography," by which he means "the celebration of the representative self as American, and of the American self as the embodiment of a prophetic universal sign" (*PO* 136).

Much like Miller, who would argue against a purely materialist understanding of the past, Bercovitch examines not only the ways in which rhetoric remains vulnerable to history, but how, as well, that "rhetoric becomes a reality" (*PO* 91). "Unregenerate readers kill the letter, reduce significance to dead fact," Bercovitch notes, suggesting the almost biblical way in which *logos* enters into and directs the outcomes of human interpreters. "Hermeneutics presupposes a reader transformed in the image of the spirit he sets out to discover" (*PO* 111). Language's power to shape reality is shown to occur through the Puritans' robust troping of inherited but malleable terms; as Bercovitch remarks, "The New England colonist not only had a private vision to convey, he had to convey it in metaphors that overturned the conventions from which these metaphors arose" (*PO* 113).

Not surprisingly, Emersonian troping in the service of "auto-American-biography" is understood as the highpoint of this tradition. "What is remarkable" about the various writers of the American Renaissance, Bercovitch notes, "is that all . . . learned from Emerson to make Romantic natural theology an expression of the national dream" (*PO* 162). Yet for Emerson to fill this particular role—for Emerson to be an author who "builds his method upon the demand for a single, certain, and comprehensive 'full sense,' diametrically opposed to invention"

(*PO* 159)—Bercovitch must focus on the early Emerson, the writer of *Nature* and "The American Scholar." The Phi Beta Kappa address especially is read as "a prophetic biography of the American self as scholar" (*PO* 168) and as "above all a testament to [Emerson's] overriding identification with the *idea* of America" (*PO* 169). This interpretation not only overlooks those early utterances by Emerson that challenge the orthodoxy of the United States, such as the 1838 address on "War" or the letter on the Cherokee Removal. It also obscures the philosopher of volatile process in the more canonical essays from roughly the same period. For Bercovitch, the early Emerson of *Nature* is most closely tied to the Puritan past, his Romanticism finely adjusted to "the tenets of early New England rhetoric" (*PO* 165), his oeuvre finally circumscribed by an "Americanism" that, in celebrating freedom, muted dissent. If Bercovitch situates this celebratory strain in the Jacksonian era and acknowledges the author's aversion to the form of grasping democracy associated with that particular presidential administration, he also notes that "[t]he rhetoric [Emerson] inherited [from the Puritans] enabled him to dissolve all differences between history and the self—as well as all differences within the self (civic, natural, prophetic)—and so to overcome political disenchantment by revealing himself as representative American" (*PO* 173).

This portrait of Emerson—which views the author less as an antagonist to the rampant materialism of a nascent democracy than as a participant in a rhetorical tradition that allowed him to resolve all antagonism into an inherited set of terms—to some extent echoes such genteel "conservative" versions of Emerson as that of Oliver Wendell Holmes, who carefully bound the author's always threatening antinomianism within the restraining mores of his time. The difference, of course, is that Bercovitch's portrait of Emerson focuses on a rhetoric that preexists the author and is understood (despite its roiling creative energies and susceptibility to revision) to paralyze dissent. In a significant moment at the end of the book, Bercovitch suggestively inserts a Marxist perspective into what had heretofore been an analysis of rhetoric:

> For well over two centuries, under the most diverse conditions, the major spokesmen for a self-proclaimed people of God subsumed the facts of social pluralism (ethnic, economic, religious, even personal) in a comprehensive national ideal, transferred the terms of conflict normally inherent in that ideal from history to rhetoric, and secured the triumph of that rhetoric by identifying it with the assertion of the representative American self. The

palpable social effects of the strategy argue the importance of ideology (in the Marxist sense) in the shaping of the United States.
The persistence of the myth is a testament to the visionary and
symbolic power of the American Puritan imagination. (*PO* 186)

The power of this conclusion lies in its divided critical stance of resistance
and receptivity, in Bercovitch's refusal to commit to either implication
discerned in the rhetoric he has studied. If the concluding gesture comes
close to a grudging admiration for the sheer force of a particular discourse
to transform social reality, the statement is hedged by the penultimate
sentence—a sentence that foretells the ideological analysis to which Bercovitch would increasingly direct his attention.

Writing in the *Partisan Review* shortly after the book's publication,
Alan Trachtenberg would discern a "minor chord" that rippled disso-
nantly throughout the text and "demystif[ied American] ideology."[33] Not
all readers heard the antimony. Sam B. Girgus recalls reading Bercovitch's
first book and believing it to concur with his own belief "that America
is exceptional."[34] Russell J. Reising would soon argue that Bercovitch's
analysis of America's myths and symbols was invariably compromised by
his fitful and wayward identification with those myths and symbols as
voiced by Emerson and the Puritans. In part, the competing receptions
of Bercovitch's first book was related to Emerson's idea that all language
is "fossil poetry"—a writerly problem Richard Poirier has described in
noting "that while we aspire to say something new, the materials at hand
indicate that whatever we say can only be understood if it is relatively
familiar." Poirier goes on to explain how the troublingly conditioned
quality of language nevertheless offers opportunities for change, how
"[e]ven in words that now seem tired or dead we can discover a desire
for transformation that once infused them. Any word, in the variety and
even contradictoriness of its meanings, gives evidence of earlier antagonistic uses, and it is this which encourages us to turn on them again, to
change or trope them further."[35]

But Bercovitch's begrudging wonderment at the U.S. rhetorical tradition and his covert ideological critique also bespeak dominant and emergent perspectives available within the field of American Studies at a moment of eroding national narratives, methodological dissatisfaction, and
increased professionalization. For young students just entering the field,
Bercovitch's approach to the colonial past and America's "classic" authors
was galvanizing. Lawrence Rosenwald recalls that from the moment he
began studying with the critic at Columbia University, he experienced a
sense that "here was something *new*. Bercovitch was really something of
a disruptor. I could read [Perry] Miller and 'get' the narrative, but Saki

came along and the whole field was suddenly, somehow, *other*. It was exhilarating and a little scary."[36]

Rosenwald's statement should be taken seriously. For if the majority of readers and students initially perceived in Bercovitch's thesis a celebratory "vision of the exemplary society that would become the model of all nations,"[37] the "minor chord" in his work threatened to undermine the very premises of American Studies. And this was even more the case in Bercovitch's second book. Unlike *The Puritan Origins of the American Self*, which was primarily interested in the rhetorical construction of an American self, *The American Jeremiad* would be more concerned with revealing the socioeconomic causes underlying that construction. Again building upon Miller's work on the Puritans, Bercovitch would rewrite the earlier critic's notion of the jeremiad as a dark and glowering id-like expression of the despairing New England Mind, portraying it instead as an essentially affirmative rhetoric designed to renovate the national mission by generating consensus. For Bercovitch, reading back through his own experiences with the "Big Words" of socialism and Zionism as well as through the tumult of the 1960s and early 1970s, America's rhetorical structures seemed to illustrate with powerful clarity Terry Eagleton's axiom that "[t]he system could be disrupted but not dismantled."[38] The jeremiad, far from a pointed cultural critique capable of producing alternatives to the social order, was seen by Bercovitch as a *product* of the system of American mythology, a cathartic ritual made in the service of that myth's regeneration, affirmation, and consummation. Taken in its entirety, *The American Jeremiad* offers a breathtaking critique of American culture and literary history, asserting that the symbolic and rhetorical form it examines "bespeaks an ideological consensus—in moral, religious, economic, social, and intellectual matters—unmatched in any other modern culture" (*AJ* 176). And in a crucial insight that would seem to completely overturn the previous critical dispensation, Bercovitch adds that "[t]he revelation of America serves to blight, and ultimately preclude, the possibility of fundamental social change" (*AJ* 179).

The theoretical problems posed by such a claim to the notions of agency and resistance—problems that might be seen to exist in a post-Vietnam critical taxonomy somewhere between Gramscian concepts of hegemony and Foucault's more restrictive version of an immanent and inescapable power—remain, for better or worse, part of our critical inheritance. But toward the antebellum writers who also comprise the final chapters of this book, Bercovitch surprisingly relaxes his critique, conceding that "all our classical writers (to varying degrees) labored against the myth as well as within it" (*AJ* 179). Meyerowitz notes that this shift in Bercovitch's position suggests that the critic "is still in the midst of his negotiation *with* the conditions and vicissitudes of an American cultural system, and *for* his own place and identity within it."[39] Within such a context we are able to hear not only the dominant strain of Bercovitch's ideological critique but also his submerged voice—another "minor chord"—enunciated, for instance, in his recognition that the writers of the American Renaissance "felt, privately, at least, as oppressed by America as liberated by it. And all of them, however captivated by the national dream, also *used* the dream to reach beyond the categories of their culture" (*AJ* 179–80). In this and many comparable passages, Bercovitch *deliberately* presents antimonies only to shuttle between them in ways that preclude his inhabiting a fixed critical position for more than a paragraph or two. In other words, a resolution to his negotiation with American culture—a culture defined and constituted in Bercovitch's analysis by the antimonies of agency and resistance—is precisely what he does *not* want.

Part of this strategy of irresolution is temperamental: the intellectual manifestation of a psyche incapable, as we have seen, of belief. But it is also the acknowledgment by a tough-minded critical sensibility that "*[i]nterpretation*," as he has elsewhere said, "*may be a trap of culture.*"[40] At its root, *The American Jeremiad* posed a serious dilemma for American Studies by undermining its methodology and premises—and hence its viability—as a field of study. It raised the question of whether it was possible for Americanists to know their subject matter when they were deeply embedded and implicated in the very object of study. But its larger claim was that the symbolic system of America always generates its own form of opposition—of which American Studies is but one variation—thereby ensuring its reabsorption into the dominant discourse and foreclosing any alternatives that might legitimately challenge it. In this exhilarating if "scary" reading, the thread of cultural criticism and outright opposition once supposed to run, for example, from Emerson to Matthiessen, strengthened the very social and political structures it had hoped to undermine. If *The Puritan Origins of the American Self* mainly focused on the rhetorical construction of selfhood, *The American Jeremiad* argued that that construction always served the hegemonic juggernaut of middle-class America. In Bercovitch's formulation, *every* attempt at dissent or opposition was *already* incorporated into the system of "America." "In all cases," Bercovitch noted, "the ideal of *American* revolution would rule out any basic challenge to the system. . . . [and] the summons to dissent . . . [inevitably] preempted the threat of radical alternatives" (*AJ* 160).

It is worth repeating, however, that the effects of this suffocating theory are mitigated in Bercovitch's discussion of canonical antebellum writers. "For our classic writers," he notes, "the symbol of America functioned as an ancestral taboo, barring them from paths that led beyond the boundaries of their culture. . . . [but t]he symbol [also] set free titanic creative energies . . . " (*AJ* 180). Still, if he acknowledges the possibility of agency in the authors he depicts, he does so in a manner that immediately places all such possibilities into larger webs of conditionality. Melville and Hawthorne play greater roles in *The American Jeremiad*, but once again the most surcharged and ambivalent case study is Emerson, whose career no longer authorizes the writings of others so much as it "exemplifies the possibilities and constrictions of the nineteenth-century jeremiad" (*AJ* 183). Emerson emerges as that figure who will exert increasing importance in Bercovitch's thinking: a test case for the possibilities of dissent in American culture, a cautionary reminder of the fatal—and ultimately unsustainable—allure of transcendence when confronted with the traps of culture. Bercovitch will come increasingly to rely on Emerson's writing to probe and even undermine his depiction of the seemingly inexhaustible power of American ideology to absorb competing views. In *The American Jeremiad,* however, he can assert that "[f]ar from pressing the conflict between individual and society, Emerson obviated all conflict whatever by defining inward revolt and social revolution in identical terms" (*AJ* 184).

Toward the end of his discussion, Bercovitch admits that "the extreme to which Emerson's pessimism could reach demands special attention" (*AJ* 190). But by situating Emerson at the center of American myth and symbol, by embedding him within the object he putatively would criticize, Bercovitch consigns him to an eternally recurring co-optation, an a priori situation inside an inescapable grid of signification wherein "continuous conflict . . . and gradual fulfillment become mutually sustaining concepts, and as such . . . lend themselves powerfully to the [socializing] strategies of the American jeremiad" (*AJ* 177).

The implications of this portrait of Emerson posed an alarming problem for Americanists. The transcendentalist, made to mean so many things during the century following his death, was suddenly representative of *all* American Scholars entrenched in the ideology generated by their object of study. To understand "our classic authors" as identifying "with America as it ought to be . . . [in] the service of society" (*AJ* 181–2) was to call into question the entire American Studies project. It was to suggest that the goal of critical opposition, long espoused by leftist or liberal participants in the myth-and-symbol school, was little more than a chimera, a wispy illusion easily absorbed by the discursive power of "America." Exemplary Americanists such as Leo Marx and Henry Nash Smith suddenly seemed in Bercovitch's analysis to have failed in their critique of U.S. culture; no longer cultural makers, they were now seen as incapable of looking beyond the ideologically saturated field they studied for genuine alternatives to the status quo. In so presenting their work, Bercovitch summarily deprived the humanistic subfield of American Studies of a central premise explicated by Matthiessen and others: that the literary (or the aesthetic, more generally) might serve to voice an Ahabian "No, in thunder" to instrumental thinking. By conceiving of power as inexhaustible and inexhaustibly capacious in its ability to generate and then absorb elements of resistance, Bercovitch nullified the animating premise behind Matthiessen's *American Renaissance* and the subsequent elaborations involving myths and symbols as techniques for recalling America to its New World mission.[41] Perhaps more important, he articulated a theory of national ideology that, in imagining opposition as only another script of power, seemed to foretell the eventual absorption and dissipation of all psychic processes, all interiority, consciousness itself.

As the leading exponent of consensus theory in American Studies, Bercovitch in the 1980s would adopt the role of tutelary spirit to a new generation of critics in several important ways. In his influential "The Problem of Ideology in American Literary History" as well as in the introduction to *Reconstructing American Literary History*, both published in 1986, he would self-consciously adopt the role of Emerson's American Scholar leading a generational revolt that would express its antifoundational critical order in the "dissensus" of the *Cambridge History of American Literature*, edited by Bercovitch. If his call for a new literary history "echoes the summons of Emerson's *American Scholar*,"[42] as he put it, and if Emerson's address itself was "conceived in a spirit of dissensus," Bercovitch's revisionist challenge would nevertheless need to avoid Emerson's mistake of denouncing "the present in order to awaken the nation to its millennial calling."[43] Indeed, the so-called New Americanists would have to keep in mind "a major problem of the new literary history": "the paradox of an antagonist literature that is somehow also culturally representative."[44]

If the general tone of these documents is the exuberant reimagining of a national literary tradition in the spirit of Brooks and the Young Americans, a more somber note occurs in the surprising dedication of *Reconstructing American Literary History* "To the memory of / F. O. Matthiessen / and Perry Miller." The dedication is not simply a gesture of respect and admiration for those figures who had made Bercovitch's project of revision possible. Rather, the commemoration of the two critics serves as a lament for the diminished capacities of art and selfhood that resulted from an understanding that culture was the site of instrumental coercion.

This recognition occurs in the inconclusive and searching registers of Bercovitch's discussion of the new literary history, as when he notes that while "the almost programmatic suspiciousness [of the New Americanists] is the negative side of ideological analysis . . . I would like to think . . . that among [the new work] is the challenge of alternative *historical* possibilities, including alternative ways of intellectual, moral, and political commitment."[45] Where such alternatives might be located, given Bercovitch's sense of the all-consuming voracity and consolidating power of the American consensus, is never decisively addressed. And this inability to suggest concrete viable alternatives takes formal shape in the odd unsettledness we experience when reading, within the space of a few pages, such apparently incongruous statements as the assertion that "there's no escape from ideology" (which assumes *no* possibility of getting outside ideology)[46]; the "question [of] whether to use culture's terms or to be *used* by them" (which posits *some* resistance within ideology's enclosure)[47]; and the call for "a cultural dialectic attuned to the power of language no less than the language of power, sensitive to the imaginative . . . while insisting on the cognitive" (which seems *almost* to renovate the aesthetic as a source of resistance).[48] Such a wobbly trajectory is not only the expression of a theorist grappling with the unsettling ontological consequences of his theory. As I have already suggested, the rapid shuttling between possible positions can be seen as a strategy for mitigating and even undermining the grossly determining aspects of that very theory.

Bercovitch will address this problem most deliberately in his examination of "Emerson, Liberalism, and the Problems of Liberal Dissent," the penultimate essay in *The Rites of Assent*.[49] In many ways, this expansive book can be seen as the summation of his thinking on American culture and literature—a prolonged meditation on the constraints and interstitial possibilities for the resistant self saturated by ideology and always threatened by co-optation. That inquiry begins with the autobiographical essay, "The Music of America," in which Bercovitch more affirmatively advances the rationale for a study of ideology when he notes that "[i]f dreams of transcendence are indices into the traps of culture, then inquiry into the trapping process may provide insight into our own and into others' actual non-transcending condition" (*RA* 5). This recognition may be "problematic, provisional, and *nourished* by the frustrating sense of boundaries" because it "denies us access to apocalypse, but it helps make our surrounding worlds visible" (*RA* 5). In a particularly revealing statement, Bercovitch links this process of inquiry to a narrative of discovery, likening his experience to Emerson's American Scholar, who "grows concentrically toward transcendence, in

an expanding circle from nature to books to representative selfhood"
(*RA* 5). Bercovitch's own discoveries, however, are best described as "un-
representative," "a series of increasingly particularized border-crossings:
first into 'America' proper; then, into the interdisciplinary field of
American Studies; and finally, into the special area of American literary
scholarship" (*RA* 5).

This outward, concentric journey is interesting for its counterintuitive
teleology—from nation to culture to the literary. Moreover, this progressive series of "border-crossings" will not only recall "Perry Miller's vocational epiphany at the mouth of the Congo River" (*RA* 25) as well as
Emerson's imagining, in *Nature*, of Columbus first viewing America, but
will be linked to the suggestion of an alternative account of discovery:

> My own America, if I may call it so, elicited a different sense of
> wonder. To put this in its proper prosaic terms, it elicited a critical
> method designed to illuminate the conflicts implicit in border-
> crossing, and to draw out their unresolved complementarities.
> I spoke of this method . . . as unrepresentative, thinking of the
> corporate American figure in Emerson's Scholar. But the contrast
> itself suggests . . . the other America hidden from view by that
> interpretation; or as I called it, appropriatively, the unincorporated
> country of my alien namesakes, Sacco and Vanzetti, a rhetorically
> United States of nonetheless mainly unresolved borders—between
> class and race, race and generation, generation and region, region
> and religion, religious and ethnic and national heritage—and
> a constantly shifting array of cultural crossings, including those
> between Jewish-Canadian marginality and Emersonian dissent.
> (*RA* 26–7)

How to square this account of demystification with an intellectual
journey from nation to literary scholarship and how to align the transition between immigrant marginality and "Emersonian dissent" are
the critical burdens of Bercovitch's penultimate essay. Emerson is saved
for a drama that prefigures not only Bercovitch's but that of American
Studies as well: a conflict that unravels in the contest over the words
individualism and *individuality*. In focusing on these words, Bercovitch
identifies a significant nodal point in the Jacksonian era, when democracy threatened to subsume political alternatives. But he also addresses,
however latently, late-twentieth-century conceptualizations of ideology,
hegemony, and agency. If his writing previously had identified a powerful ideology capable of paralyzing dissent, it did so by suggesting that
the equally powerful figure of the self-reliant individual unfettered by

social norms was in fact a *product* of this ideology: a particular model of subjectivity that served to reinforce the linked belief systems of capitalism and democracy. In this closed circuit model of consensus, the citizen is all but rendered inoperative when it comes to proposing alternative actions or thoughts that challenge this immanent power.

The implications of this theory are what roil and animate "Emerson, Liberalism, and the Problems of Liberal Dissent." In it, Emerson manages alternately to "supersede by transforming" (*RA* 283) the "tradition he inherited" (*RA* 285) and to be subsumed by the rhetoric of his culture. In many ways, this reading is a reprise—a politicized reprise—of Stephen Whicher's influential vision of a declensionary Emerson: a figure bowed by age and circumstances to shift the focus of his thinking from "Freedom" to "Fate." Emerson studies in the 1970s and 80s, defined largely by Whicher's narrative and, to a lesser extent, Harold Bloom's theories about the American "difference" in poetic influence, are apparent in Bercovitch's version of the author. What the critic inserts into the discussion is a self-consciously politicized portrait of Emerson, a thinker engaged with two concepts of the individual rooted in the Enlightenment concept of self-empowerment but taking on urgent connotations in the first half of the nineteenth century: *individuality,* or the liberating form of selfhood described by French associationists as accruing within communal social formations, and *individualism,* a version of selfish personhood associated in Emerson's time with the materialistic grasping of laissez-faire capitalism, generally, as well as, more particularly, with Jacksonian democracy. Tracing Emerson's flirtation with the first term—especially as it was deployed within the Brook Farm experiment—Bercovitch locates a moment in Emerson's journals where, poised to adopt the socialist model, poised in other words to embrace a political form antithetical to the existing order, he ultimately recoils against the outer limits of American liberal ideology and accepts instead a form of Jacksonian individualism that he hopes to invest with utopian value.

At the historical level, Bercovitch's portrait is open to several criticisms. Most importantly, he tends to see Jacksonian democracy as a totalizing and inevitable fact, when it seems more likely that for Emerson, both the nation and its government were felt to be up for grabs, in process and still susceptible to change.[50] Furthermore, Bercovitch tends to underestimate the truly prophetic force of Emerson's thinking at this time: its stated willingness to rethink all social, political, and religious forms and to ground them in a version of selfhood untethered to any prior models. All of which is to say that Bercovitch's portrait of Emerson, like any work of criticism, cannot help but be concerned with the particular issues of its originary moment. For the critic, Emerson's eventual avowal of individualism "amount[s] to a breathtaking work of culture—a wholesale appropriation of utopia, all the hopes of reform and revolution nourished on both sides of the Atlantic by the turmoil of modernization, for the American Way" (*RA* 335). Yet within the seemingly determining rhetoric of the dominant culture, Bercovitch nevertheless attempts to locate the source of agency and the possibility of social change within Emerson's thinking. Describing the author's visit to Europe during the socialist upheavals of 1848, Bercovitch remarks how

> Emerson's *abiding* utopianism demonstrates the radical energies potential in American liberal ideology. The same convictions which led him to reject socialism also impelled him a decade earlier outward to revolutionary concepts of European individuality. It was not then, or ever, a matter of transcending his culture but on the contrary of plumbing its depths. Emerson's role as prophet was to carry the basic premises of 'America' as far as they would go, to the hither verge of what was ideologically conceivable—and thereby to challenge his society. . . . (*RA* 342)

Still, if the possibility of meaningful social challenge is raised here and elsewhere, it is circumscribed throughout the essay by a further qualification:

> The appeal of Emersonian dissent lies in an extraordinary conjunction of forces: its capacity to absorb the radical communitarian visions it renounces, and its capacity to be nourished by the liberal structures it resists. It demonstrates the capacities of culture to shape the subversive in its own image, and thereby, *within limits,* to be shaped in turn by the radicalism it seeks to contain. . . . Emersonian dissent testifies . . . to the oppositional forms generated within the structures of society. (*RA* 348–9)

This version of Emerson has been remarkably influential in our time—as powerful in its shaping of our reception of the author as were earlier portraits by Brooks, Matthiessen, and Miller. Bercovitch's Emerson has achieved such widespread acceptance, moreover, because it illustrates with particular clarity the shift in American Studies whereby a prior commitment to a nationalist project has given way to what it prefers to call a "radical" critique of that project. It points to a relocation of power from political and economic sources to larger and less palpable sites located within culture itself. And it suggests how these critical and theoretical shifts might not only reenergize American Studies but would reenergize it precisely by releasing it from previous models and canons now seen as connected to a larger imperial project.

At the same time, Bercovitch's treatment of Emerson reveals how this shift in emphases has exacted an incredible expense for which we continue to pay: an expense of agency and of meaningful opposition and analysis. Regardless of how close Emerson comes to successfully altering the contours of antebellum ideology, he is ultimately and always already inscribed, in Bercovitch's account, by the power he would seek to undermine and alter. He is, in Donald E. Pease's phrase, a "non-starter."[51] Yet if this hermetic model would seem to foreclose all meaningful critique, it is worth remarking once again that Bercovitch enacts throughout his essay an Emersonian gesture of inassimilable movement, a constant shuffling and rearranging of perspectives that might serve as a staging ground for new affect and meaning. As in Emerson's work, Bercovitch's linguistic momentum ultimately serves to trouble all efforts at premediation; it can neither be satisfactorily domesticated nor transposed into available forms or categories. Like Emerson's own essays, "Emerson, Liberalism, and the Problems of Liberal Dissent" is a device meant to produce dilemmas that cannot be resolved, to generate and proliferate interpretations—so that efforts to sort Bercovitch's thought, or to fix it categorically, ultimately result in acts of bad conscience and intellectual dishonesty.

Given Bercovitch's contention that American ideology is capacious enough to generate and absorb all resistance, the question remains: can the literary intellectual effect meaningful social change? The dilemma has in many ways been anticipated by the so-called New Americanists, the very critics for whom Bercovitch's theory of consensus acted, initially, as inspiration, and later, as a model to overcome. Early in its career, Bercovitch's work came under attack by what Leo Marx has ironically called the "Old Americanists,"[52] who found its conclusions threatening to the broader project of understanding American culture. More recent critics, however, have charged that Bercovitch's professional location—within American Studies and American literary studies—prohibits him from going far enough in his critique. By focusing his analysis on a distinctive American tradition, in other words, his body of work resembles nothing so much as the totalizing ideological system he had set out to demystify. For critics such as Paul Bové and William V. Spanos, the only way to effectively combat what they perceive as a global American hegemony from within a disciplinary framework is to resituate American Studies in a postnationalist, comparativist setting that calls attention to the connections between the emergence of the discipline and the rise in American imperial aspirations during the Cold War.[53] In a typical statement, Spanos sees an unacknowledged "complicity" in "Bercovitch's 'reformist' mode of dealing with problems confronting the Americanist seeking for alternatives to the consensus-producing imperatives of the American jeremiadic discourse, specifically, his disabling delimitation of critical options to those made available by the discourse."[54]

Bercovitch has sought to answer both the question of critique and the degree to which his work "remains vestigially inscribed by the ideology of American exceptionalism even as it criticizes it and tries to transcend its confining parameters"[55] in a series of essays on critical methodology, the most developed of which is "Games of Chess: A Model of Literary and Cultural Studies."[56] A dense, allusive, and highly associative essay meant as a "polemic against the aesthetics of transcendence" (GC 17), "Games of Chess" suggests, among other things, why Bercovitch's pilgrimage has moved from American Studies to literary studies. Locating in philosophical idealism and cultural materialism a shared "platform of transcendence" that leads, teleologically, to absolute solutions and resolutions, Bercovitch advances a countervailing form in literary study, with "its principle" being "resistance to any unified system of enclosure, or (what amounts to the same thing) an astonishing vulnerability to appropriation by other systems of closure" (GC 23). Unlike cultural studies, with its disciplinary origins in the transcendently oriented social sciences, the literary, for Bercovitch, "moves forward either by rejecting the abstraction outright, or else, far more frequently and more forcefully, by accepting it only to expose its limitations" (GC 27). It does so in its insistent regard of details instead of absolutes, its particularizing of the nontranscendent grounds of lived experience. For the later Bercovitch, the work of exposure carried out by the literary is most forceful because it occurs "textually rather than programmatically, as the insidious, often surprising result of aesthetic process" (GC 27). If the canonical authors of the American Renaissance were esteemed by such critics as Matthiessen and Miller for their capacity to oppose the dominant culture, the aesthetic itself becomes for Bercovitch the grounds of resistance precisely "because the language game [played by authors] returns us to gaps between experience and explanation" (GC 27).

Equating disciplinary logic and ideology itself with the game of chess, Bercovitch rejects the "deadend endgame[s]," or "traps" of transcendentalism, in order to offer a "middle-game sacrifice" model defined by "positionality, inventiveness, and strategic combinations" (GC 31). This model, which is literary in nature, works to "decline or circumvent" the absorbing quality of consensus by particularizing the absolute and thereby inviting "us to question and challenge . . . the [totalizing] endgames" of ideology (GC 34). "[W]e are always-already more than our culture says we are, as a language is more than a disciplinary vocabulary" (GC 37). In a move that initially seems to return him, fatally, within the gravitational pull of the American myth, Bercovitch asserts that "'America' is to the modern world as the middle-game sacrifice is to the game of chess . . . an opportunity for open-ended fulfillment" (GC 52–4). This statement is followed by a carefully balanced description in which the critic draws from the United States and its "global cultural economy" a correlative language, "that astonishing complex of sacred-secular meanings developed in the modern era as a symbology of the new" (GC 54). But suddenly pulling back from the exuberant attraction of his own description, Bercovitch concedes his awareness "that the model I've just expounded looks suspiciously like an American fantasy of new beginnings—an effort to adapt the America game to a literary-and-cultural studies errand into a new millennium" and asks if that model isn't precisely "the trap to be avoided?" (GC 56).

The answer comes in a dialogic chess-like game of intellectual moves that pits various disciplinary approaches against the problem of transcendent traps: "*First, the philosophic move:* Since . . . our terms of analysis are themselves language games reproducing the forms of culture they describe, we have no foundation for objectivity, no Archimedean fulcrum outside culture for disinterested inquiry. . . . *Then, the literary cultural response:* We may have to accept that particular trap . . . ; but we can play . . . to circumvent the trap" (GC 56). Precisely how Bercovitch proposes to do this is through an Emersonian "recommencement," a term he draws from "The American Scholar" ("I greet you on the re-commencement of our literary year" [*EL* 53]) and deploys as a term within culture that, in its "endless affirmation of beginnings" (GC 56), suggests the possibility of change. Bercovitch locates the dynamics of this processual and dynamic flux in the formal particularities of an Emerson essay. The very opposite of Stanley Cavell's portrait of Thoreauvian philosophy as "written with next to no forward motion, one that culminates in each sentence,"[57] Bercovitch's Emerson inaugurates in "The American Scholar" a form "whose rhythm and logic require us to reconceive the meaning of each of its parts—section, paragraph, sentence—as a recommencement in its own right" (GC 55).

In many ways, this description recalls, in its broad understanding of revisionary action, Robert Milder's understanding of "The American Scholar" as "tapping a widespread discontent among the young and joining it to a diagnosis of the cultural, spiritual, and economic failure of America," thereby redrawing "the lines of sociohistorical reality so as to transform an age of apparent collapse . . . into one of revolutionary opportunity and to summon the marginalized intellectual to the very forefront of epochal change."[58] But the Emerson whose "recommencement" is advanced by Bercovitch ultimately seems less illuminated by prophetic visions than by a chastened sense that the ludic capacities of the literary, in directing us from abstract solutions to particular dilemmas, may help bring us back to communion with the everyday world, and from there to the "circumvention" of ideology's trap. In his strategic use of the word *circumvention*, Bercovitch leans less on its primary definition "to besiege" than on its secondary meaning to outwit with cunning and, just as importantly, "to avoid or try to avoid fulfilling, answering, or performing (duties, questions, or issues)."[59] Bercovitch's circumvention differs from the New Americanist *intervention*—that quasi-juridical mediation that posits the critic in dispute with the corporate body of "America"—not so much in its recognition that direct intervention is futile but rather in its suspicion that such acts ultimately rely on a form of transcendence, an emphasis on material determinants or ethereal speculation that mandates a *solution* to cultural problems.

If one of those problems has been the deep embeddedness of Americanists within their object of study, the solution by a number of recent critics has been an attempt to reframe the object in terms understood to be *outside* it. Put another way, if Bercovitch's model of American discourse as containing all opposition seems to reflect the increasing global hegemony of the United States, the solution to such a model and its correlative hegemony is to imagine "transnational," "postnational," "postdisciplinary," and "exilic" frameworks from which to contextualize and critique very real imbalances of power in ways imagined as somehow *beyond* the American discourse it would resist.

Bercovitch's response to such efforts is simultaneously more fatalistic and more optimistic—which may be to say more Emersonian. Recognizing that "'America' is neither new nor final, but, from start to finish, a fiercely contested middle game" of "particulars, agency, predicaments, and limitations" (GC 57), the critic suggests that all efforts to escape from its rules are illusory at best. Within this context, a switch in emphasis from the discourse of American Studies to transnational or postnational perspectives would not only risk mirroring the globalizing process through which U.S. power has been consolidated in the past decade or so, but it would also cede responsibility for the continuing and even more urgent need to analyze the durable power of an American consensus that has authorized it, even in the guise of dissensus. "And whatever end we think we see unfolding" in the game of America, Bercovitch notes, "it would be well to have a clear view of the rules we play by. For one thing, this would allow us more fully to appreciate our options within the game. For another thing, it would help us understand the unresolved predicaments that may issue (who knows?) in alternative, post-American forms of the game" (GC 56).

In this respect, Bercovitch's corpus might also be considered utopian, at least in the sense Slavoj Žižek means when he notes that "utopia has nothing to do with imagining an impossible society" but rather "the construction of a u-topic space, a social space outside the existing pa-rameter . . . of what appears to be 'possible' in the existing universe."[60] For Bercovitch, this space is created in the recommencing aesthetics of the particular and processual, a recommencing that allows for the spec-tral dissent Bercovitch himself enacts by *circumventing* the very theory he proposes. This circumvention is animated by his refusal to relinquish sheer interpretive power, his insistence on staying both in and out of the game, and it is further fueled by a recognition that new varieties of dissent might arise as the American Way is exported globally.

Haunting Bercovitch's circumvention is Emerson, who represents not only the rites of assent the critic has analyzed so perspicaciously through-out his career, but also the "right of ascent"—the implied promise, shared obversely and antagonistically by the national ideology and those who would resist it, that the self might be a commencement, a recommence-ment, a setting out through the vicissitudes of history and context toward a representative embodiment, an anguished democracy of *becoming*. But the critic's exemplary circumvention also suggests that during our pres-ent moment, when the United States has achieved an unparalleled global reach, the imperatives of the "American" Scholar remain as urgent as they were in Emerson's orginary address.

CHAPTER 7

Emerson's Ghosts

Communing with ghosts is not unprofitable to
one who listens to their tales.
— Vernon Parrington, *Main*
Currents in American Thought

Recalling a trip to Emerson's grave on May 6, 1882, Walt Whitman observed that "It is not we who come to consecrate the dead—we reverently come to receive, if so it may be, some consecration to ourselves. . . ."[1] Whitman's recollection recapitulates in many ways the opening of Moncure Conway's *Emerson at Home and Abroad,* when "From this vigil beside the grave of Emerson," the biographer recollects his first encounter with Emerson's prose—a "sentence only!"—which in turn inspired him to realize that within himself "[a] human aim had arisen; souls were to be saved."[2] Throughout this book I have suggested that the histories of American literary scholarship and American Studies have been shaped in large part by a similar impulse—a desire for consecration from beyond the grave, for Emerson, as putative originator of a national literature, to matter in ways that spoke directly to literary and cultural academics and that implied a greater social role for those academics. Nathaniel Hawthorne hints at this perdurable longing for ghostly consecration in *The Scarlet Letter* when he notes that "There is a fatality, a feeling so irresistible and inevitable that it has the force of doom, which almost invariably compels human beings to linger around and haunt, ghostlike, the spot where some great and marked event has given color to their lifetime."[3]

Of course, not all of Emerson's critics have been so powerfully haunted by the example of "The American Scholar." To offer but one example, the philosopher Stanley Cavell recalls teaching a seminar on Emerson with Sacvan Bercovitch during which "issues of the tension between the historical and the philosophical Emerson kept arising, mostly at our invitation, but sometimes to our dismay."[4] This disparity resulted because "philosophy necessarily [left] out history" for Bercovitch, "which [for him] contains the most interesting material in thinking about Emerson,"[5] while for Cavell something like the opposite was true. Emerson's efficacy in directing social action was not nearly so compelling to Cavell as was his thinking about the *process* of thinking and the related question of how to be in the world. Cavell's sustained absorption with Emerson may be seen in this light as an effort to capture the movement of the author's thought through a language always shaped by past usage, a language against which he strives to think "aversively." While history is a necessary constituent in this effort, it is, for the philosopher, always subordinate: what comes *after* prolonged reflection and engagement with Emerson's intellectual modeling. "If . . . the fact is to emphasize that Emerson went against the popular grain," Cavell argues, ". . . shouldn't this be put together with the fact of Emerson's perpetual sense that what he heard from the culture went against his grain?"[6] Cavell takes seriously, in other words, the process of thought and the affective experience of being Emerson in his attempts to explain why that thought might matter to students of philosophy and what it might mean for American thought to inherit Emerson as a philosopher. "Every word chagrins us," Cavell continues, alluding to Emerson's bristling remark in "Self-Reliance." "That is quite a fantastic confession for anyone to think to make. If you think Emerson means it (I do) then it seems to me to speak volumes about the way he writes—since he shares every word with those for whom he is fated to write. So each word he sets down is a potential cause for chagrin."[7]

Cavell's remarks, emerging primarily from the philosophical tradition, not surprisingly are made with little reference to what has been the major story of American literary studies during the past quarter century: the widening of critical and theoretical approaches accompanied by a similar expansion of the canon. Both developments are in part the products of an increased recognition of social plurality in the United States that began with the civil rights movement, the women's movement, and the 1965 Immigration Act. These interrelated transformations have not only reshaped the United States into a more culturally diverse place; they have led to a shift in American Studies and American literary criticism away from the white Anglo-American Protestant dispensation that made up their shared field of study for so long. The result has been a redirection of American literary studies toward works that reflect a more richly diverse, complex, and culturally interwoven society. This alteration in the field not only has changed the meaning of Emerson; in some cases it has called into question the desirability of maintaining Emerson at the center of—or even within—a national literary tradition; it has even thrown into question the desirability of a national literary tradition of any kind.

It is no exaggeration to say that despite the enlivening figure of philosophy, aesthetics, and cultural criticism discerned by some recent commentators, Emerson's place in American literary history has never been more vehemently contested, more questioned, more threatened. In part this has to do with the social and cultural transformations just mentioned. In part it has to do with a related and uneasy awareness of the increasing global dominance of the United States in a post–Cold War era: an alarm at the untrammeled and what Miller termed the "appalling" force of a geopolitical superpower capable of asserting its will seemingly unchallenged throughout the world. To gauge the recent shift in tone toward American literary and cultural studies we need look no farther than two telling prefixes that mark the transition from the Berlin Wall's symbolic partition of a bipolar world to the fractious, sectarian, laissez-faire dynamic of globalization that has resulted from the Wall's destruction. I refer, in the first instance, to the revisionary excitement that surrounded the collaborative project of Bercovitch and the New Americanists during the eighties. At the core of that excitement was the prefix "re-," a promissory word that seemed, after the myth-symbol school, to suggest that the entire corpus of American Studies and American literary scholarship was up for grabs, subject to change, to radical rethinking: that the American Renaissance was to be "reconsidered," for instance, that American literary history would be revised, reimagined, reconceptualized, remade, and, perhaps, revolutionized. During the past decade, in the wake of the simultaneous globalization and balkanization of the world (and, not incidentally, of literary studies), this exuberant revaluation of U.S. literature and culture has been replaced by an apocalyptic preoccupation with "post-"ness: a condition summed up in such words as postnationalism, postdisciplinarianism, postpolitics. These apocalyptic "post"-ings are conjoined with a desire for radical transformation, a yearning to tear the critical self free from the hermetic and entrapping matrix of American ideology: a deep-seated longing to so transfigure the given and administered circumstances of U.S. cultural life that the very criteria by which we might consider change would be irrevocably altered. The advocacy for a post*everything* world can be understood, at least in part, as the need to disavow contemporary circumstances in which the American Way (or at least a neoconservative version of the American Way) has declared global aspirations, a moment in which, as a recent and notorious government report asserts in an alarmingly Orwellian tone, "the American homeland is the planet."[8]

Within these new social and geopolitical configurations, Emerson's position as founder of an idealist literary and philosophical tradition believed to tacitly underwrite and even celebrate the dominance of the United States is understandably under significant reconsideration. If many New Americanists questioned the value of Matthiessen's American Renaissance as too narrow and restrictive—a Cold War version of the genteel canon of high ideality that barely concealed its desire for a normative (white, male) social order—more recent discussions would ask if *any* focus on a solely "American" literary tradition is worth continuing. At the heart of these calls to dissolve the boundaries of nation and discipline is the fear that such categories merely reinscribe a national—and globally imperialist—ideology that is not only busy shaping the world in its image but also of shaping the world in order to maintain its own self-image.[9] In this environment, it is not surprising that some critics would like to exorcise Emerson's ghost from the study of American literature, to expunge its undue influence from our collective understanding of the past, to diminish and demystify rather than continue consecrating its memory. The questions these critics pose are urgent variations of those already examined throughout this book: Is Emerson a viable figure within a new and urgently felt paradigm? Is there a recuperable presence in his work? On what grounds can we continue—would we *want* to continue—to insist upon his centrality? Are we finished with Emerson?

Before attempting to answer these questions directly, we might turn to a similar "post"-ing in Emerson's own thought and writing. I refer to "Experience" (1844), an essay of loss and hope and an attempt at what Stephen E. Whicher called a "solution . . . for the skepticism bred by the excessive claims of faith."[10] If much of American literary studies has been summoned into being and enabled by the American Scholar's preoccupation with that "curious . . . conversion" by which "experience becomes thought" (*JMN* 5: 320) and thought then is promulgated so as to alter another person's "state of mind" (*EL* 65), "Experience" is more concerned with what the deluge of daily life, the irreducible and experiential givenness of the world, might have to tell us *despite* those a priori conceptions and deeply felt desires we harbor to change that world. "Experience" is concerned, in other words, with how we might go about living when confronted with grief, unhappiness, social inertia, historical burdens, and other conditions from which we can never entirely or imaginatively extricate ourselves.

It is worth noting in this context just how many passages that eventually make their way into "Experience" have origins in the spring and summer of 1837—the period during which Emerson's efforts to compose "The American Scholar" were given dramatic emphasis by the financial crisis then roiling the nation. "Is it not pathetic that the action of men on men is so partial?" he writes in May, lamenting the fact that "[w]e never touch but at points" (*JMN* 5: 328). Or in August, just a few weeks before delivering "The American Scholar," he once again notes the baleful recognition that the autonomous self entails loss and isolation when he remarks, "As Boscovich taught that two particles of matter never touch, so it seems true that nothing can be described as it is" (*JMN* 5: 353). Images that appear in different guises in "Experience" are first tried out during this critical period as well. "Conversation among the witty & well-informed hops about from spot to spot around the surface of life" (*JMN* 5: 329), he notes in an extended passage that images social talk as a flitting bird but will return, transformed, in a more pointed and poignant observation of limited powers that describes how "[l]ike a bird which alights nowhere, but hops perpetually from bough to bough, is the Power which abides in no man and in no woman, but speaks from this one, and for another moment from that one" (*EL* 477).[11] That the partial and fragmentary experience of power, or insight, invests "the whole society" (*EL* 477) rather than the individual with a role in revealing the potential of Reason is also worked up more than once in 1837, including Emerson's entry that "[o]ne thing experience teaches, the variety of men" (*JMN* 5: 325). Even the death of Emerson's oldest son Waldo, which some commentators have taken to be the core event shaping Emerson's anguished nonbeing in "Experience," is imaginatively prefigured during the Panic of 1837, when the boy is still an infant: "Ah! My darling boy, so lately received out of heaven leave me not now! Please God, this sweet symbol of love & wisdom may be spared to rejoice, teach, & accompany me" (*JMN* 5: 293).

The point in mentioning these textual adumbrations and corollaries is not only to suggest that the despairing or skeptical tendencies in Emerson's thought are never the product of some single event—Waldo's death, for instance, or the failure of antebellum America to achieve its millennial expectations. Nor is it to suggest how the darker, brooding vision of "Experience" and some of the later essays occurs earlier in Emerson's thought than was once supposed. Rather, the comparison of passages written in the spring and summer of 1837 suggests that the project of "conversion" expressed in "The American Scholar" was for Emerson always accompanied by an often painful acceptance of the "real" world, of given actuality, as the place we inhabit. The accompanying "nausea and dismay at the yawning gap between actual and ideal experience," as Buell terms it,[12] are not only evident in "Experience" but are deeply present in the journal entries that trace and accompany the composition of "The American Scholar," when Emerson oscillates wildly from the hopeful sense that in the ruins of society a visionary spokesperson might contribute to the "upbuilding of a man" (*EL* 67) to a despairing nihilism that calls not only this millennial project but life itself into question. The famous journal passage in which Emerson declares that, in the wake of financial calamity, "The land stinks with suicide," is preceded by a stark rebuke less to himself than to the conditions of existence itself: "I wrote above that life wants worthy objects; the game is not worth the candle: It is not that I,—it is that *nobody* employs it well" (*JMN* 5: 334). And in a moment of shuddering recognition at the intractable problems of the present moment—problems made intractable because they constitute the very structures maintained by a society they nevertheless harm— Emerson's despair foretells the periodic sense of hopelessness shared in later generations by Brooks, Matthiessen, Miller, and Bercovitch.

Cavell has described Emerson's thwarted and lethargic tone at the start of "Experience" as emerging from a single morose fact: "that the world exists as it were for its own reasons."[13] As such, this intersection between skepticism and romanticism, between what in "Prudence" Emerson calls "aspiration and antagonism" (*EL* 357), has served to animate American literary criticism and American Studies throughout their comparatively brief histories. The more recent desire to circumscribe the canonical significance of Emerson—as an author and thinker who no longer conforms to global, multicultural, or radical-activist paradigms, as a figure who now seems inadequate to the task of dismantling national boundaries or imagining a postdiscipline—is structurally analogous to Emerson's own revulsion at the "grub state" of existing conditions and his simultaneous hunger for a "conversion" or metamorphosis of those conditions. And his weary confrontation with the intransigent world at the beginning of "Experience" bears more than a passing resemblance to recent depictions of the American literary tradition as embedded within a Western cultural tradition that is the first cause of the very social and human problems it supposedly longs to eradicate.

One of the things that makes "Experience" so interesting, in other words, is its effort to work through the problems and challenges that accompany the attempt to remake and reimagine the world. No longer willing to see the soul's self-determination as heroic and foreordained, no longer willing to adopt the compensatory bravado of a quasi-revolutionary politics, and, finally, no longer willing to remain aloof on the heights of idealism but hesitantly descending to the world of power, Emerson seeks in the essay to enact through language the experience of the forlorn self confronting disappointment, limitations, and the refractory quotidian of an often ungraspable existence. As readers of the essay know, he does so through a series of dialectical encounters with what he terms "the lords of life"— "Illusion, Temperament, Succession, Surface, Surprise, Reality, Subjectiveness"—by which he means those limitary aspects of human existence that frustrate and hedge all transcendent aspirations. These "lords of life" are what he will elsewhere call "necessity" (*EL* 476) and—in another great late essay—"Fate." For the moment, however, they not only expose as wildly optimistic his earlier writings on the primacy of individual consciousness; they seem to rule with an unbending severity over what Emerson had once regarded as the sovereign and unfettered Self.

Yet if the subjugation of the self to necessity is a major occasion for "Experience," it is important to point out that this occasion is presented without struggle or resistance only at the beginning of the essay. Each presentation of a "lord of life" is in fact staged so as to determine how the individual might better live within a revised understanding of a partial and fragmentary world. The section on "Illusion" is a model for this procedure. Considering the biological determinism he suspects may play some role in the spiritual rapture he craves, Emerson asks, "What cheer can the religious sentiment yield, when that is suspected to be secretly dependent on the seasons of the year, and the state of the blood?" (*EL* 474). Much like the opaque colors of mood, which can distort or screen out the rays of insight, the "state of the blood" poses enormous threats to a universal cultivation of Self-Reliance by suggesting that both the impulse toward self-sovereignty and the barriers to its full realization are encoded in our physiology and therefore largely unalterable. Biological predisposition radically attenuates hope for social progress and personal enrichment, or, as Emerson puts it, "Temperament puts all divinity to rout" (*EL* 475). But having *almost* conceded the futility of hope next to the "chuckle of the phrenologists," Emerson suddenly alters course. "Theoretic kidnappers and slave-drivers," he says, sharply criticizing these "doctors," "they esteem each man the victim of another, who winds him round his finger by knowing the law of his being. . . ." (*EL* 475). Invoking language from the social realm—the language of slavery and, more subtly, of the marketplace in general—Emerson undermines scientific claims of certitude and determinism as "theoretic" and underwritten in the final analysis by a desire for mastery, a longing to exert control over the uncertainty and flux with which he began his essay. The assertion of a predictable physiological determinism is in itself determined, he argues, though less by any physical hardwiring or biochemical imperatives than by the same conditions that are the occasion for Emerson's searching essay: the desire for grounding in the indecipherable mutations of experience. What any casual encounter with another person seems to suggest, he continues, is the *unpredictability* of human behavior. "I saw a gracious gentleman who adapts his conversation to the form of the head of the man he talks with!" Emerson notes—and the exclamation point is important, for it enacts the surprise (another "lord of life") with which we are daily presented despite our best efforts to manage and make sense of daily occurrences. "I had fancied that the value of life lay in its inscrutable possibilities; in the fact that I never know, in addressing myself to a new individual, what may befall me" (*EL* 475).

The section on "Illusion," in other words, turns the logic of limitation upon itself; it reasons patiently and broadly, in a manner that is neither sophistical nor simply contrary; and in so doing, it reveals how our suppositions and models about the world are merely that—guesses made from available evidence but always open to comparison and revision once new information is received and added to the mix. And it is precisely this habit of thought—what I take to be a distinctly *Emersonian* way of considering and convolving premises and presuppositions so as to avoid premature certainty—that may help us to better consider the threatened eclipse of the author's cultural centrality in the wake of canonical revisionism and newer trans- and postnational approaches to U.S. literary history. If this book has focused on a quartet of idiosyncratic critics who took what in hindsight appears to be a uniformly traditional view of the "major" writers, it must be reiterated that the "field imaginary" of "American" literary and cultural studies has been so expanded and complicated in recent years as to risk rendering their collective work quaint and obsolete. With a national literature now quite diverse, with a field now widened and complicated in unprecedented ways, the question to ask of Emerson is not only whether he can be reshaped for multicultural America, but whether a quasi-biographical "great figure" approach makes sense any longer.

One way of answering this question is to insist that Emerson's native and national characteristics are less his own than they are manifestations of the institutional and personal urgencies of the twentieth-century critics and scholars I have discussed throughout this work. Lawrence Buell has recently shown how Emerson fits into at least some transnational modes of inquiry. His eclectic reading in European and Asian writing, for instance, arguably influenced him far more than (say) the American sermonic tradition. Similarly, his transatlantic reputation and his reception by a younger generation of English authors have yet to be addressed and explored in anything approaching the depth of his relationship to the Concord transcendentalists. Linking Emerson to a diverse range of authors—José Martí, Charlotte Forten, Marcel Proust, D. H. Lawrence, and Olive Schreiner, among others—Buell suggests a variety of Emersonian contexts that have little or nothing to do with the author's vaunted "Americanness." Indeed, the more one returns to Emerson's work with the question of a native literary tradition in mind, the more one is struck by how little the issue seems to have interested the author in any sustained fashion. "The American Scholar"—the Ur-text of American Studies—is remarkably devoid of extended discussion or analysis of nationality and its relation to intellectual work. The title, rather, is better understood as a traditional boilerplate upon which Emerson launched into his preferred transpersonal—and transnational—topic. As Buell remarks, "Emerson himself strove . . . to advance his own vision of the human prospect in literature, in religion, in philosophy, in social theory, by pressing the claims for Self-Reliance against traditionalism and groupthink in such a way as to include in principle all humanity, not just the cultured elite to which he belonged."[14] The native Emerson advanced by practically every twentieth-century critic from Brooks to Bercovitch, in other words, needs to be seen as an image produced in large part by the historical and cultural requirements of an emerging academic specialization as well as by an increasingly dominant world power anxious to see its power manifested in a commensurate intellectual tradition.

Something of the same can be said for more recent feminist approaches to the author. If early feminist attention to Emerson's work levied a critique of his masculinist language ("Whoso would be a man must be a nonconformist" [EL 261]), women's and gender studies increasingly have brought attention to Emerson's involvement in the (transnational) nineteenth-century feminist movement as well as to the more general influence of women in his life. Phyllis Cole, to cite an exemplary case, has examined the biography and writings of Emerson's aunt, Mary Moody Emerson, and discovered a figure of almost incalculable influence in forming his thoughts and style. But Cole's work is not simply a unidirectional influence study with Emerson as the teleological end point. Her work richly illuminates the life of a singular intellect condemned to obscurity during her own life and, more importantly, serves as a kind of test case for revealing how the two most significant shapers of American Studies—Miller and Matthiessen, who ignored this important figure either through concerns with a male intellectual heritage or with the intrinsic dimensions of the literary—were blind to the literary and extraliterary role of women in Emerson's thought. Cole's research enables us to "reenvision the [Emersonian] tradition from [Mary Moody Emerson's] vantage point," a vantage that situates her pungent thinking on religion and nature "at the center of a larger circle" of literary and intellectual workers.[15] Cole's rich portrait is not simply corrective; her aim is to "suggest a wider story and tradition, a story about the intergenerational family as a culture, where books and parlors, public and private affairs, speech and silence, male and female literally cohabited."[16] In so doing, she anticipates what has come to be known as the "no more separate spheres" movement, named after Cathy N. Davidson's important special issue of *American Literature* arguing for a distancing from previous "binaric gender division[s]" in order to discuss women's writing in more productively hybridized considerations of gender and other issues.[17]

This desire to move beyond prior conceptual divisions has also informed what is by far the most heated reconsideration of Emerson in the past decade and a half: his relationship to race and the antislavery movement preceding the Civil War. As with the efforts to relate Emerson to the women's issues of his era, most discussions of Emerson and slavery focus on the period between 1844 and 1863, when the author's transcendentalism gave way to a less idealistic political pragmatism, a period in which essays on the "Emancipation in the British West Indies" (1844) and "Woman" (1855) show an author and thinker more actively engaged in the topics and concerns of the day. In recent years a handful of scholars—including Eduardo Cadava, Gregg Cane, Len Gougeon, Albert J. von Frank, and Laura Dassow Walls[18]—have come to see Emerson as relatively enlightened about issues of race and as a vociferous, if belated, opponent of slavery. Ian Finseth even more recently has revised the "simplified analytical binary in which Emerson appears as either a racist who betrayed his faith in human equality or what we might call a recovering racist who managed to overcome his retrograde views and take his place on the right side of history"[19] by discovering in Emerson a willingness to "expos[e] and challeng[e] the doctrine of Anglo-Saxon purity in his suggestion that African Americans, along with other nonwhites, will play a culturally and biologically integral role in the nation's future."[20] Despite the national focus at the end of this sentence, Finseth's study is noteworthy for its suggestive positioning of Emerson in larger transnational discussions of race. Emerson's thought and writing are seen increasingly by Finseth and others as a significant node in a larger canonical constellation shaped less by considerations of national identity than by questions of race and ethnicity.

One could expand outward the contextual circles of Emerson' relevance almost indefinitely—arguing, for instance, on behalf of the importance of his discursive participation in such enormous world-historical forces as capitalism, individualism, and social collectivity. Emerson's role and participation in transatlantic movements of religion and philosophy continue to need additional exploration. And his deeply felt response to the "holy" cause of the Civil War resonates more than ever in an era when terms such as "freedom" and "democracy" have been co-opted to wage a ghastly "global war on terror" that threatens to bankrupt the very concepts it claims to defend.

The larger point here is that much of our current critical discussion— the desire to push a history-bound field of study beyond the limitations of the aesthetic, the national, the ideological—is finally, if not exactly an Emersonian legacy, then certainly a legacy most memorably articulated by Emerson. The author found his way into the academy in part for his ability to enshrine prevalent cultural values and to serve as an organizing principle for the emerging field of American literary studies. But his greater contribution to the critics he has engaged has been his ability to problematize the cultures and academic disciplines in which he has been situated. Valued for the way he called cultural ideals and assumptions into question, Emerson became a central figure in American literary studies because he provided a fertile and powerfully contrastive language that helped institutionalize the practice of argument by which critical evaluations are created. If that language came out of Emerson's own struggles to imagine himself as a public intellectual, a writer and speaker, it also allowed students and professors to attain critical distance on their own ideological commitments. The "self-distrust" Perry Miller felt to be a critic's most valuable and exportable product is continually nourished by Emerson's thought and writing.

In the first chapter of this book I described Emerson's literary effects as the endless troping of competing discourses. I suggested, moreover, that because his writing is always a discursive hybrid—a volatile admixture of the theological, philosophical, scientific, social, and aesthetic, each energized by transitionless juxtaposition, each incorporating another ad infinitum, each troping the forms in which these discourses find themselves delivered—it repeatedly calls such discursive modes into question even as it summons us to rethink or reimagine what we mean by *politics, religion, nation, discipline.* Whether Emerson continues to haunt readers in a nation and a world likely to experience radical transformations in the next few decades is of course finally impossible to predict. To claim for him a future readership in a nation where English may not remain the dominant vernacular, for instance, would seem a form of special pleading. Whether subsequent scholars and critics of a globalizing United States and its literary tradition will find Emerson of continued relevance to their work will depend, as this book has sought to reveal, on the extent to which they find in his thought and writing answers they require *right now*. It will depend, in other words, on whether Emerson continues to open doors they scarcely knew existed, whether he continues to compel new revisions, new assumptions, new hopes: whether his writing will provide models of a world still recognizable and deemed of value. As one of the haunted—as one of Emerson's ghosts in the haunted fields of literary and cultural criticism—I can only suggest that Emerson remains valuable *to me* for the way he initiates a critical tradition that has its roots in that still-resonant call for the "conversion of society" (that quasi-theological longing for social and cultural transformation that would strive to remake the world in the nowhere of utopia) as well as its obverse (the limitary directives of experience). And I would venture to suggest he still has something to say to those who struggle to negotiate the vexed and interwoven issues of literature and social action; who feel drawn to intellectual work and, at the same time, to addressing the society in which that work is embedded; who believe these last two compulsions draw sustenance from even as they at times seem to disable each other. Emerson's continued ability to haunt us derives from his capacity to help us think better, through an enriched language, about what it means to change or solidify our experiential commitments as humans living in a community, a nation, a world. We are haunted when Emerson challenges us to better think and act—critically and affirmatively, receptively and resistantly—in our own particular historical moment.

In this way Emerson's ghost lingers, however vaporously, over every attempt we may make to become scholars—American or otherwise.

NOTES

Chapter 1

1. Geoffrey H. Hartman, *Scars of the Spirit: The Struggle Against Inauthenticity* (New York: Palgrave, 2002), p. 4. In this way, the critics I discuss have been *ghostwritten* by Emerson.
2. Winfried Fluck, "The Humanities in the Age of Expressive Individualism and Cultural Radicalism," in *The Futures of American Studies,* ed. Donald E. Pease and Robyn Wiegman (Durham, N.C.: Duke University Press, 2002), pp. 211–30.
3. Stanley Cavell, "The Philosopher in American Life," reprinted in *Emerson's Transcendental Etudes* (Stanford: Stanford University Press, 2003), p. 54. I might acknowledge here what my study *isn't*. I am less concerned in *Emerson's Ghosts* with a teleological account of Emerson studies; as a result, I leave out some of the most influential critics of the author, including O. W. Firkins, Jonathan Bishop, and Barbara Packer, all of whose work I have nonetheless profited from immensely. For wide-ranging historical accounts of Emerson studies, see Charles E. Mitchell's *Individualism and Its Discontents: Appropriations of Emerson, 1880–1950* (Amherst: University of Massachusetts Press, 1997); and Sarah Ann Wider's *The Critical Reception of Emerson: Unsettling All Things* (New York: Camden House, 2000).

4. Oliver Wendell Holmes, *Ralph Waldo Emerson* (Boston: Houghton Mifflin, 1884), p. 79.

5. A related way of saying this issues from Irving Howe: "To confront American culture is to feel oneself encircled by a thin but strong presence: a mist, a cloud, a climate. I call it Emersonian, an imprecise term but one that directs us to a dominant spirit in the national experience. Hoping to engage that spirit, I am not sure that anyone can even grasp it. How grasp the very air we breathe?" Quoted in Eduardo Cadava's *Emerson and the Climates of History* (Stanford: Stanford University Press, 1997), no page number.

6. See especially Jacques Derrida's *Specters of Marx: The State of the Debt, the Work of Mourning, and the New International*, trans. Peggy Kamuf (New York: Routledge, 1994).

7. Murray Krieger, "My Travels with the Aesthetic," in *Revenge of the Aesthetic: The Place of Literature in Theory Today*, ed. Michael P. Clark (Berkeley: University of California Press, 2000), p. 226.

8. Terry Eagleton, *The Ideology of the Aesthetic* (London: Blackwell, 1990).

9. Robert D. Richardson, *Emerson: The Mind on Fire* (Berkeley: University of California Press, 1995), p. 170.

10. Carl E. Prince, "The Great 'Riot Year': Jacksonian Democracy and Patterns of Violence in 1834," *Journal of the Early Republic* 5 (1985): 2.

11. Maurice Gonnaud, *An Uneasy Solitude: Individual and Society in the Work of Ralph Waldo Emerson*, trans. Lawrence Rosenwald (Princeton: Princeton University Press, 1987), p. 140. For convenience, I will refer henceforth to the Democratic Party, although this name was not used until around 1840.

12. For a discussion of what the words *individualism* and *individuality* meant to Emerson in the late 1830s, see Sacvan Bercovitch, "Emerson, Liberalism, and Liberal Dissent," in *Rites of Assent* (New York: Routledge, 1993), as well as the discussion of Bercovitch's article in chapter 6.

13. Richard Hofstadter and Michael Wallace, eds., *American Violence: A Documentary History* (New York: Knopf, 1971), p. 477.

14. Prince, "The Great 'Riot Year," p. 6.

15. David Grimstead, "Rioting in Its Jacksonian Setting," *American Historical Review* 77 (1972): 364.

16. Noah Webster, *The Letters of Noah Webster*, ed. Harry M. Warfel (New York: Library Publishers, 1953), p. 504. For discussions on the politics of language in antebellum America, see Kenneth Cmiel, *Democratic Eloquence: The Fight Over Popular Speech in Nineteenth-Century America* (New York: W. Morrow, 1990); Thomas Gustafson, *Representative Words: Politics, Literature, and the American Language, 1776–1865* (New York: Cambridge University Press, 1992); and David Simpson, *The Politics of American English, 1776–1850* (New York: Oxford University Press, 1986).

17. Marvin Meyers, *The Jacksonian Persuasion: Politics and Belief* (Stanford: Stanford University Press, 1957), p. 179.

18. Philip Hone, *The Diary of Philip Hone, 1828–1851*, ed. Allan Nevins, 2 vols. (New York: Dodd, Mead, 1927), pp. 122, 123, 124.

19. *The Letters of Ralph Waldo Emerson*, 10 vols, ed. Ralph L. Rusk and Eleanor Tilton (New York: Columbia University Press, 1939), vol. 1, p. 410.
20. Gay Wilson Allen, *Waldo Emerson: A Biography* (New York: Viking Press, 1981), p. 230.
21. Hone, *Diary*, p. 140.
22. *Niles Weekly Register* (November 1, 1834): 137 (emphasis added).
23. Hone, *Diary*, p. 140.
24. Giles Gunn, *Thinking Across the American Grain: Ideology, Intellect, and the New Pragmatism* (Chicago: University of Chicago Press, 1992), pp. 236, 221.
25. It should be noted that the term *hegemony* is anachronistic and almost certainly too totalizing a term for the fractious and processual nature of antebellum social polity. If culture could serve as a liberating sphere for Emerson, however, it would become suffocating in the twentieth century as it increasingly became linked to politics and business.
26. The speaker is Virgil:

> "Oh proud Christians, wretched and weary, . . . is it not plain to you that we are worms born to form the angelic butterfly and fly up to judgment without defenses?"

> Dante Alighieri, *Purgatorio*, trans. W. S. Merwin (New York: Knopf, 2000), p. 99.

27. Daniel T. O'Hara, *Lionel Trilling: The Work of Liberation* (Madison: University of Wisconsin Press, 1988), p. 54. O'Hara has since gone even farther, arguing that "for today's global elites, the aesthetic is a category to be dismissed as not serious enough for thought, and this American view is New Historicist, often put forward in a smugly critical or delighted fashion." *Empire Burlesque: The Fate of Critical Culture in Global America* (Durham, N.C.: Duke University Press, 2003), p. 54.
28. In "Emerson's Most Famous Speech" (1923), Bliss Perry interprets "The American Scholar" as proleptic advice to an emerging professoriate: "Emerson's message to the academic community would have, I think, a note of yearning," Perry remarks, implying that his subject's well-known problem of vocation might have been solved had tenure-track positions been available in the 1830s: "The historic Emerson always wished to be one of us." *The Praise of Folly and Other Papers* (Boston: Houghton Mifflin, 1923), p. 111. Other scholars would project onto the Phi Beta Kappa address personal versions of their newly imagined professional selves: Katherine Lee Bates, a vocal advocate for the separate study of American literature, seconded Emerson's claim "that the American scholar, looking to nature and to life for education more than to mere books, should be free and brave." *American Literature* (Chatauqua, N.Y.: Chautauqua Press, 1897), p. 217. For O. W. Firkins, "The American Scholar," written in an "academic" style, "contained, in epitome, the bulk of Emerson's philosophy." *Ralph Waldo*

Emerson (Boston: Houghton Mifflin, 1915), p. 71. To these and other aca-
demicians, Emerson emerged as American literary scholarship's originary
figure as well as its chief proponent. "[T]he earliest of the little group of
the founders of American literature to go through college," Brander Mat-
thews noted, Emerson had one ambition: "to be a professor of rhetoric."
See *An Introduction to the Study of American Literature,* revised ed. (New
York: American Book Co., 1918), p. 98. So quickly and pervasively assimilated into the academy was the image of a scholarly Emerson that in 1906
Leon Vincent, author of the *American Literary Masters,* could describe him
as "a professor of rhetoric" instructing a "student body" of young scholars
(Boston: Houghton Mifflin, 1906), pp. 159, 186.

29. *Emerson and the Climates of History* (Stanford: Stanford University Press,
    1997), p. 18.

30. "'Time & patience change a mulberry leaf into satin,'" he writes in Decem-
    ber, quoting from James Howells's *English Proverbs* (*JMN* 5: 371).

31. My understanding of this context is deeply indebted, here and throughout,
    to Robert Milder's "'The American Scholar' as Cultural Event," *Prospects*
    16 (1991): 99–147.

32. Kenneth S. Sacks, *Understanding Emerson: 'The American Scholar' and His
    Struggle for Self-Reliance* (Princeton: Princeton University Press, 2003),
    p. 17.

33. For an excellent recent discussion of what he calls the "radical linguistic
    turn," see Frank B. Farrell, *Why Does Literature Matter?* (Ithaca: Cornell
    University Press, 2004).

34. Helen Vendler, *Invisible Listeners: Lyric Intimacy in Herbert, Whitman, and
    Ashbery* (Princeton: Princeton University Press, 2005), p. 67. Vendler here is
    ventriloquizing what she construes to be an Ashberian theme.

35. Geoffrey H. Hartman, *The Fateful Question of Culture* (New York: Colum-
    bia University Press, 1997), p. 61.

36. In fact, the very way in which surplus is integrated into the "system" of
    his essays may be seen as reflecting capitalist logic, the transformation
    of dissensus into consensus, and any number of other socially inflected
    mechanisms.

37. My ideas on the way aesthetic language resists political discourse are greatly
    indebted to the work of Murray Krieger. For a fine summary of that work,
    see his "My Travels with the Aesthetic," pp. 208–36. Emerson's writing
    may claim to be authorized by God, nature, genius, or democracy—by self,
    Soul, or power—but it does so by calling attention to the way we invari-
    ably "err in the expression" of those things to which "a perfect faith is due"
    (*EL* 269).

38. Sigmund Freud, *Civilization and Its Discontents,* trans. and ed. James
    Strachey (New York: Norton, 1961), p. 13.

39. John Carlos Rowe, *At Emerson's Tomb: The Politics of Classic American
    Literature* (New York: Columbia University Press, 2002), p. ix.

40. Perry Miller Papers, courtesy Harvard Library, HUG 4572.7.

Chapter 2

1. John Dewey, "Ralph Waldo Emerson," *Characters and Events*, vol. 1 (New York: Holt, 1929), p. 71. Dewey's comments reiterate a longstanding tradition, evident in the *Saturday Review*'s obituary: "He philosophized like a poet, and wrote poetry like a philosopher; wherefore specialists in both kinds are disappointed with him." Printed in *Littell's Living Age* (April–June 1882), p. 570. For more on Emerson's reception at this period, see Len Gougeon, "Looking Backwards: Emerson in 1903," *Nineteenth-Century Prose* 30 (2003), pp. 50–73.

2. Edwin P. Whipple, "Emerson as a Poet," *North American Review* 135 (1882): 1.

3. Anonymous, "Ralph Waldo Emerson," *Century Magazine* 24 (1882): 457.

4. Robert Habich addresses Emerson's biographers in "Emerson's Lives," *New England Quarterly: A Historical Review of New England Life and Letters* 69 (1996): 631–79.

5. Henry James, "Emerson," in *The American Essays*, ed. Leon Edel (New York: Vintage, 1956), p. 52.

6. For a discussion of the tendency of critics to escape their interpretive responsibilities by focusing on Emerson's mystic transcendentalism, see Michael Lopez, *Emerson and Power: Creative Antagonism in Nineteenth Century* (DeKalb: Northern Illinois University Press, 1996), especially his first chapter.

7. "Mr. Emerson," reprinted in *Littell's Living Age* (April–June 1882): 567.

8. "Emerson," *The Dial* (May 1882): 1.

9. Julian Hawthorne, "Ralph Waldo Emerson," *Harper's New Monthly Magazine* 65 (1882): 309.

10. Susan Coolidge, "Concord. May 31, 1882," *Atlantic Monthly* 49 (1882): 93.

11. W. T. Harris, "Ralph Waldo Emerson," *Atlantic Monthly* 50 (1882): 252.

12. Richard H. Brodhead, *The School of Hawthorne* (New York: Oxford University Press, 1986), p. 65.

13. Oliver Wendell Holmes, *Ralph Waldo Emerson* (Boston: Houghton Mifflin, 1884), p. 104.

14. For more detailed accounts of Gilded Age culture and society, see Larzer Ziff, *The American 1890s* (1966; Lincoln: University of Nebraska Press, 1979); T. J. Jackson Lears, *No Place of Grace: Antimodernism and the Transformation of American Culture, 1880–1920* (New York: Pantheon Books, 1981); Alan Trachtenberg, *The Incorporation of America: Culture and Society in the Gilded Age* (New York: Hill and Wang, 1982); and Casey Nelson Blake, *Beloved Community: The Cultural Criticism of Randolph Bourne, Van Wyck Brooks, Waldo Frank, and Lewis Mumford* (Chapel Hill: University of North Carolina, 1990), pp. 11–28.

15. Still the authoritative biography on Holmes is Eleanor M. Tilton's *Amiable Autocrat: A Biography of Dr. Oliver Wendell Holmes* (New York: Henry Schuman, 1947). Also helpful is John T. Morse, Jr.'s *Life and Letters of Oliver Wendell Holmes*, 2 vols. (London: Sampson Low, Marston & Co., 1896).

16. Brodhead, pp. 4–5.
17. The most important nineteenth-century spokesperson for this idea, of course, was Matthew Arnold, whose description of culture as "the pursuit of our total perfection" "by getting to know, on all matters which most concern us, the best which has been thought and said in the world" might be understood as the genteel tradition's mission statement. This conception of culture meant that those American authors who sought to represent the ideal, to speak and edify the nation, were enshrined as national treasures by genteel critics, teachers, and poets. See Arnold, *Culture and Anarchy*, ed. R. H. Super (Ann Arbor: University of Michigan Press, 1965). For a more skeptical view of the genteel cultural program, see Nina Baym, "Melodramas of Beset Manhood: How Theories of American Fiction Exclude Women Writers" (1981), reprinted in *Feminism and American Literary History* (New Brunswick: Rutgers University Press, 1992), pp. 2–18.
18. For more on this belletristic aesthetics and its cultural context, see Frank Lentricchia, *Modernist Quartet* (Cambridge: Cambridge University Press, 1994), p. xii.
19. William Crary Brownell, *American Prose Masters* (Cambridge, Mass.: Harvard University Press, 1963), p. 96.
20. Edmund Clarence Stedman, "Corda Concordia. Read at the Opening Session of the Summer School of Philosophy, Concord, July 11, 1881," *The Poems of Edmund Clarence Stedman* (Boston and New York: Houghton Mifflin, 1908), p. 175.
21. George E. Woodberry, *Poems: My Country, Wild Eden, The Players' Elegy, The Northshore Watch, Odes and Sonnets* (New York: Macmillan, 1903), pp. 157–8.
22. Richard Watson Gilder, *The Poems of Richard Watson Gilder* (Boston: Houghton Mifflin, 1908), p. 138.
23. Oliver Wendell Holmes, *Ralph Waldo Emerson* (Boston: Houghton Mifflin, 1884), p. 314. Subsequent references will appear parenthetically in the text.
24. Len Gougeon, "Holmes's Emerson and the Conservative Critique of Realism," *South Atlantic Review* 59 (1994): 108.
25. George Santayana, "The Genteel Tradition and American Philosophy," *Selected Critical Writings of George Santayana*, ed. Norman Henfrey (Cambridge: Cambridge University Press, 1968), vol 2.
26. Still the most complete biography of Conway is Mary Elizabeth Curtis, *Moncure Conway, 1832–1907* (New Brunswick, N.J.: Rutgers University Press, 1952). See also John d'Entremont, *Moncure Conway, 1832–1907* (New York: Oxford University Press, 1987); Jay B. Hubbell, *The South in American Literature, 1607–1800* (Durham, N.C.: Duke University Press, 1954); and Richard Beale Davis, "Moncure Daniel Conway: Radical Southern Intellectual," *Interpretations: Studies in Language and Literature* 9 (1977): 1–6.
27. Moncure D. Conway, *Autobiography, Memories, and Experiences of Moncure Daniel Conway*, 2 vols. (Boston: Houghton Mifflin, 1904), 2: 157.

28. See Ray Allen Billington, *Frederick Jackson Turner: Historian, Scholar, Teacher* (New York: Oxford University Press, 1973), pp. 10, 24, 427.

29. Allen F. Davis, *American Heroine: The Life and Legend of Jane Addams* (New York: Oxford University Press, 1973), pp. 2, 20–1.

30. Moncure Conway, *Emerson At Home and Abroad* (Boston: James R. Osgood, 1882), p. 355. Subsequent citations will appear parenthetically in the text.

31. Conway, *Autobiography,* 1: 281, fn.

32. Joel Porte was the first to notice the way in which Conway aligned Hutchinson with Emerson in *Representative Man: Ralph Waldo Emerson in His Time* (New York: Oxford University Press, 1979), p. 345, fn. 3.

33. James Elliot Cabot, *A Memoir of Ralph Waldo Emerson*, 2 vols. (Boston: Houghton Mifflin, 1887), 1: iii–iv. Subsequent citations will appear parenthetically in the text.

34. Horace Scudder, "Emerson's Genius," *Atlantic Monthly* 60 (1887): 566–72. My discussion of Cabot is indebted to the fine scholarly work of Nancy Craig Simmons, including her "Arranging the Sybilline Leaves: James Elliot Cabot's Work as Emerson's Literary Executor," in *Studies in the American Renaissance, 1983,* ed. Joel Myerson (Charlottesville: University Press of Virginia), pp. 333–89; "Philosophical Biographer: James Elliot Cabot and *A Memoir of Ralph Waldo Emerson,*" in *Studies in the American Renaissance, 1987,* ed. Joel Myerson (Charlottesville: University Press of Virginia) pp. 365–92; "The 'Autobiographical Sketch' of James Elliot Cabot," *Harvard Library Bulletin* 30 (1982): 117–52; and "Speaking of Emerson: Two Unpublished Letters Exchanged Between John Jay Chapman and James Elliot Cabot," *Harvard Library Bulletin* 31 (1983): 185–7.

35. Quoted in Simmons, "Emerson's Literary Executor," p. 337.

36. Stanley Cavell's thirty-year engagement with Emerson is an exemplary example of discerning in the author a philosophical tradition that *isn't* pragmatic.

37. For example, in "Philosophical Biographer" Simmons remarks that Cabot "stressed the conservative elements in Emerson's enterprise, depicting his career as one more stage in the unfolding of the universal mind rather than an iconoclastic break with the past. Cabot had watched Emerson carefully cultivating acceptance, working within the tradition, not against it. Cabot had no wish to destroy this image," p. 373.

38. William Graham Sumner, "Sociology" (1881), in Perry Miller, *American Thought: Civil War to World War I* (New York: Holt, Rinehart and Winston, 1963), p. 80.

39. See, for instance, John Guillory, *Cultural Capital: The Problem of Literary Canon Formation* (Chicago: University of Chicago Press, 1993).

40. Simmons, "Speaking of Emerson," pp. 181–2.

41. John Jay Chapman, "Emerson, Sixty Years Later," reprinted in *The Selected Writings of John Jay Chapman,* ed. Jacques Barzun (New York: Funk & Wagnalls, 1957), p. 190. Subsequent citations will appear parenthetically in the text.

42. Quoted in Morse, p. 60.
43. Chapman's point of view was informed more by the cosmopolitanism of New York, where he was born and spent many of his adult years. His letter is quoted in M. A. DeWolfe, *John Jay Chapman and His Letters* (Boston: Houghton Mifflin, 1937), p. 123. Other useful discussions of Chapman include Richard B. Hovey, *John Jay Chapman: An American Mind* (New York: Columbia University Press, 1959); and Edmund Wilson, "The Mute and the Open Strings," in *The Triple Thinkers* (New York: Oxford University Press, 1948), pp. 133–64. Also helpful is Jacques Barzun's introduction to *The Selected Writings of John Jay Chapman* (New York: Farrar, Straus & Cudahy, 1957), pp. v–xxi.
44. Theodore F. Wolfe, *Literary Shrines: The Haunts of Some Famous American Authors* (Philadelphia: L. P. Lippincott, 1895), p. 45.
45. Quoted in Hovey, p. 91.
46. John Jay Chapman, *Practical Agitation* (New York: Charles Scribner's Sons, 1900; reprint 1970), p. 92.
47. John Jay Chapman, *Practical Agitation*, p. 101.
48. John Jay Chapman, *Practical Agitation*, p. 93.
49. Quoted in Hovey, p. 120.
50. Simmons, "Speaking of Emerson," pp. 182–3.
51. Simmons, "Speaking of Emerson," p. 182.
52. Richard Poirier, *The Renewal of Literature: Emersonian Reflections* (New York: Random House, 1987), p. 90.

Chapter 3

1. *Van Wyck Brooks: The Early Years, A Selection from His Works, 1908–1925*, ed. Claire Sprague, rev. ed. (Boston: Northeastern University Press, 1993), p. 83. All further quotations from *The Wine of the Puritans*, *America's Coming-of-Age*, and "On Creating a Usable Past" will be from this edition; page numbers will be given in parenthesis in the text and designated by *VWB*. Useful discussions of the life and career of Brooks include James R. Vitelli, *Van Wyck Brooks* (New York: Twayne Publishers, 1966); William Wasserstrom, *The Legacy of Van Wyck Brooks: A Study of Maladies and Motives* (Carbondale: Southern Illinois University Press, 1971); James Hoopes, *Van Wyck Brooks: In Search of American Culture* (Amherst: University of Massachusetts Press, 1977); Raymond Nelson, *Van Wyck Brooks: A Writer's Life* (New York: E. P. Dutton, 1981); T. J. Jackson Lears, *No Place of Grace: Antimodernism and the Transformation of American Culture, 1880–1920* (New York: Pantheon Books, 1981), pp. 251–7; Casey Nelson Blake, *Beloved Community: The Cultural Criticism of Randolph Bourne, Van Wyck Brooks, Waldo Frank, and Lewis Mumford* (Chapel Hill: University of North Carolina, 1990); Claire Sprague, introduction, *Van Wyck Brooks: The Early Years, A Selection from His Works, 1908–1925*, pp. xvii–lix; as well as Brooks's own *Autobiography* (New York: E. P. Dutton, 1965). For more general discussion of the literary movement Brooks and his contemporaries

represented, see Malcolm Cowley, "The Revolt Against Gentility," in *After the Genteel Tradition: American Writers, 1910–1930*, ed. Malcolm Cowley (Carbondale: Southern Illinois University Press, 1964); Howard Mumford Jones, *The Theory of American Literature* (Ithaca: Cornell University Press, 1965); Daniel Aaron, *Writers on the Left: Episodes in American Literary Communism* (New York: Harcourt, Brace and World, 1961); Richard Ruland, *The Rediscovery of American Literature: Premises of Critical Taste, 1900–1940* (Cambridge, Mass.: Harvard University Press, 1967); and Kermit Vanderbilt, *American Literature and the Academy: The Roots, Growth, and Maturity of a Profession* (Philadelphia: University of Pennsylvania Press, 1986).

2. Quoted in *VWB*, p. lv.

3. Quoted in Hoopes, *Van Wyck Brooks: In Search of American Culture*, p. 174.

4. Hoopes, p. 10.

5. Quoted in Hoopes, p. 23.

6. Hoopes, p. 28.

7. Brooks's Journal (3–4 December 1904), Van Wyck Brooks Papers, courtesy Special Collections, Van Pelt Library, University of Pennsylvania. About the sanctified space of American culture, Brooks notes, "Apparently both [Concord and Lexington] are ashamed of being in the 20th century." The next day he notes about the Old Manse that it "stood . . . the very picture of desolation."

8. In fact, the courses offered by these two professors were among the only ones Brooks excelled in.

9. Journal, 3 December 1904. Van Wyck Brooks Papers.

10. The high point of the process of genteel sanctification of Emerson ensured, Eric Cheyfitz has argued, that "what emerged into the memory of American literary history was a wholly disembodied Emerson: Emerson the Idealist, the Romantic, the Transcendentalist." See Cheyfitz's forward to Maurice Gonnaud, *An Uneasy Solitude: Individual and Society in the Work of Ralph Waldo Emerson*, p. ix.

11. Eliot, "Emerson as Seer," *Atlantic Monthly* 91 (1903): 855.

12. Santayana, "Emerson the Poet," in *Santayana on America*, ed. Richard Lyon (New York: Harcourt Brace, and World, 1968), p. 275.

13. Cooke, "The Emerson Centennial," *New England Magazine*, New Series, 28 (1903): 255.

14. Thomas, "Emerson," *The Critic* 42 (1903): 388.

15. Lee, *The Critic* 42 (1903): 418.

16. Paul Elmer More, "Emerson," in *Cambridge History of American Literature*, vol. 2, ed. William P. Trent, John Erskine, Stuart P. Sherman, and Carl Van Doren (New York: MacMillan, 1917), p. 173.

17. George E. Woodberry, *Ralph Waldo Emerson* (Boston: Houghton Mifflin, 1907), p. 176.

18. Quoted in Eric Sigg, *The American T. S. Eliot: A Study of the Early Writings* (Cambridge: Cambridge University Press, 1989), p. 149.

19. What should be stressed here is the way in which Brooks's argument prefigures Santayana's "genteel tradition."

20. See *The Correspondence of Emerson and Carlyle*, ed. Joseph Slater (New York: Columbia University Press, 1964), pp. 370–1. This countertradition also includes Melville's debunking portrait of Emerson in *The Confidence Man*, Lowell's more representative caricature in "A Fable for Critics" (1848), as well as the famous Christopher Cranch cartoon of Emerson as a long-legged transparent eyeball blithely striding the countryside.

21. Henry James, "Emerson," reprinted in *The American Essays of Henry James*, ed. Leon Edel (New York: Vintage, 1956), p. 61

22. Casey Nelson Blake, *Beloved Community*, p. 18. "[D]ependent on his mother, indifferent and covertly contemptuous of his father," T. J. Jackson Lears adds, Brooks at an early age constructed a refuge from business by imagining a career in literature; see *No Place of Grace*, p. 251. Yet as James Hoopes has noted, despite Brooks's efforts to thwart "the sense that as a male he was condemned to the brutal world of business which had ruined his father" by mastering his mother's "cultural training," "there must have been resentment that he refused to consider a career in business"; Hoopes, p. 21. It was a deeply felt sense of the sexual division of labor in upper-class Plainfield that accounted for the young Brooks's vision of art and culture as alternately ethereal and practical, abstract and of this world.

23. Mumford, "Introduction: The Beginnings of a Friendship," in *The Van Wyck Brooks/Lewis Mumford Letters*, ed. Robert Spiller (New York: E. P. Dutton, 1970), p. 4.

24. J. David Hoeveler, Jr., *The New Humanism: A Critique of Modern America, 1900–1940* (Charlottesville: University Press of Virginia, 1977), pp. 84–5.

25. T. S. Eliot, untitled review of vol. 2 of Trent, Erskine, Sherman, and Van Doren, eds., *Cambridge History of American Literature*, in *Athenaeum* 464 (25 April 1919): 238.

26. Bromwich, *A Choice of Inheritance: Self and Community from Edmund Burke to Robert Frost* (Cambridge, Mass.: Harvard University Press, 1989), pp. 153–4.

27. Charles E. Mitchell, *Individualism and Its Discontents: Appropriations of Emerson, 1880–1950* (Amherst: University of Massachusetts Press, 1997), p. 51.

28. Although, as Claire Sprague asserts, Brooks's insistence that the past "has no objective reality" (*VWB* 220) is far more radical than contemporary revisionist polemics; see p. xxiii.

29. Russell J. Reising, *The Unusable Past: Theory and the Study of American Literature* (New York: Methuen, 1986), p. 223.

30. Paul Jay, *Contingency Blues: The Search for Foundations in American Criticism* (Madison: University of Wisconsin Press, 1997), p. 71.

31. Warner Berthoff, *The Ferment of Realism: American Literature, 1884–1919*, (New York: Free Press, 1965), p. 287.

32. Waldo Frank, *Our America* (New York: Boni and Liverwright, 1919), pp. 151, 71.

33. Van Wyck Brooks, *The Life of Emerson* (New York: E. P. Dutton, 1932), p. 299. Subsequent citations from this work will appear parenthetically in the text as *Life*.

34. Mitchell, *Individualism and Its Discontents*, p. 52.

35. *Brooks/Mumford Letters*, p. 33.

36. See, for instance, Wasserstrom, *The Legacy of Van Wyck Brooks*, p. 57.

37. Vitelli, *Guide*, p. x.

38. In *Brooks/Mumford Letters*, p. 27. The passage Mumford's note refers to begins: "I am going through a little Reconstruction Period of my own just at the moment."

39. Edmund Wilson, "Mr. Brooks's Second Phase," *New Republic* 103 (30 September 1940): 452–4.

40. Mark Roydon Winchell, *Cleanth Brooks and the Rise of Modern Criticism* (Charlottesville: University Press of Virginia, 1996), p. 273.

41. See Peter Carafiol, *The American Ideal: Literary History as Worldly Activity* (New York: Oxford University Press, 1991), especially pp. 63–70.

42. Richard Ruland and Malcolm Bradbury, *From Puritanism to Postmodernism: A History of American Literature* (New York: Viking, 1991), p. 269.

43. Ruland and Bradbury, pp. 272–3.

44. This dilemma by no means ended soon; for a discussion of Lionel Trilling's efforts to reconcile the opposing trends, see John Rodden, *The Politics of Literary Reputation: The Making and Claiming of 'St. George' Orwell* (New York: Oxford University Press, 1989), pp. 80–93.

45. Wilson, "Imaginary Conversations: II Mr. Van Wyck Brooks and Mr. Scott Fitzgerald," *New Republic* 37 (April 30, 1924): 249–54.

46. The phrases are those of Raymond Nelson, *Van Wyck Brooks*, p. 144.

47. Wilson, "Ezra Pound's Patchwork," *New Republic* (April 19, 1922). Repr. in *The Shores of Light* (New York: Farrar, Straus & Young, 1952), p. 48.

48. Wilson, "The Pilgrimage of Henry James," *New Republic* 42 (May 6, 1925): 283–6.

49. *Brooks/Mumford Letters*, p. 27.

50. *Brooks/Mumford Letters*, p. 27.

51. *Brooks/Mumford Letters*, p. 33.

52. *Brooks/Mumford Letters*, p. 33.

53. Quoted in Hoopes, p. 174.

54. *Brooks/Mumford Letters*, p. 33.

55. The phrase is Ruland and Bradbury's, p. 273.

56. Spiller, commenting in *Brooks/Mumford Letters*, p. 64.

57. Vitelli, *Van Wyck Brooks*, p. 111.

58. Quoted in Hoopes, p. 174.

59. Quoted in Hoopes, p. 174.

60. Krieger, "My Travels with the Aesthetic," p. 228.

61. *Brooks/Mumford Letters*, p. 26.
62. Bliss Perry would refer to Brooks's work as "a charming picture of Emerson among his Concord friends" in *Emerson Today* (Princeton: Princeton University Press, 1931), p. 11.
63. Schappes, "Review of The Life of Emerson," *The Symposium: A Critical Review* 3 (1932): 540–7.
64. Perry Miller, "From Edwards to Emerson," in *Errand into the Wilderness* (Cambridge, Mass.: Harvard University Press, 1956), p. 198.
65. Given this point of view, it is not surprising that the one contemporary writer Brooks seems to have followed with particular interest was John Dos Passos, whose combination of aestheticisim and radicalism caused the critic to remark "that few things were more interesting than the development of this remarkable writer," *Autobiography*, p. 585.
66. Vitelli, p. 116.
67. Blake, p. 239.
68. The formulation is James M. Albrecht's in "Saying Yes and Saying No: Individualist Ethics in Ellison, Burke, and Emerson," *PMLA* 113 (1999): 48.
69. Lewis Mumford, *The Golden Day: A Study of American Literature and Culture* (New York: Norton, 1926). All subsequent citations will appear parenthetically in the text as *GD*.
70. Blake, p. 220.
71. Howard Mumford Jones, *The Theory of American Literature*, p. 141.
72. Lionel Trilling, "Parrington, Mr. Smith, and Reality," *Partisan Review* 8 (1940): 24–40.
73. Richard Ruland, *The Rediscovery of American Literature: Premises of Critical Taste, 1900–1940*, p. 186. As part-time editor at Harcourt Brace, Brooks was instrumental in publishing Parrington's work.
74. Parrington, *Main Currents in American Thought: The Beginning of Critical Realism in America, 1860–1920*, vol. III (New York: Harcourt Brace, 1958), p. xx. All subsequent citations will appear parenthetically in the text as *MC* and refer to the second volume, *Main Currents in American Thought: The Romantic Revolution in America, 1800–1860* (New York: Harcourt Brace, 1954).
75. David R. Shumway, *Creating American Civilization: A Genealogy of American Literature as an Academic Discipline* (Minneapolis: University of Minnesota Press, 1994), p. 165.
76. Much like the early Brooks, Parrington understands Emerson primarily as an important harbinger of Whitman, whose democratic realism was occasionally lit by "romantic splendor" (*MC* 69).
77. Frank, *Our America*, pp. 195–7.
78. Mary M. Colum, "An American Critic: Van Wyck Brooks," *Dial* 76 (1926): 33–41.
79. Paul Rosenfeld, "Van Wyck Brooks," in *Port of New York: Essays on Fourteen American Moderns* (New York: Harcourt Brace, 1924), pp. 19–63.
80. *Brooks/Mumford Letters*, p. 103. Mumford adds as an afterthought, "(Of course, I mean 'complete' for our generation: the work is never completed.)"

81. The phrase is Ruland's, p. 9.
82. Quoted in Blake, p. 246.
83. The substitutive relationship of absence and loss is experienced by the victim of trauma, according to Dominick LaCapra, *Writing History, Writing Trauma* (Baltimore: Johns Hopkins University Press, 2001). "When absence is converted into loss," LaCapra notes, "one increases the likelihood of misplaced nostalgia or utopian politics in quest of a new totality or fully unified community." But when the opposite happens—when loss is converted into absence—"one faces the impasse of endless melancholy, impossible mourning, and interminable aporia in which any process of working through the past and its historical losses is foreclosed or prematurely aborted" (46).
84. Letter, Eleanor Stimson Brooks to Lewis Mumford, 18 March 1929, Van Wyck Brooks Papers.
85. Letter, Charles Brooks to Van Wyck Brooks, 25 March 1931, Van Wyck Brooks Papers.

Chapter 4

1. Louis Hyde, ed., *Rat and Devil: Journal Letters of F. O. Matthiessen and Russell Cheney* (Hamden, Conn.: Archon Books, 1978), p. 246. Further references are cited in the text as *RD*. A veritable corpus of Matthiessen criticism has arisen in the past two decades. See Jonathan Arac, "F. O. Matthiessen: Authorizing an American Reniassance," pp. 90–112; and Donald E. Pease, "*Moby-Dick* and the Cold War," pp. 113–55, both in *The American Renaissance Reconsidered,* ed. Walter Benn Michaels and Donald E. Pease (Baltimore: Johns Hopkins University Press, 1985); Eric Cheyfitz, "Matthiessen's *American Renaissance:* Circumscribing the Revolution," *American Quarterly* 41 (1989): 341–61; James W. Tuttleton, "Politics and Art in the Criticism of F. O. Matthiessen," *New Criterion* 7 (1989): 4–13; David Bergman, "F. O. Matthiessen: The Critic as Homosexual," *Raritan* 9 (1990): 62–82; Marc Dolan, "The 'Wholeness' of the Whale: Melville, Matthiessen, and the Semiotics of Critical Revisionism," *Arizona Quarterly* 48 (1992): 27–58. Biographical accounts of Matthiessen include Leo Marx, "The Teacher," pp. 205–11; Bernard Bowron, "The Making of an American Scholar," pp. 212–22; Henry Nash Smith, "American Renaissance," pp. 223–8; Paul M. Sweezy, "Labor and Political Activities," pp. 229–43; and John Rackliffe, "Notes for a Character Study," 244–60, all in a special issue of the *Monthly Review* 2 (1950), as well as Kenneth S. Lynn, "F. O. Matthiessen," in *Masters: Portraits of Great Teachers,* ed. Joseph Epstein (New York: Basic Books, 1981), pp. 103–18. Book length studies include Giles Gunn, *F. O. Matthiessen: the Critical Achievement* (Seattle: University of Washington Press, 1975); Frederick C. Stern, *F. O. Matthiessen: Christian Socialist as Critic* (Chapel Hill: University of North Carolina Press, 1981); and William E. Cain, *F. O. Matthiessen and the Politics of Criticism* (Madison: University of Wisconsin Press, 1988). The most illuminating recent

studies have extended earlier discussion of Matthiessen's homosexuality as source and inspiration of his critical practice; see especially Henry Abelove's fine discussion in *Deep Gossip* (Minneapolis: University of Minnesota Press, 2003); and Jay Grossman, "The Canon in the Closet: Matthiessen's Whitman, Whitman's Matthiessen," *American Literature* 70 (1998): 799–832.

2. Wilson O. Clough to Matthiessen, December 1941, Matthiessen Papers, courtesy of Yale Collection of American Literature, Beinecke Library, ZA MS.206.

3. I'm indebted for this formulation to Henry Abelove, *Deep Gossip*, p. 61.

4. Ralph Waldo Emerson, "Ode, Inscribed to W. H. Channing," *Collected Poems and Translations,* ed. Harold Bloom and Paul Kane (New York: Library of America), p. 63.

5. Robert Spiller, *Late Harvest: Essays and Addresses in American Literature and Culture* (Westport, Conn.: Greenwood Press, 1981), p. 105. "Historical logic," according to Spiller, put Emerson "at the heart of the movement."

6. In "The Making of an American Scholar," *Monthly Review,* p. 213; hereafter cited parenthetically in the text as *MR.*

7. F. O. Matthiessen, *American Renaissance: Art and Expression in the Age of Emerson and Whitman* (London and Toronto: Oxford University Press, 1941), p. xvi. Hereafter cited parenthetically in the text as *AR.*

8. Specifically, such symptoms accord with Freud's classic statement on grief and depression in "Mourning and Melancholy," *The Standard Edition of the Complete Psychological Works of Sigmund Freud,* vol. 14, ed. James Strachey (London: Hogarth Press, 1953), pp. 243–58. Describing melancholia as the byproduct of an overzealous critical faculty, Freud charts the course by which the libido, forcibly withdrawn from a departed object—whether "a loved person, or . . . the loss of some abstraction . . . such as one's country, liberty, an ideal, and so on" (243)—becomes internalized. Setting up the lost object as part of itself, the ego is then free to reproach it with scathing ruthlessness, taking revenge on the original object by describing that part of its (newly internalized) self as unworthy. Freud puts it succinctly: "The shadow of the object is on the ego." Taken to its logical extreme, the revenge against the unrequited and now-internalized object is suicide, that "overcoming of the instinct which compels every living thing to cling to life" (246).

9. Ruland, *Rediscovery of American Literature*, p. 232.

10. Sacks, *Understanding Emerson* (Princeton: Princeton University Press, 2003), p. 16.

11. *Harvard Crimson,* Sept. 28, 1933, no page number.

12. *Harvard Advocate,* January 29, 1950, p. 341.

13. The "Oxford Letter" exists in a typescript prepared by George Abbott White. Matthiessen Papers, ZA MS.206. All quotations are from the typescript.

14. See Leo Marx, "'Double Consciousness' and the Cultural Politics of an American Critic," in *The Pilot and the Passenger: Essays on Literature, Technology, and Culture in the United States* (New York: Oxford University Press, 1988), pp. 239–60.

15. Edmund S. Morgan, telephone interview, 21 March 2003.
16. Pearl Kazin Bell, untitled recollection of Matthiessen, *The American Scholar* 72 (2003): 121.
17. For more on Mumford's work, see the previous chapter.
18. Matthiessen, *The Responsibilities of the Critic: Essays and Reviews by F. O. Matthiessen*, ed. John Rackliffe (New York: Oxford University Press, 1952), p. 254.
19. Matthiessen, *Russell Cheney, 1881–1945: A Record of His Work, with Notes by F. O. Matthiessen* (New York: Oxford University Press, 1947), p. 39. Hereafter cited within the text as *RC*.
20. I borrow this phrase, with ironic intentions, from John Carlos Rowe, who has somewhat controversially argued that Emerson's transcendentalism or "aesthetic dissent" "reveals itself to be at fundamental odds with social reforms." Matthiessen, as I hope I've suggested, would vehemently disagree with the absolutism of such an assertion. See Rowe, *At Emerson's Tomb*, p. 21.
21. J. C. Levenson, letter to author, 9 April 2003.
22. That Matthiessen believed such concerns were of central importance to Cheney is evident in the selection of letters he chose to highlight in *Russell Cheney*.
23. Mumford, *Golden Day*, pp. 104–5.
24. Matthiessen, *Responsibilities*, p. 247.
25. Krieger, "My Travels with the Aesthetic," pp. 208–36.
26. Matthiessen, *Responsibilities*, p. 181.
27. Sacks, *Understanding Emerson*, p. 70.
28. Eric Chefitz, "A Common Emerson: Ralph Waldo in an Ethnohistorical Context," *Nineteenth-Century Prose* 30 (2003): 255.
29. Matthiessen, *Responsibilities*, p. 160.
30. For an engaging account of the political and aesthetic accomplishments of the Popular Front, including a brief consideration of Matthiessen's role in it, see Michael Denning, *The Cultural Front: The Laboring of American Culture in the Twentieth Century* (New York: Verso, 1996).
31. Untitled manuscript, written during World War II. Matthiessen Papers, ZA MS.206.
32. Undated letter (from the midthirties) Matthiessen Papers, ZA MS.206.
33. Quoted in John Lydenberg, ed., *A Symposium on Political Activism and the Academic Conscience: The Harvard Experience, 1936–1941* (Hobart and William Smith Colleges, 1977), p. 6.
34. Matthiessen Papers, ZA MS.206.
35. As I have already suggested, Matthiessen's dual commitments to social action and aesthetic formalism have come to be seen as a doomed entanglement between two competing, if deeply experienced, ideologies. Such readings, provocative as they are, overlook the reasons that a purely instrumental approach to writing was problematic to Matthiessen. They also ignore the way in which his aesthetic analysis, formed within the particular circumstances of his relationship to Cheney, is actually deployed throughout the book. If

our own contemporary critical praxis insists upon reading the past and its artifacts as the staging ground for contestatory social values—that is, as a politically charged symbolic field open to appropriation—it is worth noting that this mode of reading was available to Matthiessen as well. At times, he comes close to aligning himself with a politicized reading of literature, as when he states in his introduction that "[a]n artist's use of language is the most sensitive index to cultural history, since a man can articulate only what he is, and what he has been made by the society of which he is a willing or unwilling part" (*AR* xv). But we would do well to read this sentence again. Contained within its opening is a cautionary note, an implied warning that reductive politicized readings too often occur through the willful elision of a text's specific internal features and of an author's particular imaginative explorations—both of which, by attempting to create new modes of thinking and of being, might affect culture, but in ways inevitably difficult to anticipate.

In refusing to attach purely instrumental values to a given text and to honor rather that text's often baffling autonomy, Matthiessen in many ways mirrors Emerson's own complex understanding of the relationship between thought and action. Emerson's famously ambivalent stance toward political activism (the locus of contemporary critical obsession) is simultaneously a desire to do *something* to further progressive social change without relinquishing his first principle that one has always to disregard received opinion and to listen instead to the voice within, that "if a single man plant himself indomitably on his instincts, and there abide, the huge world will come around to him" (*EL* 70). If this position at times recalls John Ashbery's "fence-sitting as an aesthetic principle," it also insists upon honoring the complex and unpredictable interactions of consciousness and the circumstanced world, language and action, and it does so without any illusions about the frequent inadequacy of intellectual work in a democratic society. See Ashbery, "Soonest Mended," *Selected Poems* (New York: Penguin, 1986), p. 88.

While Matthiessen was certainly less conflicted than Emerson about overt political activity outside his critical practice, as a literary historian he strives to countenance the full range of motives and effects within a literary work and to understand it both "as the most sensitive index to cultural history" (*AR* xv) *and* as containing its own "subtle principle of life" that "can be gained only through direct experience of it, again and again" (*AR* xi). Such a critical project—to understand History and Literature (not accidentally the name of the program that drew him from his beloved Yale to Harvard) as coexistent and mutually influencing—suggests a temperamental impatience with homogenous argumentation and criticism based upon a priori assumptions. It suggests, moreover, his willingness to inspire, rather than preclude, interpretive speculation: to release imaginative energies that might assault contemporary pieties and help construct a new world not entirely reducible to ideological structures. If art is action, as critics such as Granville Hicks argued during the thirties, it is, for Matthiessen, nevertheless a broader and subtler form of action than could be accounted for in Marxist criticism, and to claim otherwise was, for him, to engage in intellectual dishonesty. In writing *American Renaissance,* Matthiessen continually bumps up against questions that engage us still: To what extent are literature and social change related? What kinds of practical effects can be expected from a sensitive response to American literature and its possibilities for social renovation? And to what degree are thought and action mutually contributive or debasing factors? Given these fundamental questions, Emerson was the logical place to begin his masterwork, not only the creative spark against or with whom his authors reacted, but the uncanny embodiment of those contradictions haunting America's cultural critics.

36. Michael Lopez, "*The Conduct of Life:* Emerson's Anatomy of Power," in *The Cambridge Companion to Emerson,* ed. Joel Porte and Saundra Morris (Cambridge: Cambridge University Press, 1999), p. 245.

37. John Michael, "Democracy, Aesthetics, Individualism: Emerson as Public Intellectual," *Nineteenth-Century Prose* 30 (2003): 197.

38. Mark Edmundson, *Towards Reading Freud: Self-Creation in Milton, Wordsworth, Emerson, and Sigmund Freud* (Princeton: Princeton University Press, 1990), p. 134. This view is similar to Richard Poirier's understanding of Emerson as laboring against inherited traditions of language and thought.

39. For more on this transition in Emerson's thought, see T. Gregory Garvey's "Emerson's Political Spirit and the Problem of Language," in *The Emerson Dilemma: Essays on Emerson and Social Reform,* ed. T. Gregory Garvey (Athens: University of Georgia Press, 2001), pp. 14–34.

40. See, for instance, "Democracy at Harvard," in the June 1938 issue of *The Nation,* p. 662, for a representative discussion.

41. Matthiessen Papers, ZA MS.206.

42. Matthiessen Papers, ZA MS.444.

43. 11 January 1935, Matthiessen Papers, ZA MS.444.

44. Richard H. Pells, *Radical Visions and American Dreams: Culture and Social Thought in the Depression Years* (New York: Harper & Row, 1973), p. 293.

45. Such a shift is signaled not only by his brief consideration of the title of the book as *Democracy in Literature* but by his willingness to drop the second half of an introductory statement that read, "These standards are the inevitable and right extension of Emerson's demands upon *The American Scholar into an age where the central problems to be solved are collective rather than individual"* (quoted. in *MR,* p. 224; emphasis added).

46. Jonathan Franzen, "Perchance to Dream: In an Age of Images, a Reason to Write Novels," *Harper's* 92 (1996): 51.

47. Gerald Graff, *Professing Literature: An Institutional History* (Chicago and London: The University of Chicago Press, 1987), p. 219.

48. Gunn, *F. O. Matthiessen,* p. 106.

49. For the same reason, Matthiessen fails to see the "radical" Emerson of "Man the Reformer" and "The Young American."

50. While my discussion of an early transcendental and a later tragic Emerson might, as Michael Lopez notes, overly schematize the writing, producing a "rise-and-fall pattern" that "gives Emerson's career the symmetry of classical tragedy," it nevertheless helps shed light on the selection process behind Matthiessen's strangely decentered center of the American literary canon. See Lopez, "*The Conduct of Life*," p. 244.

51. Donald E. Pease, "Negative Interpellations: From Oklahoma City to the Trilling-Matthiessen Transmission," *boundary 2* 23 (1996): 1–33. Pease's truly remarkable insight, the foundation for my own reading of Matthiessen's interpretation of *White-Jacket*, is primarily concerned with the Althusserian concept of a Repressive Apparatus as it is ratified, among other places in American culture, through conservative talk radio. My view of Matthiessen's work differs in that I see *American Renaissance* far more as a document produced by the utopian ideals and the dissolution of those ideals during the 1930s rather than as a work to be read back through the political ligature of the Cold War. However, in working out Matthiessen's reading of *White-Jacket* in more detail, I see my discussion intensifying Pease's insight.

52. Richard Chase, *Herman Melville: A Critical Study* (New York: MacMillan, 1949), p. 21.

53. John Samson, *White Lies: Melville's Narratives of Facts* (Ithaca: Cornell University Press, 1989), p. 129.

54. Herman Melville, *White-Jacket, or The World in a Man-of-War,* vol. 5, *The Writings of Herman Melville,* ed. Harrison Hayford, Hershel Parker, and G. Thomas Tanselle (Evanston and Chicago: Northwestern University Press, 1970), p. 392. Subsequent citation will appear in the text as *WJ*.

55. Apparently upon doctor's orders, he and Cheney would soon find an apartment together in Boston, thereby remedying the winter isolation of coastal Maine.

56. William James, "Address at the Centenary of Ralph Waldo Emerson, May 25 1903," *Writings 1902–1910* (New York: Library of America, 1987), p. 1124.

57. Jonathan Arac, *Critical Genealogies: Historical Situations for Postmodern Literary Studies* (New York: Columbia University Press, 1989), p. 167.

58. Cheyfitz, "Matthiessen's *American Renaissance,*" p. 349.

59. Richard Poirier, "Human, All Too Inhuman," *The New Republic* (Feb. 2, 1987): 30.

60. Kay Redfield Jamison, *Night Falls Fast: Understanding Suicide* (New York: Knopf, 1999), p. 130.

61. Jamison, *Night Falls Fast,* p. 19.

62. In this, of course, he shares a fascinating parallel with Brooks.

63. Particularly poignant in this regard is a Sept. 20, 1948 issue of *Time* found in Matthiessen's bureau with a review of his last book, *From the Heart of Europe,* entitled "Innocent Abroad": "Harvard Professor Francis Otto Matthiessen is a bald, mild-mannered little bachelor who thinks the job of U.S. intellectuals is to 'rediscover and rearticulate' the needs for Socialism. . . .

Seldom has the gullibility and wishful thinking of pinkish academic intellectuals been so perfectly exposed as in [his] little book" p. 112–14.

Chapter 5

1. The discussion is wide and various, but the following recent works have
   been influential to my own understanding of the topic: Bruce Robbins, "Espionage as Vocation: Raymond Williams' Loyalties," in *Intellectuals: Aes-
   thetics, Politics, Academics,* ed. Bruce Robbins (Minneapolis: University of
   Minnesota Press, 1990), and *Secular Vocations: Intellectuals, Professionalism,
   Culture* (London: Verso, 1993); Edward W. Said, *Representations of the Intellectual* (New York: Pantheon Books, 1994); Helen Small, ed., *The Public
   Intellectual* (Malden, Mass.: Blackwell, 2002); and Richard A. Posner, *Public
   Intellectuals: A Study of Decline, with New Preface and Epilogue* (Cambridge,
   Mass.: Harvard University Press, 2003).
2. David Farber, "Intellectuals and Democracy: Academics in Paradise/Emer-
   son's Vocation," *American Literary History* 12 (2000): 794.
3. Lawrence Buell, *Emerson* (Cambridge, Mass.: Harvard University Press,
   2003), p. 43.
4. An early portrait of Miller can be found in the elegiac "Perry Miller and
   the American Mind," a special edition of the *Harvard Review* 2:12 (1964).
   Other important discussions of Miller include David A. Hollinger, "Perry
   Miller and Philosophical History" *History and Theory* 7 (1968): 189–202;
   Francis T. Butts, "The Myth of Perry Miller," *American Historical Review* 87
   (1982): 665–94; Arne Delfs, "Anxieties and Influence: Perry Miller and Sacvan Bercovitch," *New England Quarterly* 70 (1997): 601–15; and Michael G.
   Murphey, "Perry Miller and American Studies," *American Studies* 42 (2001):
   5–18. While I diverge sharply from Nicholas Guyatt in my reading of Miller,
   his "'An Instrument of National Policy': Perry Miller and the Cold War,"
   Journal of American Studies 36 (2002): 107–49, has proved most useful in my
   own research, especially regarding Miller's postwar activities.
5. Edmund S. Morgan, telephone interview, 21 March 2003.
6. J. C. Levenson, correspondence, 9 April 2003.
7. David Levin, "Perry Miller at Harvard," *The Southern Review* 19 (Autumn
   1983): 816.
8. Perry Miller, *Errand into the Wilderness* (Cambridge, Mass.: Harvard University Press, 1956), p. vii. Further references to this book, which contains
   "From Edwards to Emerson," are cited in the text as *EW.* For a fine reading
   of Miller's introduction, see Amy Kaplan, "'Left Alone in America': The
   Absence of Empire in the Study of American Culture," in *Cultures of United
   States Imperialism,* ed. Amy Kaplan and Donald E. Pease (Durham, N.C.:
   Duke University Press, 1993), pp. 3–21.
9. T. S. McMillin, *Our Preposterous Use of Literature: Emerson and the Nature
   of Reading,* pp. 103–4. For more on Emerson's centrality to the American
   literary canon, see David R. Shumway, "Emerson and the Shape of Ameri-

can Literature," in *Disciplining English: Alternative Histories, Critical Perspectives,* ed. David R. Shumway and Craig Dionne (Albany: State University of New York Press, 2002), pp. 115–34.

10. Edward W. Said, *Representations of the Intellectual,* p. xii.

11. Charles McLaughlin, telephone interview, 16 May 2003.

12. "Transcendentalism," a lecture delivered 22 July 1960, at Gonzaga College, typescript, Miller Papers, courtesy Harvard Library, HUG 4572.15, p. 1. Miller destroyed nearly all of his correspondence and was estranged from his family, according to William Hutchison (e-mail, 4 April 2003). Much of my biographical information is pieced together from disparate comments he made to students over the years.

13. See Michael G. Murphey, "Perry Miller and American Studies," pp. 5–18.

14. George Herron, "The Message of Jesus to Men of Wealth," Christian Union 42 (December 11, 1890): 804–5.

15. Herron, *The Menace of Peace* (New York: Mitchell Kennerly, 1917), p. 58.

16. Kenneth S. Lynn, "Perry Miller," *The American Scholar* 52 (1983): 221–70.

17. Lynn, "Perry Miller," p. 225.

18. Quoted in Perry Miller, *The Responsibility of Mind in a Civilization of Machines,* ed. James Crowel and Sanford Stearl (Amherst: University of Massachusetts Press, 1979), p. 2.

19. Perry Miller, *The New England Mind: The Seventeenth Century* (Cambridge, Mass.: Harvard University Press, 1939), p. 8.

20. David M. Robinson makes a similar point when he notes that "[t]he inscrutability of an unapproachable God seemed [to Miller] to cohere with a contemporary alienation before threatening and certainly inexplicable conditions of existence." "The Road Not Taken: From Edwards, Through Chauncy, to Emerson," *Arizona Quarterly* 48 (1992): 50.

21. Friedrich Nietzsche, "The Use and Abuse of History," *Thoughts Out of Season,* trans. Adrian Collins (New York: Russell & Russell, 1964), p. 26.

22. That Miller understood and appreciated the value of economic analysis is apparent not only in his conclusion to *The New England Mind: The Seventeenth Century* but also in his review article on "Charles A. Beard," *The Nation* (25 Sept. 1948): 344–6.

23. Perry Miller, *Orthodoxy in Massachusetts, 1630–1650* (Boston: Beacon Press, 1965), p. xi.

24. Miller, *Orthodoxy,* p. xviii.

25. Miller, *The New England Mind: The Seventeenth Century,* p. 15.

26. Robinson, "The Road Not Taken: From Edwards, Through Chauncy, to Emerson," p. 45.

27. For a discussion of the "democratic revival" underway in the academy during 1939, see Philip Gleason, "World War II and the Development of American Studies" *American Quarterly* 36 (1984): 343–58.

28. John, Lydenberg, ed., *A Symposium on Political Activism and the Academic Conscience: The Harvard Experience, 1936–1941* (Hobart and William Smith Colleges, 1977), p. vi.

29. Leo Marx, *A Symposium on Political Activism and the Academic Conscience*, pp. 32–3.

30. MacLeish's statements, which appeared as "The Irresponsibles," *The Nation* 150 (18 May 1940): 618–23, are discussed in Kermit Vanderbilt, *American Literature and the Academy: The Roots, Growth, and Maturity of a Profession*, pp. 463–4.

31. MacLeish, "Irresponsibles," p. 620. Ironically, MacLeish anticipates postwar and Cold War discussion that portrayed communist orthodoxy as inherently at odds with academic freedom.

32. MacLeish, "Irresponsibles," p. 618.

33. Miller, "Correspondence on 'The Irresponsibles,'" *The Nation* 150 (1 June 1940): 681.

34. *Symposium*, pp. 5, 66.

35. Leo Marx, e-mail correspondence, 19 March 2003.

36. Miller's reading of Emerson as a young radical who grew increasingly complacent with age was extremely influential—shaping his student Stephen E. Whicher's important book on Emerson, *Freedom and Fate*, for instance. But this version of Emerson has been hotly contested in recent years, no more persuasively so than by Len Gougeon, among the first to find in the later Emerson a political reformer committed especially to the cause of abolition; see especially Len Gougeon, *Virtue's Hero: Emerson, Antislavery, and Reform* (Athens: University of Georgia Press, 1990). Miller's focus on the younger Emerson is the result not only of his identifying a parallel between the transcendental revolt against the Unitarian establishment and his own disagreement with Harvard's political left. It is also the product of his larger commitment to the social efficacy of thought and, one suspects, his temperamental affinity for youthful revolt.

37. *Symposium*, p. 29.

38. See the second chapter.

39. The ability of Emerson's early transcendental rhetoric to effect any social change whatsoever has recently been challenged by John Carlos Rowe, who asserts that "Transcendentalism reveals itself to be at fundamental odds with the social reforms regarding slavery and women's rights." Rowe, *At Emerson's Tomb*, p. 21. Rowe has been challenged on a number of fronts, most trenchantly perhaps by Harold K. Bush (in T. Gregory Garvey's *The Emerson Dilemma*), who considers such polarized readings of Emerson as either "Transcendentalist or social reformer" to ignore how his rhetoric attempts to join both realms and to thereby conjure into existence a "political religion" still capable of goading us to action; see "Emerson, John Brown, and 'Doing the Word': The Enactment of Political Religion at Harpers Ferry, 1859," in *The Emerson Dilemma*, p. 211. Additional discussion of this topic was carried out in the Summer-Fall double issue of *Nineteenth-Century Prose* 30 (2003), especially Eric Chefitz, "A Common Emerson: Ralph Waldo in an Ethnohistorical Context," pp. 250–81; John Michael, "Democracy, Aesthetics, Individualism: Emerson as Public Intellectual,"

pp. 195–226; and Joel Porte, "Emerson and the Refounding of America," pp. 227–49.

40. David Levin, "Perry Miller at Harvard," p. 805.

41. Rowe, *At Emerson's Tomb*, p. 21.

42. MacLeish, "Words Are Not Enough," *The Nation* 156 (March 13, 1943):368.

43. Kenneth Murdock, "Correspondence on 'The Irresponsibles,'" *The Nation*, 681.

44. From undated letters in the Perry Miller-Kenneth Murdock Correspondence, Miller Papers, HUG 4572.7.

45. Guyatt, "'An Instrument of National Policy,'" p. 116.

46. Undated, Perry Miller-Kenneth Murdock Correspondence, HUG 4572.7.

47. See especially Robert Milder's "The Radical Emerson?" in *The Cambridge Companion to Ralph Waldo Emerson*, ed. Joel Porte and Saundra Morris (Cambridge: Cambridge University Press, 1999), pp. 49–75.

48. Guyatt, pp. 132–3.

49. Bruce Robbins, "Espionage as Vocation," p. 286.

50. F. O. Matthiessen Papers, ZA MS.206. The letter is dated 13 January 1943.

51. Guyatt, p. 117.

52. Guyatt, p. 117.

53. 16 April 1944, F. O. Matthiessen Papers, ZA MS.206.

54. Vanderbilt, p. 538.

55. Quoted in David R. Shumway, *Creating American Civilization*, p. 312.

56. Donald E. Pease, *Visionary Compacts: American Renaissance Writings in Cultural Context* (Madison: University of Wisconsin Press, 1987), p. 244.

57. Guyatt, p. 122.

58. "'The American people are talking democracy over again,' was the way Benson Y. Landis put it in introducing a lengthy reading list on the subject of democracy that was published by the American Library Association in January, 1940." See Gleason, "World War II and the Development of American Studies," p. 346.

59. Daniel J. Boorstin, *The Genius of American Politics* (Chicago: University of Chicago Press, 1953), p. 1.

60. Boorstin, p. 162.

61. Boorstin, p. 194.

62. See Eric Bentley, ed., *Thirty Years of Treason: Excerpts from Hearings before the House Committee on Un-American Activities, 1938–1968* (New York: Viking Press, 1971), pp. 601–12.

63. Ellen Schrecker, *No Ivory Tower: McCarthyism and the Universities* (Oxford: Oxford University Press, 1986), p. 93.

64. Schrecker, p. 218.

65. Quoted in Guyatt, p. 127.

66. Miller, "Emersonian Genius and the American Democracy," reprinted in *Nature's Nation* (Cambridge, Mass.: Belknap Press of Harvard, 1967), p. 163. Further references to this article are cited in the text as *NN*. Miller's discussion of Emerson and the problem of democracy is informed to some

extent by Daniel Aaron's *Men of Good Hope: A Story of American Progressives* (Oxford: Oxford University Press, 1951), p. 16, in which Aaron notes:

> Like John Adams and Thomas Jefferson, Emerson believed in a natural aristocracy, although his *aristoi* bore little resemblance to Jefferson's. Society divided itself into the men of understanding and the men of Reason. The former, the most numerous and the most ordinary, lived in 'a world of pig-lead' and acted as if 'rooted and grounded in adamant.' Sunk in this profound materialism, they lacked the imaginative penetration of the true aristocrats, the men of Reason, who plumbed the spiritual reality behind the world of fact. The men of Reason—poets, seers, philosophers, scholars—the passive doers, served humanity as the geography of the 'super-sensible regions' and inspired 'an audacious mental outlook.' They formed no inflexible caste, but they wonderfully 'liberated' the cramped average afraid to trust itself.

67. Cushing Strout, correspondence, 19 March 2003.
68. Sacvan Bercovitch, *The American Jeremiad* (Madison: University of Wisconsin Press, 1978), p. 184.
69. Milder, "The Radical Emerson?" p. 59.
70. Miller, "Foundations of American Democracy," delivered 5 and 6 May 1953 at Baldwin Goddard College, typescript, Miller Papers, HUG 4572.15, p. 17.
71. Miller, "Foundations of American Democracy," p. 24.
72. Miller, *Responsibility*, p. 140.
73. Jesper Rosenmeier, telephone interview, May 19, 2003.
74. Miller, *Responsibility*, p. 86.
75. Miller, *Responsibility*, p. 189.
76. Miller, "Emerson's 'American Scholar' Today," delivered in 1955 (no date) at Goddard College, typescript, Miller Papers, HUG 4572.15, pp. 3, 6.
77. Miller, *Responsibility*, p. 189.
78. Miller, "New England's Transcendentalism: Native or Imported?" reprinted in *Emerson's Prose and Poetry*, ed. Joel Porte and Saundra Morris (New York: Norton, 2001), p. 670.
79. Miller, "Emerson's 'American Scholar' Today," p. 23.
80. Miller, "Transcendentalism," pp. 1–2.
81. Miller, "Emerson's 'American Scholar' Today," p. 2.
82. Miller, "Emerson's 'American Scholar' Today," pp. 9, 22.
83. Miller, "Emerson's 'American Scholar' Today," p. 23.
84. Miller, "Emerson's 'American Scholar' Today," p. 23.
85. Miller, "Emerson's 'American Scholar' Today," p. 25.
86. Robbins, *Secular Vocations*, p. 23.
87. Robbins, *Secular Vocations*, p. 23.
88. Miller, "New England's Transcendentalism," pp. 670–1.
89. Miller, "New England's Transcendentalism," p. 678.
90. Miller, "New England's Transcendentalism," p. 678.

91. Miller, "Transcendentalism," p. 12.

92. Miller, "The American Humanities in an Industrial Civilization," lecture from a seminar at the University of Massachusetts, 6 July 1956, typescript, Miller Papers, HUG 4572.15, p. 4.

Chapter 6

1. Among the best discussions of Bercovitch and his work are Carol Colatrella and Joseph Alkana, eds., *Cohesion and Dissent in America* (Albany: SUNY Press, 1994); Frederick Crews, "Whose American Renaissance?" in *The Critics Bear It Away: American Fiction and the Academy* (New York: Random House, 1992), pp. 16–46; Arne Delfs, "Anxieties of Influence: Perry Miller and Sacvan Bercovitch," *New England Quarterly* 70 (1997): 601–15; David Harlan, "A People Blinded from Birth: American History according to Sacvan Bercovitch," *Journal of American History* 78 (1991): 949–71; Susanne Klingenstein, *Enlarging America: The Cultural Work of Jewish Literary Scholars, 1930–1990* (Syracuse: Syracuse University Press, 1998), pp. 347–406; Rael Meyerowitz, *Transferring to America: Jewish Interpretations of American Dreams* (Albany: SUNY Press, 1995), pp. 215–60; Russell J. Reising, *The Unusable Past: Theory and the Study of American Literature*, pp. 74–91; and Alan Trachtenberg, "The Writer in America," *Partisan Review* 46 (1977): 466–75.

2. Quoted in Kenneth Lynn, "Perry Miller," *The American Scholar* 52 (1983): 221.

3. Gerald Graff, *Professing Literature: An Institutional History* (Chicago and London: The University of Chicago Press, 1987), p. 219.

4. This reading of culture has a long and well-known critical genealogy that includes Max Horkheimer and Theodor W. Adorno's analysis of "The Culture Industry" as a vitiating force of democracy (see especially "The Culture Industry: Enlightenment as Mass Deception," in *Dialectic of Enlightenment*, trans. John Cumming [New York: Continuum, 1991], pp. 120–67); Gramsci's ideas about hegemony; continental structuralism and poststructuralism; and the contributions, through such figures as Raymond Williams and Stuart Hall, of an English-based cultural studies (see, for instance, Williams, "Advertising: The Magic System," in *The Cultural Studies Reader*, ed. Simon During [London and New York: Routledge, 1992], pp. 410–23).

5. Philip Roth, "Writing American Fiction," in *Reading Myself and Others* (New York: Farrar, Straus and Giroux, 1975), pp. 117–35.

6. Lawrence Buell, "Are We Post-American Studies?" in *Field Work: Sites in Literary and Cultural Studies*, ed. Marjorie Garber, Paul B. Franklin et al. (New York: Routledge, 1996), pp. 87–93.

7. I put quotes around the term because it has become in recent years something of a catch-all, referring to everything from the early Puritan conception of a "city on a hill," the antebellum dedication to a "Nation for Liberty," to Louis Hartz's sense of the uniqueness of U.S. liberalism.

Future studies on American exceptionalist discourse will need to tease out these various (and occasionally competing) meanings, to historicize and distinguish what is meant by exceptional by a given author at a given time. One recent example: after the attacks of September 11, 2001, and the War in Iraq, the issue of exceptionalism has taken on renewed philosophical and political importance; see especially Giorgio Agamben's reworking of Carl Schmitt's ideas about exceptionalism in *Homo Sacer: Sovereign Power and Bare Life*, trans. Daniel Heller-Roazen (Stanford: Stanford University Press, 1998), and *State of Exception*, trans. Kevin Attell (Chicago: University of Chicago Press, 2005).

8. Sacvan Bercovitch, e-mail, 21 January 2005.

9. As Wai Chee Dimock notes, "Emerson (more so than any of the Puritan figures) exemplifies for [Bercovitch] the contrary impulses of American literature, and American society as a whole," e-mail, 14 February 2005.

10. Sacvan Bercovitch, *The Rites of Assent: Transformations in the Symbolic Construction of America* (New York and London: Routledge, 1993), pp. 308, 190. Subsequent citations will appear parenthetically in the text as *RA*.

11. *The Puritan Origins of the American Self* (New Haven: Yale University Press, 1975), p. 162. Subsequent citations will appear parenthetically in the text as *PO*.

12. *The American Jeremiad* (Madison: University of Wisconsin Press, 1978), p. 203. Subsequent citations will appear parenthetically in the text as *AJ*.

13. "What you might remember in classifying me," he writes, "is that I'm not American, but (if I had to name identities) Jewish and Canadian—a wandering Jew and (as a Canadian) the product of 'a country without a mythology' (as a Canadian poet put it) . . . [a]n immigrant dissenting Canadian-Jewish (emphasis on the Jewish) Emersonian," correspondence, 22 July 2005.

14. *The Letters of Ralph Waldo* Emerson, 10 vols., ed. Ralph L. Rusk and Eleanor Tilton (New York: Columbia University Press, 1939), vol. 2, p. 325.

15. Quoted in Klingenstein, *Enlarging America*, fn. 72.

16. Sacvan Bercovitch, correspondence, 22 July 2005.

17. Sacvan Bercovitch, correspondence to Robert Milder, 26 December 1995. Used by permission of the author.

18. Quoted in Robert Adams, *Life and Work of Alexander Bercovitch, Artist* (Montreal: Editions Marlowe, 1988), p. 88.

19. It is worth noting that like Emerson, Bercovitch symbolically refashioned his inherited identity by substituting his middle name for his first (Joshua).

20. Both quotes, the first from Bercovitch and the second by Robert Adams, are in Klingenstein, *Enlarging America*, pp. 361, 360.

21. The phrase, which Bercovitch most often uses with reference to Emerson, is Harold Bloom's. See Bercovitch, "Emerson the Prophet: Romanticism, Puritanism, and Auto-American-Biography," in *Emerson: Prophecy, Metamorphosis, and Influence* (New York: Columbia University Press, 1975), p. 1.

22. Klingenstein, *Enlarging America*, p. 363.

23. "Sacvan Bercovitch: Cross-Cultural Adventures, An Interview with Giuseppe Nori," http:/www.aisna.org/rsajournal5/Bercovitch/html. Consulted 19 January 2005.

24. See *The Melville Log: A Documentary Life of Herman Melville, 1819–1891*, ed. Jay Leyda, vol. 2 (New York: Gordian Press, 1969), p. 529.

25. "Sacvan Bercovitch: Cross-Cultural Adventures."

26. Klingenstein, *Enlarging America*, p. 375.

27. Klingenstein, *Enlarging America*, p. 375.

28. Meyerowitz, *Transferring to America*, p. 226.

29. This schema fits three of his four book-length studies: *Puritan Origins, American Jeremiad,* and *Rites of Assent.* His book on Hawthorne is the anomaly.

30. This sense is enhanced by Bercovitch's remark in the introduction that he is at work on a full-scale revaluation of Emerson. "I never did get to write that book on Emerson," Bercovitch admits. "I taught courses instead." E-mail, 22 January 2005.

31. Bercovitch, "Emerson the Prophet," p. 29.

32. Michael Denning points out that Bercovitch's project, exemplified in the passage on Emerson, was "grounded [in] an influential and powerful version of American exceptionalism" that located an embryonic ideological consensus in the rhetoric of the Puritans. See Denning, *Culture in the Age of Three Worlds* (London: Verso, 2004), p. 183.

33. Alan Trachtenberg, "The Writer as America," *Partisan Review* 46 (1977): 474.

34. Sam B. Girgus, telephone interview, 15 February 2005.

35. Richard Poirier, *The Renewal of Literature: Emersonian Reflections* (New York: Random House, 1987), p. 138.

36. Lawrence Rosenwald, telephone interview, 24 January 2005.

37. This reading is from Lyndall Gordon, Bercovitch's first graduate student, in *Shared Lives* (New York: W. W. Norton, 1992), p. 181

38. Terry Eagleton, *After Theory* (New York: Basic Books, 2003), p. 51.

39. Meyerowitz, p. 230.

40. Sacvan Bercovitch, "Deadpan Huck," *The Kenyon Review* 24 (Summer/Fall 2002): 90–134.

41. Fluck sees in this intervention—which is rooted in the larger premises of poststructuralism—the emergence of cultural studies and the rise of race and gender studies as efforts to escape the Foucauldian "prison house of power."

42. Introduction, *Reconstructing American Literary History*, Harvard English Studies, 13 (Cambridge: Harvard University Press, 1986), p. vii.

43. "The Problem of Ideology in American Literary History," *Critical Inquiry* 12 (Summer 1986): 650, 645.

44. "The Problem of Ideology in American Literary History," 642.

45. "Afterward," *Ideology and Classic American Literature,* co-edited with Myra Jehlen (Cambridge: Cambridge University Press, 1986), p. 439.

46. "The Problem of Ideology in American Literary History," p. 636.

47. "The Problem of Ideology in American Literary History," p. 649.

48. "The Problem of Ideology in American Literary History," p. 639.

49. The essay was first published as "Emerson, Individualism, and the Ambiguities of Dissent," *South Atlantic Quarterly* 89 (Summer 1990): 623–62.

50. Robert Milder makes a similar claim in "The Radical Emerson?" in *The Cambridge Companion to Ralph Waldo Emerson.*

51. In conversation, 20 June 2005.

52. See Leo Marx, "On Recovering the 'Ur' Theory of American Studies," *American Literary History* 17 (Spring 2005): 118–34.

53. See Paul Bové, "Notes Toward a Politics of 'American' Studies," in *In the Wake of Theory* (Hanover, N.H.: Wesleyan University Press); pp. 48–66, and William Spanos, "American Studies in the 'Age of the World Picture,'" *The Futures of American Studies,* ed. Donald E. Pease and Robyn Wiegman (Durham, N.C.: Duke University Press, 2002).

54. Spanos, "American Studies in the 'Age of the World Picture,'" p. 390. It is worth noting that the summer institute out of which this collection arose— "The Futures of American Studies"—has recently been renamed "Outside American Studies."

55. Spanos, p. 388.

56. Bercovitch, "Games of Chess: A Model of Literary and Cultural Studies," in *Centuries' End, Narrative Means,* ed. Robert Newman (Stanford: Stanford University Press, 1996). Hereafter cited parenthetically within text as GC. See also "The Function of the Literary in a Time of Cultural Studies," in *"Culture" and the Problem of the Disciplines,* ed. John Carlos Rowe (New York: Columbia University Press, 1998), pp. 69–86.

57. Stanley Cavell, "The Philosopher in American Life," collected in *Emerson's Transcendental Etudes* (Stanford: Stanford University Press, 2003), p. 50.

58. Milder, *Reimagining Thoreau* (Cambridge: Cambridge University Press, 1995), p. 14.

59. This definition comes from http://dictionary.reference.com/search?q= circumvent.

60. Slavoj Žižek, *Iraq: The Borrowed Kettle* (New York: Verso, 2004), p. 123.

Chapter 7

1. Whitman, *Complete Poetry and Collected Prose,* ed. Justin Kaplan (New York: Library of America, 1982), p. 922.

2. Conway, *Emerson at Home and Abroad,* pp. 3–4.

3. Nathaniel Hawthorne, *The Scarlet Letter,* ed. William Charvat and Fredson Bowers, et al., vol. 1 of *The Centenary Edition of the Works of Nathaniel Hawthorne* (Columbus: Ohio State University Press, 1962), pp. 79–80.

4. Cavell, *Emerson's Transcendental Etudes,* p. 5. Cavell's "aversive" Emerson, a philosopher of language and a philosophical precursor to Nietzsche and the later Heidegger and Wittgenstein, is one highlight in the renewed focus on Emerson's thought. The other is of Emerson as anticipator of pragmatism as it was initiated by such late-nineteenth-century figures as William James, Charles Saunders Peirce, and John Dewey (who nevertheless would

comment, at Emerson's centennial celebration, that philosophers "extol his keen, calm art and speak with some depreciation of his metaphysic"). Louis Menand has suggested that the revival of interest in pragmatism has resulted from the conclusion of the Cold War and its contest of ideas between competing superpowers (See *The Metaphysical Club* [New York: Farrar, Straus & Giroux, 2001], p. 440). In this shifting paradigm, Emerson's later work, especially the ruminations on power and practical action in *The Conduct of Life* (1860), has found a niche in an emergent intellectual history previously suppressed. Of his earlier essays, "Circles" is an especially important example of Emerson's idea of the provisional nature of "truth." While Menand's efforts to trace the connections between Emerson and what he calls the "Metaphysical Club" are only the most recent, Cornel West was among the earliest to cast Emerson in the role of proto-pragmatist, finding in the author a figure who "creates a style of cultural criticism which . . . deploys a set of rhetorical strategies that attempt both to legitimize and criticize America, and situates his project within and among the refined and reformist elements of the middle class. . . ." (*The American Evasion of Philosophy: A Genealogy of Pragmatism* [Madison: University of Wisconsin Press, 1989], p. 41).

That Emerson's particular aesthetic practice might have a "pragmatic" aspect—that his notion in "The Poet" and elsewhere that expression might provoke action—is one of the principal arguments of Richard Poirier, perhaps the best close reader of Emerson in the past quarter century. For Poirier, literary practice is the site of a struggle between "a fully developed consciousness of self and the socially accepted styles by which that self can get expressed" (*A World Elsewhere*, p. 28). In the case of Emerson, this means we should pay particular attention to the manner in which historically determined language is both the enabling and constricting condition of utterance, the inevitable grounds against which new thought and language necessarily occur. "Any word," Poirier writes, indulging in what he calls an "Emersonian conjecture," "in the variety and even contradictoriness of its meanings, gives evidence of earlier antagonistic uses, and it is this which encourages us to turn on them again, to change or trope them further" (*The Renewal of Literature*, p. 138). What Poirier finds most interesting in Emerson's essays is their awareness of the ability to reshape context through the malleable aspect of inherited language. Still, he cautions, Emerson's writing is not to be regarded as "in itself an effective form of action. . . . At best, it can help us to deal more critically and effectively than we otherwise might with rhetorics outside literature. . . ." (*The Renewal of Literature*, p. 48). One of the ways it helps us is to call into question what Poirier terms the "imponderables" of any call for social reformation, imponderables that include how such reformation might inhibit our ability to understand the world, how individuals are to recognize a new order of things, and who gets to authorize any calls for a new order in the first place (*The Renewal of Literature*, p. 78).

The interest in Emerson's language and its constrained but pragmatic relation to action is also the basis for Eduardo Cadava's *Emerson and the Climates of History,* one of the most searching examinations of Emerson's writing in the past decade. Cadava's study might be taken as an exemplary model of the poststructuralist concern with discursive systems and their relationship to power and politics. Within this concern, Emerson is less an aesthetician than a political writer, a prose stylist whose language is always freighted by traces of historical context. This traversal of history through writing is not a passive operation, however. Noting that "all of Emerson's writings" "are to be read as eminently political acts, even when they are articulated in linguistic or philosophical terms rather than in explicitly political ones," Cadava refocuses attention to the language of nature and weather in Emerson's writing so as to suggest that it bears greater cultural signification than might initially appear. He can arrive at this point, in part, because he understands that "if Emerson's language works to change language, it does so in order to change much more than language—it does so because it seeks to produce something new and singular," and because, for Cadava, "language and representation . . . are inseparable from the transformative, and hence political, power at the heart of Emerson's writing." (See Eduardo Cadava, *Emerson and the Climates of History* [Stanford: Stanford University Press, 1997], pp. 62, 20, 18.) While Poirier and Cadava share an interest in the relationship between language and power, thought and action, Cadava's post-Foucauldian portrait of Emerson ultimately makes greater claims for the shaping power of language in the social realm.

None of these critics, each of whom has offered exemplary and important readings of Emerson, may be said to be overly concerned with "The American Scholar."

5. Stanley Cavell, e-mail, 9 January 2006.

6. Cavell, e-mail, 9 January 2006.

7. Cavell, e-mail, 9 January 2006. For a more skeptical approach to Cavell's version of Emerson, especially as it regards the political ramifications of Emersonian individualism, see Cary Wolfe, "Alone in America: Cavell, Emerson, and the Politics of Individualism," *New Literary History* 25 (1994): 137–57.

8. *9/11 Commission Report,* p. 362.

9. Of course, for those who would seek to break the frame of American Studies and engage in transnational or transcultural viewpoints, a similar criticism can be made; doesn't such work merely reflect an expansionist imperial project, as well?

10. Whicher, *Freedom and Fate,* p. 123.

11. No better example illustrates the compositional method of Emerson: the way he mines previous journal entries and reinvests them with fresh meanings.

12. Buell, *Emerson,* p. 126.

13. Cavell, *Emerson's Transcendental Etudes,* p. 112.

14. See especially Buell, "Emersonian Poetics," *Emerson,* pp. 107–57, 331.

15. Phyllis Cole, *Mary Moody Emerson and the Origins of Transcendentalism: A Family History* (New York: Oxford University Press, 1998), p. 7.

16. Cole, *Mary Moody Emerson,* p. 10. Other recent treatments of Emerson and issues of women's rights include Jeffrey A. Steele, "The Limits of Political Sympathy: Emerson, Fuller, and Women's Rights" and Cole's own "Pain and Protest in the Emerson Family," both in *The Emerson Dilemma,* as well as Christina Zwarg, *Feminist Conversations: Fuller, Emerson, and the Play of Reading* (Ithaca: Cornell University Press, 1995).

17. See Cathy N. Davidson, "Preface," *American Literature* 70 (1998): 456.

18. See Len Gougeon, *Virtue's Hero;* Cadava, *Emerson and the Climates of History;* Gregg Cane, *Race, Citizenship, and Law in American Literature* (Cambridge: Cambridge University Press, 2003); Albert J. von Frank, *The Trials of Anthony Burns: Freedom and Slavery in Emerson's Boston* (Cambridge, Mass.: Harvard University Press, 1998); and Laura Dassow Walls, *Emerson's Life in Science: The Culture of Truth* (Ithaca: Cornell University Press, 2003).

19. Ian Finseth, "Evolution, Cosmopolitanism, and Emerson's Antislavery Politics," *American Literature* 77 (2005): 729–30.

20. Finseth, "Evolution, Cosmopolitanism, and Emerson's Antislavery Politics," p. 749.

INDEX